PSYCHOLOGY

SYMBOLISM

AND

THE SACRED

PSYCHOLOGY
SYMBOLISM
AND
THE SACRED

Confronting Religious Dysfunction in a

Changing World

Second Edition: Revised and Updated 2007

Perspectives on the Meaning of Life

by

Stephen T. Manning

CheckPoint
Press

OTHER BOOKS BY THIS AUTHOR

The Color of Truth Volume I: Patterns in Light

The Color of Truth Volume II: Parallels in Life

The Color of Truth Volume III: Principles to Live By

Psychology, Symbolism, and the Sacred (2nd Ed. 2006)
ISBN-10: 0-9551503-7-X   ISBN-13: 978-0-9551503-7-1
Published by CheckPoint Press, Ireland

CheckPoint Press
Books with Something to Say..

CHECKPOINT PRESS
DOOAGH
ACHILL IS.
CO. MAYO
REPUBLIC OF IRELAND

WEBSITES: CHECKPOINTPRESS.COM & COLOR-OF-TRUTH.COM

EMAIL: EDITOR@CHECKPOINTPRESS.COM

TABLE OF CONTENTS

PART I: DIAGNOSIS AND ASSESSMENT

Immorality or Insanity? (4) Fundamentalism (8) The Role of Psychology
(12) Solutions and Cures (18)

Religious Personality Types (23) Authoritarian and Humanistic Religion
(31) Education or Indoctrination? (34) In Conclusion (41)

Social Benefits of Religion (45) The True Religious Experience (47)
Extraneous Origins (48) Identifying the Origin (49) Synthetic Religious
Experiences (50) Environmental and Subjective Causes (51) Psychosis
and Psychomancy (54) Individual Features of Collective Problems (54)

PART II: THERAPEUTIC FOUNDATIONS

Subjectivity, Objectivity, and Taxonomies (63) Universal Truth Theory (67)
Phenomenological Evaluations (69) Reductive Classifications (70)
Universality (71)

The Psyche and The Soul (85) A Divided Mind (86)

A Psychology of Religion (92) Religious Terminology (94) The Religious
Theory (95) The Freudian Theory (98) Jungian Archetypes (99) Delving
deeper (102) The Psychospiritual Theory (107)

PART III: A UNIVERSAL SYNCHRONICITY

PART IV: CONCLUSIONS AND APPLICATIONS

DIAGRAMS & ILLUSTRATIONS: PAGES 109-120

Diagram 1: Structures of Psycho-Spiritual Theories
Diagram 2: Psychological and Religious Concepts
Diagram 3: Stages of Psychospiritual Interpretation
Diagram 4: Conceptual Values of White, Blue, and Red
Diagram 5: Properties of the Color Spectrum
Diagram 6: The Electromagnetic Spectrum
Diagram 7: Conceptual Triads – White, Blue, Red
Diagram 8: Fire, Water, Air, and Earth
Diagram 9: Symbolic Elements of the Greek Soul
Diagram 10: Atomic Structure
Diagram 11: Chakras
Diagram 12: The Cosmic Circle
Diagram 13: The Individual Triad
Diagram 14: The Hindu Trimurti
Diagram 15: Triadic Correlations in Eastern Traditions
Diagram 16: Political Colors of the Arab League c. 1960
Diagram 17: The Arab – Israeli, Cain and Abel Dynamic
Diagram 18: The Papacy and the Holy Roman Emperors
Diagram 19: Flags of France, Austria, Prussia, and Germany in 1918
Diagram 20: Traditional Colors of the Kingdom of France
Diagram 21: 'The Allies' and the 'Central Powers' during World War I
Diagram 22: The Asian Dynamic
Diagram 23: The Twelve Red/White/Blue Nations of the Allied Forces
Diagram 24: Eight More Allied Nations
Diagram 25: The Remarkable Display of Post WWII Historical Symbolism
Diagram 26: Opposing Forces; WWI, WWII, Korean, & Cold War
Diagram 27: The Three Subdivisions of the Red Archetype
Diagram 28: Traditional Islamic Symbolism
Diagram 29: Solar and Lunar Symbolism in Religion
Diagram 30: Jesus and Mary as Archetypes
Diagram 31: Monotheism's Triple-Triadic Archetype
Diagram 32: The Progressions of Truth

TABLES

SYNOPSES OF UNIVERSAL SYMBOLS

TECHNICAL FOREWORD

Although a separate book in its own right, *Psychology, Symbolism, and the Sacred* is one of seven planned books by this author in the 'Perspectives on the Meaning of Life' series. Accordingly, the reader may expect to see certain key discussions repeated throughout the series. Part Three of this book in particular contains materials previously covered in *The Color of Truth Volume I: Patterns in Light*. Those who have already read that book may therefore choose to skip Part Three which, to all intents and purposes is a summation of the phenomenon of the newly-discovered Triadic Archetype, as illustrated in the center section. If so inclined, new readers are invited to peruse the color-of-truth.com website as a foundation for this, and other speculative topics covered herein.

Based on materials from a PhD doctoral dissertation, this work was primarily designed for the academic sphere. Certain specialist terms may therefore be unfamiliar to the lay reader. Accordingly this 2nd 2007 Edition includes a running glossary and chapter sub-titles for ease of reference. Selected discussions have also been updated from the 2004 edition, most notably the inclusion of Chapter Thirteen: A Triadic Social Theory.

As to the content; it is important to emphasise that this is a scientific work inasmuch as it advocates a *'radical empiricism'* [1](please see footnote) and as such is primarily concerned with the facts. But this is also a book about faith and beliefs. Accordingly, despite the fact (and equally *because* of the fact) that we are broaching traditionally 'unscientific' topics such as religion and the soul – this presentation will, and indeed *must* be delivered from an entirely scientific perspective. That is to say; when dealing with metaphysical concepts such as 'spirituality,' 'religious beliefs' or 'the

---

[1] "To be radical, an empiricism must neither admit into its constructions any element that is not directly experienced, nor exclude from them any element that is directly experienced." *Essays in Radical Empiricism*, by William James. P 40. Ch. 2 (1912).

conscience' for example, we will remain firmly in the 'radically-empirical' arena, drawing conclusions solely from systematic and logical observations and from the previous findings of sociologists and psychologists such as Freud, Jung, Fromm, James, Moore, Allport, Hood, Spilka and many others in their insightful work in this area.

However, any scholarly paper that presumes to address a topic as ineffable and noumenal as religion must of necessity indulge in a little philosophical and theoretical dabbling – if only to explain certain features of religious perspectives in relation to the field of science. Therefore, whilst acknowledging semantic limitations and differing opinions on the topic, but in order to avoid excessive ambiguities about what exactly is meant by the term 'religion' in this book, let us abridge the multidimensional term 'religion' to refer here to:

> The properties or attributes of any philosophically or theologically-based system of collective activity that furnishes adherents with a set of life-principles and beliefs that include metaphysical features, and / or a divine or transcendent object of devotion—as foundational life values and goals.

Although perhaps appearing to exclude certain philosophical, ethical, or ritual-based non-theistic traditions that undoubtedly carry 'religious' properties, including Buddhism, Confucianism, Taoism or Freemasonry for example; this definition will help maintain focus on the central theme of this book which, although making occasional reference to other religious traditions, is mainly concerned with the psychology and symbolism of Western Christianity, Judaism and Islam – the 'big three'.

The use of capital letters in words that refer to 'God' or 'The Great Unknown' or 'Ultimate Reality' or perceived causes and / or effects of such including 'The Way', 'The Divine', 'The Truth' or 'True' are respectfully used in this presentation in philosophical recognition of an 'Absolute Origin' or 'Source' of cosmic realities. Although this is usually the domain of theology and philosophy and therefore will not be *directly* addressed in isolation in this presentation, the fact that these concepts and definitions feature so prominently in religious thinking obviously requires that we refer to them – indeed, such references are key to a full understanding of the subject matter. Therefore, terms such as those listed above will feature more prominently in our discussion as the presentation progresses. Equally, because this book is concerned with a general vs. specific psychological approach to religion and religious behaviors; when unnamed or non-specified reference is made to 'The Church', 'the Church', or 'churches', the reader should understand this to include any or all of the world's faith traditions, religions, sects, groups or denominations, including theistic and non-theistic belief systems alike. Although such generalizations may indeed overlook the exceptions to any given rule, the reader is respectfully invited to consider the logistical limitations of presenting such a short book on such a long and involved topic.

Due to the global market, this book may be written in either American or European English. The reader is therefore kindly invited to allow for any apparent inconsistencies of spelling or grammar. In addition, wherever the text uses technical terms specific to psychology and religion 'inverted commas' and / or *italics* will be used to identify or emphasize words of ambiguous meanings or of special import. If further explanations are required, they will be footnoted to page's end and/or listed in the *Running Glossary* at the rear of the book. All direct quotes from other sources or references to other authors or sources will be marked in Arabic numerals and comprehensively noted at the end of Part Four.

Flag illustrations are courtesy of the Flags of the World (FOTW) website, and are cataloged along with tables, diagrams, and illustrations on pages vii and viii. Other diagrams included are duly referenced or are of the author's design. The symbol '♣' will be inserted followed by the number of the respective diagram in the center section. In grayscale editions the reader can access the free 16-page full-color *Diagrams and Illustrations Section* by visiting *http://color-of-truth.com* and following the respective links.

Gratitude is respectfully extended to all those whose writings or opinions are referenced in this work. Under the international 'fair rules' copyright doctrine as per *The Chicago Manual of Style* 15th Ed. 4.75-4.84, reference is duly made in the text as well as in the Bibliography at the rear of the book. In their first mention or when accompanying direct quotes, the titles of any such referenced works or websites will be written *in italics*. Apologies are offered if any references have been omitted either in error or due to absent sources. An alphabetized bibliography of sources and referenced works may be found at the back of the book.

INTRODUCTION

A lthough much of this book is investigative and critical in nature, it is also restorative and optimistic, and springs from a hopeful enthusiasm that scientific truth, when applied to problems of any type or description, will ultimately prove productive and beneficial.

This declared confidence in scientific truth should not however be interpreted as a denial of the possible existence of other truth forms – forms that have yet to be tangibly experienced, clearly understood, or translated into empirical language. Indeed, a good portion of this paper is directed towards the interpretation of such ubiquitous phenomena as mystical experiences, cultural and religious symbolism, and assorted metaphysical occurrences whose hidden truths remain in large part veiled from the speculations of the scientific mind.

Based upon the principle that increased understanding and access to truth will always benefit mankind; the methodical and tenacious pursuit of hidden knowledge and its subsequent translation into common language is an enterprise that should be honored, encouraged and applauded. Seen in this light, rational truth becomes a bridge; a connection between the known and the unknown; the natural and the supernatural; the theory and the proof – or disproof. Thus, rational truth offers a better way to a better collective future. A stable and reliable bridge-of-knowledge so-to-speak, over that seemingly bottomless chasm of ignorance and superstition that has so long haunted humanity.

But building bridges, even purely philosophical ones, is trying work. Fraught with hidden dangers, foundation work for interdisciplinary bridge-building is often slow and tentative, for a 'bridge' that is anchored in competing ideologies strengthens only with the passage of time and the march of courageous pioneers. Unfortunately, far too many choose to withdraw to familiar albeit infecund territory, rather than risk the personal challenge of discovery that accompanies the genuine quest for truth.

Arguably, this historical reluctance to foray beyond the comfort zones of our own familiar cultures is at the root of many of humanity's most persistent problems, namely ethnic, religious, and geopolitical tensions that have all but strangled humanity's collective potential. Seeped in myth and superstition, and exercising many forms of suppression and censorship over the masses, sectarian ideologies have thus given rise to some of history's most sinister social institutions. Traditionally feeding off the relative ignorance of the population; the only proven antidote to this disquieting subjugation of the human spirit has been the full and honest exposure of the facts through the illuminating light of science. Naturally, albeit regrettably, this has brought the religious world and the world of science into regular conflict, as each battles – in their own particular ways – to establish the historical authority of their respective ideologies.

Based upon new discoveries in both arenas, this book attempts to advance the bridge building process between, (i) the field of science, with its facts and data, experiments and empirical principles; and (ii) the often-opposing sphere of religion, with its mystical hypotheses, philosophies, rituals, beliefs and practices, that in combination so often stretch the human mind in two apparently different directions; the logical-factual vs. the spiritual-emotional respectively. As history testifies all too well, attempts to reconcile these two positions have been fraught with frustration, mutual suspicion, and not a little enmity, not least of all because of a historic inability – especially since Renaissance times – to envision how two (apparently) diametrically-opposed ideologies could possibly coexist harmoniously, without compromising their fundamental philosophies and principles. For indeed, each does appear to hold a different perspective on 'Truth.' On the one hand, empiricism prevails. Whilst on the other, such intangibles as revelation, mystical encounters, and religious dogma and doctrines are accepted by religious adherents with equal, if not more merit as representative of the essential 'meaning of life'. Unfortunately, especially in the Western world advocates of the two perspectives – being equally passionate about their chosen positions – regularly find themselves utterly opposed, and in the subsequent vacillating debate the diverging extremes of intellectual intransigence and religious dogmatism are fuelled and fortified, resulting in an increasingly impoverished sphere of conceptual collaboration. But as eager fingers tap out their opinions and discoveries, and insights and beliefs on millions of computers worldwide, the great unknowns that have previously fostered so many acrimonious debates are slowly but surely being exposed to the helping and healing light of self-evident, scientific truths – truths that simply bear witness unto themselves.

By first identifying, and then uncompromisingly confronting the social evils that arise out of religious excesses, this book will attempt to demonstrate how the wise and discerning application of existing scientific knowledge – in conjunction with new empirical discoveries and established religious proofs [2] – will succeed in establishing a foundational 'language' of accepted realities common to both religion and science even as they occupy apparently opposing positions in the religion-science divide.

In attempting this bridge building (or bridge developing) enterprise, there is unspoken recognition of the existence of sufficient stable territory to support the construction of bridging discussions in the first place: On the scientific side, factual evidence is witness unto itself. On the religious side, despite significant (but decreasing) scientific opinion to the contrary, the reality of the 'personal (or True) religious experience' as an observable fact is accepted – (the proofs of which will be discussed in due course). It is upon this combined scientific base, and employing recent exciting discoveries in the history and language of universal symbolism that we will begin the mutual bridging translation of religious beliefs and scientific facts.

Following in the footsteps of such giants of psychology as Sigmund Freud, Carl Gustav Jung, and William James, and with occasional reference to *The Color of Truth* series of books by this author, we will explore findings on the personal and collective unconscious, the psyche, archetypes, and noumenal realities, and re-evaluate in the light of new discoveries and scholarship how such may be applied in remedial, preventative, and developmental psychology – specifically pertaining to religion-related disorders at both the individual and collective level. Introducing a new 'psychospiritual' theory as a foundation for such work, we will pursue a marriage of corresponding truths between both science and religion – chiefly as applied to current, Western and Middle-Eastern monotheistic spheres such as in contemporary Christian, Jewish, and Muslim societies.

However, our optimism and confidence in presenting these dynamic bridging suggestions is tempered with the sober awareness that over the centuries a considerable amount of superfluous, unproductive, and destructive dross has accumulated particularly on the religious side of the

---

[2] 'Established religious proofs' refers to the accumulated scientific data on the substantial effects of religious faith; Carl G. Jung's archetypes; the existence of the conscience etc..

divide – and not only because of the improvability of many of religion's claims. This includes institutionalized corporate and political dross that currently threatens not only to obscure and even suffocate many of the virtuous founding principles of religion, but dross that simply cannot be used as any foundation for scientific bridge building. Comparable to the parallel, obstructive, and ultimately unscientific viewpoints of certain ultra-empiricists who would deny religion's very right to exist, much that is designated as 'religion' today is far from authentic and needs to be exposed as such, because nothing of true worth can fruitfully prevail upon false or insubstantial foundations. Accordingly, a good portion of Part One will be devoted to clarifying (perhaps a little audaciously) what genuine religion *is not* as well as what it is – to be accomplished of course in clear, frank, and unequivocal terms. All the while of course, acknowledging that religion at the individual level is often an intimate and very private condition that defies absolute definitions. For this reason, we will concentrate chiefly upon general-collective expressions of religious adherence and their social consequences, translating such into hypothetical individual cases only as serves our exploratory needs.

Upon this introduction we may now establish the book's main objectives: The first is to shed new light upon the nature and character of a variety of modern religion-related behaviors and psychological conditions; individual and collective; healthy and unhealthy; functional and dysfunctional; subtle and obvious – later to propose a tenable solution to the increasingly disturbing manifestations of religious obsession, addiction, and extremism that overshadow us all.

A second goal of this book is to introduce the reader to a revolutionary exposé of universal symbolism that effectively and pragmatically connects the spheres of psychology, anthropology, religion, physics, art, and political history (amongst others) – upon which base we can re-examine the fractured condition of many of these human disciplines in relation to a universal 'whole'. [3]

A third concurrent goal is to present the above evidence and observations in such a manner as to scientifically delineate and separate 'the True' (with a capital 'T') from 'the false' in religion, thus exposing the original true heart of the 'genuine religious experience' common to all traditional faiths. By doing so we will help cultivate, and ultimately balance

---

[3] The full exposition of this discovery is covered in *The Color of Truth* series by this author

the creeds of sincere believers by applying scientific knowledge specific to their tradition, personal calling, or personal beliefs.

The fourth, interconnected, and very important goal of this work is to suggest a general means of approach by which practicing psychiatrists, psychologists, therapists, social workers, counselors, teachers, mentors, ministers.. and any other inspired individuals besides, may reconnect with the very 'soul' of humanistic psychology (as-it-were) and in so doing, become the desperately needed 'true doctors of the soul' that sadly, are so few in number in so many of today's religious institutions.

In summation: By raising awareness of the *psychosomatic*[4] characteristics of religion and the moral and ethical attributes of psychology respectively, and then evaluating this information against a cohesive backdrop of universal symbolism, it is hoped that a foundation of mutually-recognizable territory can be established from where we may pursue a balanced quest for both empirical and metaphysical truths.

In this conceptual bridge-building and truth-seeking process that ultimately aims at a progressive convergence between the two fields, three main theoretical outcomes may be anticipated: Firstly; that that which is currently wanting will be (provisionally) identified. Secondly; that that which is superfluous will be exposed, and thirdly; that many existing confusions and misunderstandings will be resolved – at least theoretically and tentatively. The resulting clarity of purpose and direction in the fields of religion, sociology, and psychology will be of particular interest to those of us who continue to believe that the ultimate objective of both science and religion is to advance humanity's awareness of 'Universal Truth' – preferably in dynamic cooperation, but certainly within an atmosphere of mutual respect and understanding. In short, collaboration through education and respect, rather than confrontation through ignorance and suspicion.

And if one viewpoint must occasionally surrender to the other (as is always the case with true education), then let it occur with the grace and humility deserving of those who have made the pursuit of Truth their first and earnest goal . . . and who still have the courage to allow Truth to be her own witness.

Stephen T. Manning PhD
Autumn / Winter 2006

---

[4] Psychosomatic; the influence of the mind on the body – particularly in regards to disease

PART ONE

DIAGNOSIS AND ASSESSMENT

A provisional review of the current state of religion in Western and Middle-Eastern spheres, drawing specific attention to the individual characteristics of collective religious behaviors; both fruitful and destructive; functional and dysfunctional; and an overview of the effects of religious institutions' operational polices on their officers and members

CHAPTER ONE

A SOCIAL PATHOLOGY

*A frank and uncompromising appraisal of some of the more disturbing
aspects of institutionalized religion in our world today*

Everyone is affected by religion. Whether believer, *agnostic,*[*] *atheist* [†]
or undecided, or whether simply living in sweet oblivion of the
whole religious debate, one cannot live in the world today and not be
affected by the peaks and swells of religious opinion. No different to
primeval times when religious superstitions and beliefs shaped the social
and economic policies of ancient civilizations, modern cultures and politics
are equally permeated by religion in many shapes and forms.

Increasingly however, many forms of modern religious expression
are seen as being a blight on civilization rather than a blessing. Surely no
one will dispute the curse of radical fundamentalism; the hubristic
exploitations of authoritarian clergy; or the disempowering ignorance that
accompanies so many of our longstanding, superstition-based orthodoxies?
But despite many theoretical and political attempts to do so, mankind has
yet to successfully and substantially separate the religious and the political
world. Indeed, religion's perennial durability in relation to the historical rise
and fall of civilizations adds considerable weight to the contrary argument;
that separation from the political world is *not* the solution to any perceived
'religious problem' but rather, that a fruitful symbiotic union between
religion and politics based upon universal ethical and moral principles is the
choice of wisdom that will best serve humanity in the long run. Implied in
this argument of course, is the clear understanding that it is the *best* of both

---

[*] Agnostic; ('a'-without / 'gnösis'-knowledge) – one who accepts the *possibility* that God
exists, but believes there can be no formal proof thereof
[†] Atheist; ('a'-without / 'theos'-of God) – one who denies the existence of God(s)

worlds that should be combined. In such a union the various faith traditions would bring their accumulated human resources and social wisdom to bear, with such stridently proclaimed principles as the universal 'Golden Rule' (loving one's neighbor) forming the moral backbone of social ethics and corporate enterprise. Political science meanwhile, would provide the pragmatic structural foundations, thus grounding both religion and politics in a true and 'Godly' humanitarianism. Political enthusiasm would provide the drive, and religious virtue would supply the guidance. In other words, it would be (a) the moral fortitude and social wisdom, and (b) the noble ambitions and scientific structure of both religion and politics respectively that would be partnered in any such productive merger.

However, and speaking frankly and uncompromisingly; in viewing the recent spate of atrocities committed in the name of religious beliefs or under religious sanction or protection; anyone could justifiably conclude that popular religion is losing its virtue – if not its very reason. Despite the fact that acts of prejudice, immorality, and criminal violence have all-too-often been sanctioned by duplicitous clerics lurking insidiously in the alcoves of history, surely the current Pandora's box of sexual depravity, corporate corruption, and maniacal religious zeal that infests modern religious institutions is cause for special concern? From acts of mindless terror carried out by suicidal zealots upon unsuspecting civilians; to the plague of chronic sexual abuse perpetrated upon innocent children by trusted clerics; or even to the slick displays of overt religious piety that mask the reprehensible complacency of self-involved religious groups – any general psychological assessment of the current state of institutionalized religion must surely include a *diagnosis* [*] of at least partial gross dysfunction and compromised morality; if not downright madness. Whatever the final clinical diagnosis, the fact that institutionalized religion is suffering an unparalleled *pathogenesis* [†] is surely beyond question.

Immorality or Insanity?

Sadly, the issue of rescuing the religious world's suffocating morality comes second to the task of restoring its sanity. For without the foundation of reason, any brave efforts to restore a functioning morality are doomed to founder in the emotive confusion common to the uneducated religious mindset – a mindset historically vulnerable to prevailing superstitions and the manipulations of the wicked. Certainly, as long as religionists claim the

---

[*] Diagnosis; assessment; evaluation; critical analysis of the nature of something
[†] Pathogenesis; the development of a diseased or morbid condition

authority to designate as 'truth' that which escapes logical or scientific scrutiny, incidences of unscrupulous or delusional-based exploitation of the less well-educated are likely to continue. Indeed, it is only through appealing to reason that we may begin to separate the sheep from the wolves so-to-speak, identifying the innocent and the poorly-informed from those that would perpetrate, and seek to profit immorally from deliberate and calculated manipulations.

As we are painfully discovering today, social diseases such as the aforementioned scourges of maniacal terrorism, clerical sexual abuse, and other devious orchestrations that have arisen from the perversion of religious ideals are far from being either harmless or isolated phenomena. Selective ignorance, fear of others, suppression of 'outside' learning, guilt and superstition, and 'absolute' religious convictions; each are aberrations of the spiritual quest which, sociologically and historically speaking at least, appear designed to exploit the trusting masses.

Whether these aberrations are, (i) the products of the sincere but distorted beliefs of religionists; (ii) whether they stem from psychological disorders; or (iii), are deliberate deceptions orchestrated for evil purposes; religion thus manifested infects society with the gravest forms of social cancer. Whilst admittedly not exclusive to religious institutions, there can be no doubt that the more insidious forms of social corruption are those fashioned under the guise of holiness. The active promotion of separatist ideologies in our churches, schools, temples, and mosques only serves to fuel deep mutual suspicions – leading inevitably to increased human misery through the agencies of bigotry, prejudice, elitism and fanaticism. Like dark clouds gathering on the horizon, these ominous signs of social decay can no longer be ignored. Nor can they be treated in seclusion. Increasingly manifested on a global scale these problems cry out for urgent attention and resolution. The question is.... who is up to the task?

Well first of all, not institutionalized religion as we know it today. Because these and similar problems are now so *endemic** to, and prevalent within the field of religion that they effectively preclude religion's ability to cure itself. In the case of *paedophile†* clerics for example, the hubristic manipulations and deceptions of senior clergy who covered up these appalling crimes bears pejorative testament to the chronic preeminence of selfish personal, political and economic issues over matters of morality, ethics, or true spirituality in the higher echelons of authority in the world's

---

* Endemic; prevalent in a particular location, place, or people
† Paedophile; an adult who is sexually attracted to children

largest Christian Church.[*] Despite frantic attempts to minimize public exposure, one can be assured that the policy choices made by Bishops and Cardinals were not simple nor innocent "errors of judgment" in any way, shape or form, but were calculated decisions designed to protect the prestige of the institutionalized Church and her officers at the direct expense of their trusting victims. This included the unspoken policy of ostracizing and isolating the immediate victims of sexual abuse at the very time they most needed spiritual and emotional support. Indeed, October 2006 saw the BBC TV's exposure of a longstanding 'top secret' Vatican document known as *Crimen Sollicitationis* designed to all intents and purposes to protect the institutionalized church and her officers – paedophiles or not – at the expense of whomever or whatever challenged it. This included the obstruction of any civil authorities that tried to bring criminal priests to justice. Even more disturbing perhaps is the fact that it was the current Pope, in his role as Cardinal Ratzinger, who enforced this immoral policy for over twenty years.

So too the laity as a whole, who for decades were deliberately kept ignorant of the criminal nature of so many priests. Quoting psychiatrist M. Scott Peck's clinical definition of evil, we read; "...the use of power to destroy the spiritual growth of others for the purpose of defending and preserving the integrity of our own sick selves."[1] Even today, efforts continue within the hierarchy of the Catholic Church to undermine disclosure and accountability measures. How indeed does any church defend the use of such morally-evasive and psychologically-destructive policies against the victims of her corrupt officers? Does 'corporate survival' ever justify such actions in any organization – let alone in an institution that claims moral authority over millions? Indeed, how many founding principles can be debased, and how much decay and corruption can exist before vital integrity is lost and a religion is declared morally bankrupt? Must a religious institution that claims to be founded upon the highest moral principles and beliefs descend into utter evil before we begin to take note?

The awful phenomenon of the State-and-Church run Industrial Schools system springs to mind as yet another of the more blatant examples of clerical conspiracy and child abuse on a massive scale. Similar institutions operated in Australia and Canada for decades, but it was in Ireland – arguably *the* most integrated State-Church political system in mid twentieth century Europe – where the greatest horrors took place. Whether

---

[*] The lay-Catholic website *"Survivors First"* reports that two-thirds of U.S. Bishops have been implicated either participating in, or illegally covering up cases of clerical sexual abuse

or not virtuous officers of the system could operate in such an environment without being aware of what was going on remains debatable. But it is now clear that the most awful physical and emotional abuses were visited upon the less-fortunates of society; orphans, the poor, unmarried mothers and the mentally handicapped all suffered terribly at the hands of a brutal and inhumane system. Once again, trusted individuals; priests, nuns, police, judges and politicians – the very pillars of the community – either actively colluded in suppression of these crimes or, chose 'not to have known anything.' Although publicly displayed as models of charity and social conscience, those running these awful institutions showed little compassion or mercy to their charges, and even less remorse when confronted with their crimes. Like so many of those unnamed children's graves lying still-unclaimed amongst the ruins, dark and disturbing secrets stayed buried for decades – and continue to do so. Whatever the original intention, it was never true religion or morals that fueled these institutions. Rather inhumane exploitations and shameless profiteering on a massive scale.

And what about religious extremism, especially in its more militant forms such as we witness almost daily in atrocities supposedly committed 'in the name of God', or of Allah? In the case of religious fanaticism expressed in acts of mass murder and terrorism, who is going to argue that such devastation can ever be tolerated as acceptable or justified 'expressions of religious belief?' Whatever the source of the destructive energies that motivate this bloodthirsty insanity, surely no one will deny that if such atrocities are ever to be defined in a religious context, then most certainly, it is "religion gone mad!"

In our third opening example of what I term 'gross religious dysfunction' we noted the far more subtle but equally, if not more destructive phenomenon of pseudo, or pretentious religion. This refers to those *insalubrious* * forms of popular religion that are either so vacuous, or self-involved, that at best they are little more than cliquey social clubs – and at worst, breeding grounds for prejudice and bigotry. Using dramatic speakers or high-tech multimedia shows to captivate the spellbound audience, and replete with all the trappings and affectations of piety, high-impact religious presentations collude to stimulate the emotions, often, whilst suffocating the soul – and in the process, prevent so many from experiencing their own and each other's humanity at a profound (or should we say 'truly religious') level. In an insidious pretense that amounts to little more than religious commercialism, all the signs, symbols, and sacred

---

* Insalubrious; unwholesome; unsavory; unhealthy

rituals of genuine piety are proffered for a price – a price that also buys an untroubled conscience for another week or two. Despite their often very public religious affectations, these are the very ones who constitute Karl Menninger's "common enemy"[2] who, in the words of Norman Cousins are;

> ...those whose only concern in life is that it stay in one piece during his own lifetime... up to his hips in success... (who) not only believes in his own helplessness, but actually worships it (assuming) that there are mammoth forces at work which the individual cannot comprehend much less alter or direct. [3]

In surrounding ourselves with enough like-minded others, we thus collude to sanctify the cult of 'me' by making it a cult of 'we'. Now safely nested amongst those 'chosen' others, we indulge our sanctimonious complacency in the knowledge that there is at least some safety (or public credibility) in numbers.

Token membership of the collective thus nullifies the sense of personal responsibility and, having surrendered my conscience to the group I can now luxuriate in the conviction that I, at least, am 'saved'. It is due to such apathy, ignorance, and denial of social conscience that much that is wrong with the world prevails. No different to the man in the street who conveniently "sees nothing" and does nothing when a crime is committed, pseudo-religion thus defined offers a neatly packaged, conscience-numbing narcotic in lieu of the disquieting but ultimately rewarding genuine religious experience. Wanting the image and benefits of respectability without earning them honestly with a sincere commitment to truth, religion thus packaged is the answer to the moral coward's prayers.

Fundamentalism
Equally problematic of course are those intense forms of popular religion usually labeled 'fundamentalist', 'literalist', or 'exclusivist' and which differ from the aforementioned suicidal fanatics only inasmuch as their dogmatic beliefs haven't quite carried them into the arena of militant extremism yet. Indeed, it is just one short conceptual step from dogmatic fundamentalism to militant extremism. The social environment in the United States today for instance – (incidentally the birthplace of modern Protestant fundamentalism) – has like most Western societies, sufficient economic, political, and intellectual breadth to accommodate a broad variety of religious and political opinions *without* any particular group feeling the need to forcefully

impose its position upon others. But in societies with limited 'breadth' (as here defined) such as authoritarian cultures or in economically-depressed regions for example, strict religious devotion is often identified by the masses as the panacea for all their socio-political problems. But whether in so-called 'enlightened' or still-developing societies, the fundamentalist ideology rooted in absolutism, elitism, and sectarianism remains the same. The cycle of fear, superstition, ignorance, and finally aggression seems constant throughout, and not even the so-called civilized world is safe from its effects. For even as the threat of Islamic terrorism takes root in the minds and hearts of Middle Americans, apocalyptic ministers pander enthusiastically to their fears. Blending home-grown religious beliefs with a naïve but passionate patriotism, melodramatic 'Reverends' generate increasingly radical forms of Christian fundamentalism that may, one day become the very fulfillment of their own apocalyptic projections.

These socially-acceptable forms of religious narrow-mindedness subtly depress an individual's self esteem to the point of fostering total dependence upon 'the Church,' her officers, and/or her sacraments and symbols – in direct opposition to promoting a truly universal, or united spirituality for instance. Carrying all the hallmarks of ritualized addiction, the associated obsessive behaviors are rarely seen as dysfunctional, having been repeatedly sanctified as admirable and even 'holy' within the group paradigm. Whether ritually formalized or simply implied through the repetition of unremitting religious teachings, the constant reaffirmation either of sectarian elitism, or of the individual's worthlessness when separated from specific denominational 'grace' is not only a manipulatively-selective and misleading interpretation of holy scripture, but is often conveniently and insidiously skewed by leadership to effect maximum psychological control over a trusting or (relatively) ignorant membership.

Denominational enthusiasts often mistakenly refer to the growing popularity and prevalence of such partisan beliefs as proof of their truth and value – a belief inadvertently given support in the 1930s by psychoanalyst Carl Jung when he declared; "A creed is always the result and fruit of many minds and many centuries, purified from all the oddities, shortcomings and flaws of individual experience."[4]

Although Jung's statement was presented in specific support of his *hypothesis*[*] of a *universal, subliminal archetypal symbolism*,[†] it has often

---

[*] Hypothesis; a tentative explanation; a theory; an assumption
[†] Hypothesis that suggests we are influenced by 'unknown' phenomena in the realm of the collective unconscious

been read to imply a scientific endorsement of the infallibility of certain religious creeds based purely upon their longevity and durability, and upon the mistaken presumption that more minds equals more objectivity – equals more truth; (inasmuch as such is the result of the collective vs. individual thought process). Many scholars have since rightly criticized this viewpoint for apparently sanctioning the scientific integrity of the highly-questionable creed-making process. This includes the distinguished psychoanalyst Erich Fromm who in the 1950s, refers specifically to Jung's remarks in his work on psychoanalysis and religion where, referring indirectly to Nazi fascism he says;

> Jung seems to mean that something *objective*[*] is more valid and true than something that is merely *subjective*[†]. His criterion for the difference between subjective and objective depends on whether an idea occurs only to one individual or is established by a society. But have we not been witness ourselves of a *"folie a millions,"* of the madness of whole groups in our own age? Have we not seen that millions of people, misguided by their irrational passions, can believe in ideas which are not less delusional and irrational than the products of a single individual?

Fromm goes on to add; "..it is a sociological relativism which makes social acceptance of an idea the criterion of its validity, truth, or 'objectivity'." When we consider the mass opinion-shaping effects of religious beliefs against the historical backdrop of institutionalized religion's belligerent resistance to concede to empirical facts, or, to reverse or amend erroneous doctrines in the face of undeniable truths, then Fromm's point is clearly made.[‡] That is; that mere popular acceptance of any given ideology will never suffice as proof of its universal integrity, at least not until the general collective wisdom and moral integrity of the populace has been assured. Otherwise, we are faced with the troubling prospect of conceding the inherent values of such institutions as the Inquisition, slavery, anti-Semitism, apartheid, or even Nazism; each of which was disturbingly popular in its day – endorsed and accepted by a predominantly church-going public.

---

[*] Objective; (in this context) of the collective – [see glossary for full explanation]

[†] Subjective; (in this context) of the individual – [see glossary for full explanation]

[‡] In 1982 the Catholic Church finally acknowledged Galileo & Copernicus' findings about planetary rotation some 360 years after the Inquisition suppressed their 'heretical' findings

10

Against the damning historical evidence of the acceptance of these social aberrations in so-called 'civilized' Christian societies, perhaps it is a little less surprising to read Milton Rokeach's 1968 article on the *"Paradoxes of Religious Belief"* wherein he cites the research findings of sociologists Clifford Kirkpatrick and Gordon Allport in declaring:

> ..the devout tended to be slightly less humanitarian and had more punitive attitudes towards criminals, delinquents, prostitutes, homosexuals, and those who might seem in need of psychological counseling or psychiatric treatment.[5]

Rokeach adds:
> In my own research I have found that, on the average, those who identify themselves as belonging to a religious organization express more intolerance toward racial and ethnic groups (other than their own) than do non-believers – or even communists.[6]

Finally, from Allport's *The Nature of Prejudice (1970):* "On the average, church goers and professedly religious people have considerably more prejudice than do non-church goers and non-believers."[7]

Perhaps contemporary researchers have learnt since to couch their findings in somewhat more diplomatic language, but the naked facts remain for all to see: Religionists in general tend towards exclusive and prejudicial thinking; and although Rokeach did in fact suggest that more research was needed before forming firm conclusions, even in 1968 the data showed a direct correlation between religion and bigotry in society – and how much more virulent is it today?

Instead of being passionate truth-seekers, we have, in many cases become either apathetic conformists or obsessive, factional religious addicts. In the latter case, may have failed to recognize the remedial origins of religion and, no different to alcoholics or drug addicts, abuse their chosen spiritual 'medication' far beyond its healthy designs. This addictive mindset is not of course exclusive to religion, pervading modern society in many other narcissistic forms including individualism, commercialism, and tribalistic nationalism, but it is not to these other social forms that we turn for spiritual and moral guidance. It is established religion that consistently lays claim to a unique and exclusive expertise in matters concerning individual and social conscience.

When we relate this fact to our previous conclusions concerning the general state of institutionalized religion today, we get a highly disturbing report that if applied to just one individual client, would surely give even the most stout-hearted psychologist the heebie-jeebies. Viewing the report from a social, political, and even a providential viewpoint, the list reads like a clinical definition of social depravity: Moral corruption; murderous fanaticism; public deception; piety for sale; corporate criminality; ritualized addiction; exclusive factionalism; exploitation and abuse of the masses; religion as moral cowardice; superstition, fear, and prejudice and bigotry. With religion thus defined as our moral guide the forecast for the future of society looks bleak indeed. But what then of psychology?

The Role of Psychology
Well, the obvious implication is that somehow all these factors amount to a collective *psychopathology*[*] that will benefit from the application of remedial, preventative, or developmental psychology. This is not only the opinion of this writer, but was also implied in Rokeach's comments in his 1960 book *The Open and Closed Mind* where, in contrast to the prevailing assertions of religious institutions "that religious people have greater peace of mind" he reported the following findings concerning the connections between "mental disturbances" and religion:

> ..that people with formal religious affiliation are more anxious. Believers, compared with non-believers, complain more often of working under great tension, sleeping fitfully, and similar symptoms. On a test designed to measure manifest anxiety, believers generally scored higher than non-believers.[8]

This anxiety is (in my opinion) undoubtedly linked to the authoritarian constructs – particularly of certain mainstream *monotheistic*[†] traditions, which continue to promote the concept of the individual's utter worthlessness. Disempowered and disfranchised by such morbid beliefs yet equally captivated and enthralled by them, religionists thus afflicted exist in a constant, albeit subliminal state of anxiety and addiction, which in turn fuels the development of debilitating *neuroses*.[‡] In short, they live in a state

---

[*] Psychopathology; study of the origin and development of personality disorders
[†] Monotheistic; ('mono'-one, 'theos'-God); the doctrine or belief that there is only one God
[‡] Neurosis; any of various mental or emotional disorders arising from no apparent organic lesion, involving symptoms such as insecurity, anxiety, depression, and irrational fears

of fear, not love; and whether they are consciously aware of it or not, the 'god' that they mold from this fabric, being a product (or invention) of their fear, can do no other than continue to feed their neuroses.

Ritualizing those neuroses into acceptable social norms in the form of religious beliefs and practices may serve to temporarily contain the problem at the individual level. But in the long run, the individual neurosis can only suffer its own existence by coagulating into a socially-acceptable collective form (in this case the church) – thus providing the adherent with a perceived sense of safety and security, along with a false sense of mental and emotional well-being. Through the agency of authoritarian or exclusive religious beliefs the individual neurosis is thus fuelled, sanctified, justified, and ultimately transformed into a collective *psychosis.*[*] Dogmatic religious convictions soon replace healthy questions with false 'absolutes' and the world-at-large, now seen as being populated by hostile or heathen 'others' further justifies the continued cycle of neurosis-and-psychosis. American psychiatrist Thomas Szasz neatly summarizes the neurotic-psychotic dynamic as follows:

> Doubt is to certainty as neurosis is to psychosis. The neurotic is in doubt and has fears about persons and things; the psychotic has convictions and makes claims about them. In short, the neurotic has problems, the psychotic has solutions.[9]

Attached as we so often are to our fears and superstitions, what well-rounded neurotic would ever turn down the opportunity to be part of a larger collective; wherein one's fears are not only elevated to divine status, but where one is (conditionally) guaranteed the ultimate safety – a place in heaven!

In the case of obsessive religionists suffering from paranoia and/or delusions, the presence of 'holy' terminology and rituals surrounding their particular obsession or addiction not only allows the afflicted adherent to live in a state of denial of their condition, but what is far worse, actually gives them license (in their own minds) to play out their religious superiority complexes with devastating results on society. As recent events testify, attaching the word 'Allah' or 'Jesus' to an addictive delusion neither sanctifies, justifies, nor cures it. Instead, the cloak of ritual piety only serves

---

[*] Psychosis; A severe mental disorder, characterized by derangement of personality, loss of contact with reality, and causing deterioration of normal social functioning

to mask a festering social condition whose results are anything but holy. In the resulting fog of pseudo-religiousness the borders between reality and delusion become increasingly blurred, and our world really does become a more fearful place. 'God' and 'Truth' are reduced to mere subjective justifications for all manner of social evils. Our ethical and moral responsibilities to each other are thus displaced, ironically and tragically, by unethical and immoral so-called 'religious beliefs'.

The same dangerous brew emerges when passionate political agendas are interpreted through misaligned religious beliefs. Indeed, a great many religious doctrines are clearly psychologically skewed to effect an addictive and obsessive response – often resulting in paranoid delusions and morbid fascinations – which in turn fuel suppressive authoritarianism, fundamentalism, and militant sectarianism; and as long as such conditions persist we can be quite sure that we have not yet reached a condition of good spiritual health – let alone good mental health.

Erich Fromm addressed the role of psychoanalysis in respect to religious delusions when he said;

> To help man discern truth from falsehood in himself is the basic aim of psychoanalysis, a therapeutic method which is an empirical application of the statement, *'The Truth Shall make You Free'.*[10]

This may well be true, but the real question is; does the religious world truly want to engage in a truth-process that challenges dearly held beliefs? Longstanding religious beliefs do not often submit to logic or persuasion gracefully. Most faith traditions are generational, having been passed from parents to children as part of the family culture. Hence, inasmuch as religion has successfully fused with the local culture we may expect all manner of emotions and passions to be present in the religious debate. How for example do we begin to differentiate between the various nostalgic rememberings of family, faith and culture? How do we challenge the veracity of one aspect of our experience without implicating the others? Were all those happy Christmases just a cozy family tradition; a cultural tradition; or a religious tradition?... and should we ever conclude that the religious aspect is questionable in any way – will that not also raise other, very uncomfortable questions about family, culture, and personal identity?

In the patriotic defense of nostalgia, we have inadvertently given life and credibility to many emotive religious constructs whose only true reality lies amongst our fond rememberings and hopeful expectations. For the most part modern religious beliefs are no more than the institutionalized products of our collective fears, tinged with nostalgia and romantic myth, and endorsed by longstanding traditions – generation after generation. Above all though (with a few notable exceptions), popular mainstream religion thrives on fear: Fear of God, of the devil and hell, of sin, of evil, and of all those suspicious 'others' who are not of our own persuasion. Ultimately, we are simply reflecting our own fear of ourselves, of a terrible and incomprehensible God, and of the mysterious universe that surrounds us. Religion conveniently provides the locus and the symbol-forms that justify these fears, which in turn fuel the collective neurosis and subsequent addictive psychosis known by some as 'religious elitism'. Hence the so-called "relationship of faith" towards an authoritarian, small-minded, fear-inspiring god has little if anything to do with any Ultimate Reality, Universal Truth, or a True Loving God. In reality, such neurotic dependency upon a projected delusion is not only mentally unsound, but in the ultimate irony, also constitutes technical idolatry – the breaking of the first commandment; "Thou shall not have other gods before me" (Ex. 20:3).

The 'false god' label has of course traditionally been reserved *by* mainstream religions for 'heathen' cultures; for secular vices such as the craving for power, prestige, and possessions; or addictions to alcohol, drugs, money or sex. But what most religionists fail to recognize is when their own religion becomes just such a sinful addiction, and when their prosthetic god becomes no more than a justification for their sickness. Passion for ritual and forms, and the strident defense of dogma and doctrine become increasingly more important than any personal adherence to the founding principles of justice, truth, and mercy – arguably the very heart of the Divine. 'Faith' becomes a rationalization for partisan perspectives that may or may not embrace a variety of delusions that, anywhere outside of a church or mosque would be considered downright silly, if not also somewhat sinister. Worst of all perhaps is the fact that true mystical spirituality stands little chance of expression in an environment so driven by neurotic egos and pseudo-spiritual mythologies. Faced with the disappointments and drudgery of ordinary lives, many religionists understandably find comfort and solace in their religious beliefs, escaping into their own private fantasyland complete with private angels, saints, and personal saviors, until sooner-or-later they elevate those particular beliefs above existential reality. The sincerity of such religionists is not under question – only their disturbing willingness to put religion before people, and beliefs before experience; by worshiping religious forms and mysteries over religion's universal founding principles. *Orthodoxy*[*] before *orthopraxis*[†] in other words; religiousness before compassion.

I John 4:20 sums it up in these words; "If a man say, I love God, and hates his brother, he is a liar..." Or, in Hosea 6:6; "For I desired mercy and not sacrifice; and the knowledge of God more than burnt offerings." Love trumps religiousness every time – even in God's book (so-to-speak). Consequently, those Christians who separate and elevate their religion above the interests of their neighbors – even the heathen ones – are in breach of core Bible teachings, as of course are all religious devotees who fail to grasp the humanistic principles at the heart of their respective scriptures. For without exception, all the major faiths including Judaism, Christianity, Islam, Hinduism, Buddhism, Sikhism, Taoism and Confucianism list the aforementioned 'Golden Rule' (love your neighbor) as a founding tenet.

So, although showing great religious enthusiasm for their own chosen tradition, the true spiritual piety of those who interpret their religion either in an elitist, discriminatory, or *preternatural*[‡] manner is seriously under question. One might even be forgiven for questioning their sanity, for in a primarily sensory world, if spirituality and religion do not ultimately relate back to the psychical and physical planes, then what indeed is it all about – and why indeed are we all here? If one's religion does not relate directly to one's daily interactions with one's neighbors (meaning all of humankind of course), then clearly it contradicts that most primary of instructions to 'love one's neighbor as oneself'. This is not to discredit genuine ascetic mysticism per se, where devotees spend years – perhaps even a lifetime – in meditative states (we will discuss this later), but where is the real humanity in the formula one might ask? Are we not told that we are beings of spirit, *and* mind, *and* body... and that the body is the supposed 'temple of the Holy Spirit?' Salvation in its various forms (redemption, restoration, renewal, rebirth, the way, or nirvana) happens through the understandings and resultant *actions* of men and women in their daily lives here on Earth. Latent 'graces' may or may not be a factor in different cases but even so, authentic spiritual guides have always encouraged a living, breathing morality that is played out upon this earthly stage where people battle their own personal 'false gods' daily in spirit, mind and body.

Secular culture has always been labeled the wellspring of such 'false gods' – particularly by religionists – but why indeed should religious culture

---

[*] Orthodox; adhering to the accepted tradition
[†] Orthopraxis; the activity of putting ones faith into action
[‡] Preternatural; beyond nature; supernatural

be any different? Surely it is during any given agency's rise to popularity that temptations and vices develop and take root? As history testifies all too well, the more a religion panders to political or commercial forces the less able it is to lead morally. Expediency and integrity make very poor bedfellows. Thus, true virtue is often replaced by a surrogate spirituality that is mostly religious rites and rituals; is more preaching than practice; and more talk than truth-in-action; and before we know it, another generation of well-indoctrinated devotees set forth upon their passionate crusade to convert the world to their chosen collective psychosis. Sadly however, when devoid of the cardinal virtues of truth, love, and justice or, in the absence of a genuine spirituality, *esoteric** religious beliefs are no more than evidence of a deep psychological need to escape existential reality.

In his recent book *When Religion Becomes Evil* Dr. Charles Kimball, a respected theologian and Middle-East expert bravely summarizes the five warning signs of corruption in religion as; *"(i) Absolute Truth Claims, (ii) Blind Obedience, (iii) Establishing the 'Ideal' Time, (iv) The End Justifies Any Means, and (v) Declaring Holy War."* With just a little introspection, all of these pernicious developments can be seen as they really are without their pious disguises. All are non-virtuous, arrogant and *portentous†* constructs, and as such have no place in the genuine spiritual quest or, in the practice of genuine religion. Individual neuroses, when banded together in fraternities of ignorance, will invariably produce false prophets and false principles. Indeed the bigger it gets, the more pressing the urge for the giant collective neurosis to spend itself on the subjugation or destruction of all 'others' whose view of the world may differ from 'ours'. The founding religious principles of love, truth, and humility are thus surreptitiously displaced by fear, dogmatism, and arrogance – all masquerading as religious piety of course – and yet we wonder why our societies seem ever less like heaven, and more like hell on earth.

Thus we may affirm a clinical correlation between certain common religious attitudes, beliefs and practices, and various mental disturbances and social illnesses; and between religion and a debilitating truth-discernment deficiency, which if nothing else provides the professional basis for psychology to offer its opinions and suggestions... for obviously, all of these collective trends and tendencies are fuelled by *individual* human thoughts and minds, and as we can clearly observe, not all of those minds are functioning productively. But casting judgments is the easy part...

---

* Esoteric; intended for, or only understood by a particular group
† Portentous; ominous, threatening, foreboding, weighty; marked by a pretentious pomposity

17

Solutions and Cures

Refreshing though it might be to imagine a religious world stripped of all its perverse, destructive and illusory forms; the fact remains that we can no more 'cure' the religious world of its collective ignorance and neuroses through criticism and attack – than we can cure a private client suffering from similar psychological disabilities through castigation. As all good therapists know, the road to change is often slow and difficult, and requires a great deal of patience, wisdom and compassion on the part of the counselor. The client must first be coaxed into that place where the heart and the mind are open to trust and to learn respectively. Then and only then can the process of true education and healing begin. Compassionate understanding on the part of both healer and patient should always precede correction. In the case of the client-patient this compassion must of course also be directed towards themselves, which requires a mature and objective grasp of the problem(s). The very nature of the problem often being that of presumed religious ascendancy however; the afflicted religionist must first be reinvested with a core sense of humility and willingness to reform. Ironically, it is in the ethical application of these universal 'religious' principles of humility, spiritual rebirth, and true brotherly love that we stand the best chance of freeing the minds of society from the fear-generating indoctrinations of many contemporary religious groups.

Clearly, the time of institutionalized religion's supposed monopoly as guardians of spiritual and moral truth is drawing to a close. Sectarian doctrines ring ever-more hollow to the genuinely well-educated and the astute, and conservative clerical hierarchies are increasingly seen as spent and jaded, if not downright corrupt. The time has come for a new meritocracy of moral leadership, rooted in a truly global moral spirituality, and schooled in international ethics, sociology and psychology – to now step forwards and take the reins of moral leadership.

But to be fair, social scientists too will have their biases, prejudices, and leanings, not least amongst which is an excessive preoccupation with empirical classifications. This tendency to classify (a) reductively and (b) *phenomenologically*[*] is symptomatic of a failure or reluctance to think truly 'universally' inasmuch as it excludes certain non-empirical truth forms, and is therefore similar in many ways to the roots of sectarian thinking. Because science has traditionally been preoccupied with physical realities, fact-based categories and classification systems have emerged to identify those realities. But psychology on the other hand – (being a science of the mind) –

---

[*] Phenomenology; a realism-based system of philosophy

18

must deal with less tangible constructs and processes and therefore struggles somewhat to use existing scientific terms to encompass its data. When coupled with an understandable concern that their work may be declared "pseudoscience" or "quackery" by the scientific establishment (as with the eminent psychiatrist Carl Jung for example), one begins to understand the political dynamics – and the challenges thereof – when psychologists broach new material. Ongoing debates contest the validity of new fields such as transpersonal psychology for instance, primarily because this particular discipline explores reported instances of mystical religious experiences, New Age beliefs, social myth and superstition and so on. Where indeed does genuine science end and religious speculations begin one might ask? Hopefully, our explorations in this work will help tackle this problematic area.

Meanwhile, whilst accepting the obvious necessity of categoric boundaries in the learning, research, and therapeutic processes, social scientists need to acknowledge the natural inclination towards safety and security within social and professional groups: A tendency which in turn can foster the reinforcing of personal egos and professional paradigms, thus tuning the mind to the Loreleic[*] whisperings of prejudicial discriminations. As a result, one's profession can become for the practitioner just another (only this time empirical) pseudo-religious denomination – with many of the attitudes and excesses of dogmatic orthodoxies: (i) a well-educated elite – usually male-dominated – in positions of high authority; (ii) a belief system (only this time scientific) with more-or-less 'absolute' parameters and guidelines; and (iii) a relatively poorly-informed client-base in positions of some dependence. The same basic dynamics are in place in both religious and academic institutions as we can see. As American writer Henry Canby noted in the 1930s concerning teachers and educators; "Arrogance, pedantry, and dogmatism ...(are) the occupational diseases of those who spend their lives directing the intellects of the young".[11] The same might be said of the relationship between clergy and the needy, the naïve, and the trusting; surely a definition of the bulk of traditional churchgoers?

As for psychology, doctors and counselors too must resist the urge to control and dominate in a specialized culture where, just like religious hierarchies, professional elitism is ever present. On the other hand however, and regardless of our occupation, if our innermost aspirations lead us in the principled direction of truly being '*all* that we can be' then our professional inclinations will naturally lean towards an ethic of inclusive and

---

[*] In Germanic legend, Lorelei was a seductive female siren who lured sailors to their deaths

humanitarian expansionism, rather than an insular reinforcing of our personal-or-collective, professional, political, religious, ethnic or national identities. Because as we shall soon see, such artificial divisions – when not serving the purposes of true education – ultimately only breed strife and unhappiness. The healthier viewpoint of course is to see one's profession as a mere fragment of a greater collective whole, and to understand one's own vocation in context thereof. Sadly, it is precisely the absence of such 'holistic' thinking particularly amongst certain contemporary religions that fosters what I call this "social pathology" – this communal disease – this shared psychopathology that is at the dark heart of religious dysfunction in society today. Comprising elitism, sectarianism, absolutism, dogmatism, and other forms of antisocial behavior couched in religious language and forms, it is my sincere belief that each individual so engrossed must first acknowledge the basic facts of their condition before any promise of a cure. Obviously, this being primarily a psychological problem, it should be psychologists who take the lead in establishing a cure.

If psychologists then are to take a traditional counseling approach to the matter of chronic religious dysfunction; the subject(s) and subject matter must first be examined in context with the surrounding environment in order to make an accurate diagnosis and determine the cause of the disturbance. Those who undertake this task will of necessity be possessed of a high level of theological understanding as well as having a thorough knowledge of the religious world's structures and relational dynamics, in addition to a background in therapeutic psychology. And although this may narrow the field of potential operatives somewhat, any less preparation would be insufficient to the task – for to find a solution, one must of course truly understand the problem. Once the cause of the problem is scientifically established, the next task is to determine the appropriate response which will always, in every case, involve the dynamics of wisdom, understanding and compassion. Once again and rather ironically, chiefly 'religious' virtues.

But before we get too far ahead of ourselves, we should first take a closer look at those commonly-accepted religious behaviors that undoubtedly qualify for clinical psychological assessment, during which process hoping to assess with some measure of accuracy the personalities, characters and motivations of those types of individuals to be found at the heart of these collective forms of mental disturbance.

Of course, the million-dollar question remains; are such persons mentally disturbed *because* they are religious... Or are they *religious* because they are mentally disturbed? Either way, there is certainly plenty of material here for the courageous psychologist to tackle.

CHAPTER TWO

PSYCHOPATHIC SECTARIANISM

Wherein we extend our discussion into the workings of contemporary religion with a view to identifying and separating the 'true' from the false, and the functional from the dysfunctional, in the religious world today

In reviewing the aforementioned collective problems within contemporary religious institutions including; (i) moral and corporate corruption; (ii) murderous fanaticism; (iii) religion as moral cowardice; (iv) prejudice and bigotry; and (v) blinkered fundamentalism, we uncover one particularly disturbing common denominator that fuels these social evils in one way or another; namely, psychopathic sectarianism. Although this may seem like an overly-dramatic use of the adjective 'psychopathic,' with a dictionary definition of; "Relating to or affected with an antisocial personality disorder that is usually characterized by aggressive, perverted, criminal or amoral behavior"[1] ..we can see that the term 'psychopathic' is indeed quite appropriate to those social attitudes, conditions or institutions that manifest aggression, perversion, criminality and immorality, against other individuals or groups.

The word 'sectarianism' on the other hand is described as "the bigoted adherence to a factional viewpoint"[2] and although perhaps not wholly or directly responsible for all of the abovementioned problems, the sectarian environment certainly provides the fuel and authority for their execution. Born of a perversion of the original family ethic that provides security and unity, sectarianism uses its collective strength for destructive rather than constructive purposes. Exemplified in the political world by the use of partisan political associations that abuse unitive power to cripple an opponent's endeavors – regardless of any such opponent's motivations or potential service to the community-at-large – the same destructive principle emerges in aggressive nationalism which, by forcefully advancing national self-interests at the expense of *other* nations, is a gross perversion of true patriotism. In subtle contrast, true patriotism is manifested in an individual's *personal sacrifice* for their nation. Of course, the greater patriotic act is to be willing to sacrifice oneself for the benefit of humanity and for the world at large, such as seen in the inspiring lives of true humanists; Dr. Martin Luther King, Mohandas Gandhi or Mother Theresa for example.

These same principles also apply in religious politics and practice. The truly virtuous are those who are prepared to sacrifice their own personal desires for the sake of the common good; the community, or the Church at large. Whilst the sectarians on the other hand, are equally prepared to sacrifice just about everyone *else* to protect, or advance their own group's objectives and beliefs. It is this juvenile perception of outside 'others' either as enemies or dangerous competitors that separates the sectarians from the humanitarians at the fundamental level. Thus the 'Golden Rule' that advocates 'love of one's fellow man' in all of his unique forms is reduced to a polity of fear and suspicion. Instead of unconditional love, sectarianism promotes a narrow-minded and selective state of ignorance and, through the process of religious indoctrination also fosters an insidious denial of the essential functions of the mind or spirit, namely; universal perceptions, cognitions, growth, and personal discovery. The most sinister of religious contradictions, sectarianism is thus responsible – directly or indirectly – for spawning all manner of neurotic and psychotic phenomena; social elitism, cultural enmity, ethnic violence, and institutionalized bigotry and corruption being amongst the most prevalent forms. The natural process of intellectual discovery is usually strictly limited by creedal restraints – artificial constraints that have habitually outlawed critical opinions or 'universal-type' thinking. In such a manner, superstition, myth and legend are often declared 'truth', whilst genuine scientific truths are regularly declared heresy! By blocking true growth, knowledge and universal awareness in the individual, religious sectarianism is in essence an offense against the very soul and mind of mankind, as well as against the concept of the 'universal family'. By any clinical or academic definition, religious sectarianism thus defined is undoubtedly a social disease of mammoth proportions.

But if religious sectarianism is the disease, what then are the root causes, motivations, and projected future outcomes of such a social disease? In forming a *prognosis*,* we certainly need to consider the more sinister implications of deliberate covert objectives, as well as the individual psychological temperaments of the general religious population.

---

* Prognosis; a prediction of the probable course or outcome of a disease

22

Religious Personality Types

Whichever way we approach the issue, it first needs to be acknowledged that each of the aforementioned collective problems are not simply impersonal theoretical groupings, but are comprised of living, breathing, thinking people – and it is here that we move from collective symptoms of religious dysfunction into observing individual contributions to the same. Because interwoven into those five general classifications of 'social dysfunction' noted at the beginning of this chapter, are several overlapping categories of personality types that tend to gravitate towards one type of religion or another for a variety of personal or environmental reasons.

Over the years, several attempts have been made by sociologists and psychologists to chart the different religious character or behavior types, with the most prevalent classifications hinging upon the 1950s and 1960s 'Intrinsic' and 'Extrinsic' classifications of Allport, Ross, Hunt and King, with the later 'Quest Religion' classification added by psychologist C.D. Batson in 1993 and collectively abridged and summarized here by this author as:

- **INTRINSIC:** Unselfish, devout, committed, altruistic, faith-based, non-prejudicial
- **EXTRINSIC**: Selfish, expedient, ethnocentric, utilitarian, superficial, prejudicial
- **QUESTING**: Open-minded, non-traditional, assiduous truth-seeker, moral, ethical [3]

By way of further clarification, 'intrinsic' implies that the loyal adherent has taken the core principles of their faith tradition deeply to heart, and thus finds their religious motivations from 'deep within'. 'Extrinsic' on the other hand infers a personality type who sees religious affiliation as an extension (as opposed to a negation) of the ego or, who maintains religious involvement as a justification for various forms of self-centered, materialistic, or even militant behavior. 'Questers' as the name implies tend to reject or look beyond those aspects of traditional orthodoxies that somehow fail to address key issues in society, or human spirituality. Perhaps the 'truest' of all religiously-inclined persons, determined questers are rarely welcomed by established institutions, which usually see them as a threat.

Ironically, nearly all religious movements including the many denominational offshoots of the major traditions (Judaism, Hinduism, Buddhism, Christianity and Islam) were themselves founded by just such 'questers'. From Abraham to Zoroaster; Buddha to the Bab; Mohammad to

Martin Luther; or from Jesus to Joseph Smith. Personal foibles aside, the one thing they all had in common was a singular inspired determination to advance beyond the limited religious orthodoxies of their day. How their respective religious movements managed in many cases, to regress from their inspired beginnings into extrinsic, sectarian states will be discussed in due course. For now suffice to recognize that science had seen the need to identify differing types of modern religious approaches as much as forty years ago, even then noticing a distinction between more, or less 'genuine' forms of religious expression. Clearly, the aforementioned 'extrinsic' classification most closely aligns with our findings so far on overt sectarian tendencies. However subsequent critiques of Allport's system concluded that although very useful as a general classification system, the extrinsic-intrinsic findings were somewhat inadequate as indicators of other important features of religious behavior. What those pioneering classifications do not tell us for instance, is how prevalent a particular behavior type is in relation to others in the religious community or, what the individual motivations are for the same. It was also discovered that being either committal or non-committal towards one's faith – (a feature that helped separate extrinsic and intrinsic types) – did not necessarily parallel individual prejudice ratings, thus complicating the conclusion-finding aspect of related studies.

Another critique of Allport's system was that it did not accurately differentiate between intensity of orthodoxy and/or depth of knowledge – a concern, like the issue of prejudice, that features prominently in our discussion here on the causes of sectarianism and is therefore important data to have if one is trying to find the real roots of the sectarian mindset. In short, these insightful findings although extremely useful, do not quite get at the heart of the problem. Therefore for the purposes of this work; whilst using Allport and Batson's 'Intrinsic, Extrinsic,' and 'Quest' classifications as a primary reference, we must also adopt our own classifications of 'problematic religious behaviors' that reflect, (i) personal, (ii) collective, and (iii) environmental, causes, motivations and goals, that in combination fuel the chronic persistence of pathological sectarianism in religious societies.

We will begin our examination by identifying three overlapping classes or social groups that feature specifically or significantly in the formation, promotion and development of sectarian religion, and the partisan environments they foster. These we tentatively name here; (A) injudicious idealists, (B) facile intemperates, and (C) corporate ego-materialists – to be clarified shortly. The reader will of course excuse the necessary generalizations as we attempt to categorize what is ultimately a very complex mix of personal, social, and environmental factors.

A: Injudicious Idealists (the credulous)

This first category is loosely affiliated with the aforementioned 'intrinsic' class, and despite the fact that individuals therein may display many virtuous traits, comprises the principal demographic for why sectarianism flourishes in religion today. Simply put, that cause is *'injudicious idealism'* or 'non-discerning romanticism' or maybe even 'spiritual naiveté'. As a category, this usually comprises relatively unsophisticated people with a limited or selective religious education, who are affiliated with a given religious tradition for any number of personal or environmental reasons that revolve around their own personal circumstances.

Those circumstances may stem from cultural or traditional sources that connect the individual to a particular religion. Having a longstanding family affiliation with a specific church for instance; the 'faith of my fathers'. Or, living in a social or geographic region that precludes exposure to other faiths so that one is simply not aware of alternatives: Growing up in Islamic Saudi Arabia, or Roman Catholic Ireland, or the Protestant 'Bible belt' in the United States for instance. Or, not granting credibility to other faith traditions due to a misguided belief that they are 'in error,' and therefore need conversion or damnation – as the case may be.

Often motivated by an intense and sincere idealism, such persons tend to focus their quixotic urgings upon religious hero-objects such as the Messiah, the Buddha, the Bible or Torah, the Qur'an, mythologized saints or prophets, theological precepts, or even local or regional church leaders – as opposed to concentrating upon, and nurturing universal principles of truth and justice generally promoted (at least at source) by their respective religious traditions. In other words, local or personal-cultural concerns tend to outrank more universal ideologies. This is not to say that such are not 'good' people per se, especially in the social-moral sense, but that the order of their priorities lends itself to favoring partisan, vs. universal structures and paradigms. Whatever wonderful virtues they possess as individuals (and they often do) – come second to their denominational loyalties. Usually considering themselves of little or no intrinsic worth if separated from their church or belief systems, such persons can do little else but commit to a desperate and ultimately debilitating dependence upon their tradition's central figures and doctrinal premises. Feeling a certain sense of muted security as 'unworthy' members of an exclusive group, many live out their lives of faith vicariously, choosing to see no daylight between the human or theoretical 'objects' of their faith tradition – and the road to salvation. Many in this grouping have been raised exclusively in one particular tradition, but some may also have experienced 'conversion' or 'spiritual experiences' in some form or another. Often, such 'spiritual' experiences are mistakenly assumed by the devotee to be a mystical confirmation of the singular validity of their current religious affiliation, and in a state that may only be described as 'holy enthusiasm' they invest themselves sincerely and wholeheartedly into their religious membership.

Similar feelings of attachment are also forged through emotional and/or psychological stimuli mistaken (or interpreted) as 'spiritual' events. Believing that they are truly amongst the 'chosen people,' such persons not only surrender willingly and unquestioningly to the dictates of their church, but also actively interpret the world through their church's single-minded religious perspective, and rarely if ever consider looking elsewhere for their spiritual needs. Indeed, any such spiritual searching might be considered an act of unforgivable disloyalty – earning the erring questers the appropriate reprimands, sanctions, punishments, or even total ostracism.

At the same time however, the loyal ranks of such groups can produce 'genuine' albeit denominational saints, who invest their lives righteously and wholeheartedly in the service of others – albeit typically usually for those of their own ilk. But on the darker side, beliefs and convictions can become so strong in the mind of the adherent that *any* action becomes 'reasonable' in their defense. This is where many militant excesses take root and how dogmatism, fundamentalism, and exclusivity become integral parts of any given tradition. The Crusades and the Inquisition for instance were born of just such excesses, and similar exclusivist leanings are sadly self-evident in far too many modern religious movements. Even in the best cases, the irritating tendency of such religionists to presume a condescending authority over the 'misguided' devotees of other faith traditions never really goes away. Indeed, this sense of pious exclusivity cannot exist without the presence of un-chosen 'others' who, through their continued idolatrous practices and heretical beliefs, supply the primary justification for the necessary establishment of 'orthodox' denominations. Without such divisive orthodoxies of course, there would be no need for 'soldiers' in defense of the faith. Whether those soldiers be crusaders, evangelists, jihadists, or terrorists is secondary to the fact that they are almost invariably the unwitting puppets of religious or religio-political leaders whose motives and methods of operation are often far from holy.

Therefore; (i) partly because of their relative naiveté in matters of religion and spirituality; (ii) because they constitute the bulk of the exploited masses, and (iii) due to their steadfast but partisan idealism; this category of religious adherents that (often unwittingly) constitutes the greatest numbers of partisan religionists worldwide – we will label *'injudicious idealists'*.

B: Facile Intemperates (the apathetic)

Amongst other things the word 'facile' means intellectually lazy, superficial, and insincere. 'Intemperate' in the sense implied here alludes to a unique form of self-indulgence usually only found in the palaces of dictators and despots or; amongst those who believe they have holy license to indulge their *parochial** dispositions. The term 'facile intemperates' thus conjures up an image of a shallowly hedonistic, but potentially dangerous group of people whose attitudes and urges center chiefly around self-gratification. Often worldly-wise and holding the reins of social influence, their main reason for membership in any particular religious group is to maintain a status quo that serves their own personal, social or political ambitions.

Already alluded to in our remarks concerning pseudo-religion, this second category of religious personality-types compares in many ways to Allport's aforementioned 'extrinsic' group. These are those who would 'shop' for a convenient or self-serving religion and, having found one that meets their needs, will then nominally accept its doctrines and suppositions without any great urge to substantial verification. In contrast to the aforementioned *injudicious idealists* (A) who, because of their active and sincere involvement in their respective faith traditions can at times be exploited by the institution, *facile intemperates* (B) will suffer no such inconvenience. In this case, their church is there to serve *them* – and *not* the other way round. The primary concern is not the essential truth of a doctrine, but rather how well any particular tradition suits them, or entertains them – a sort of pick-your-own-god scenario – whereby 'God' or His ministers are evaluated against a self-centered socio-political framework, and are best advised not to make too many demands of the membership. The 'virtues' that hold this group together thus revolve around a rather grand charade between leaders and congregation, whereby each reinforces the public 'integrity' of the other – contented and secure amongst so many like-minded others. But ultimately, in regard to matters of social conscience the predominant attitude is one of selective indifference.

This insidious combination of selfishness and moral apathy thus creates a sort of non-culture that allows any underlying partisan attitudes to proliferate unchecked – both within and outside of the group. At the benign end of the scale we find a mushy sort of liberal 'religion' that is too innocuous to either offend, or change lives. At the more dangerous end of the scale however, fringe movements with political or commercial objectives can flourish under the 'holy' sanction of self-appointed prophets

---

* Parochial; narrowly restricted in scope or outlook

and pseudo-evangelists who cater to the mob just as surely as the mob caters to them. In each case, the real problem lies in the fact that the term 'religious' has been hijacked by morally-indolent self-seekers and has been applied to agencies and institutions that at very best lack fundamental morals and integrity, and at worst can be described as downright evil. Although occasionally serving as breeding grounds for more active radicals (such as the overtly 'Christian' Ku Klux Klan for instance) in comparison to the other two groupings, militant extremists and fanatics are relatively rare amongst facile intemperates, not least of all because comfort-of-conscience and collective indolence are usually the centrally governing ethic: Being a radical fundamentalist simply requires too much effort. Accordingly it is no great coincidence that we find the majority of such 'churches' in affluent communities in the developed West.

In *The Psychology of Religion* (1996), we read the following comments attributed to Robert Belah concerning the "generalized religious atmosphere" in America:

> Americans are supposed to believe without question and know enough not to think too deeply about these issues. This is a habitual religion, a mechanical religion, a convenient religion. It is a faith to which all are expected to give reverent assent, but one that will not otherwise interfere with people's personal lives. It is a religion of unthinking, automatic habit.[4]

In more benign cases the shape and form of such "habitual, mechanical, and convenient" religion is dictated purely by prevailing social whims and as such is well suited to its superficial membership. But left unsaid by Belah perhaps is the fact that whilst such persons are preoccupied with their own insular worlds, they remain mostly indifferent to moral matters of global concern. The threats presented by the growth of religious extremism born out of global economic imbalances and political oppression for example, remained a distant problem until their own private worlds were directly and drastically affected, such as with the shocking legacy of the 9/11 tragedy in New York. Suddenly, everybody in the West knew how to really pray. Suddenly too, everybody wanted to know about Islam, and terrorism, and anything else remotely associated with the attack. The sad part is that it took such an act of violence to waken up public consciousness.

Such radical extremism doesn't develop in a void. It also requires the 'active' apathy of the silent masses – the collusion of the unconcerned. When disinterested and privileged communities place personal comforts before universal moral principles, the conditions that give rise to radical religious militancy are inevitably born.

In relation to the development of sectarianism; this grouping (B), being more concerned with their own personal issues are therefore less likely to be collectively driven than their more manageable counterparts (A), inasmuch as the trite institutions that they tend to be drawn to must cater first and foremost to that which motivates their prospective clientele. Indeed, it is in the collusion between leaders and membership to satisfy *and* sanctify their collective selfishness that the germs of a sort-of elitist sectarianism are bred. But this is a materialistic form of sectarianism whose only 'ideals' are those that protect the shallow interests of the group. All the same, this self-centered type of religion can still foster strong loyalties amongst those who come to rely upon the structure of the group for a sense of social identity; for social or political networking; for emotional or financial support, or for other opportunities for personal gain. Indeed, in such cases the collective apathy towards 'outside' spiritual or moral concerns actually begins to pay dividends, inasmuch as this fortifies (by default) the insular, privileged and narcissistic structures of such communities. Due then to the self-indulgent and morally-superficial leanings of this socially-apathetic category, we will label this second, quasi-religious grouping *'facile intemperates'*.

C: Corporate Ego-Materialists (the exploiters)

This third category comprises those career religionists who stand to benefit the most personally, materially or egoistically – from sectarian divisions within religion as a whole. Here we find the cardinal immoral driving force for the deliberate propagation of sectarian religiosity. This group consists chiefly of manipulative ecclesiasts or related authority figures such as denominational educators or church-affiliated politicians, who have long since understood that their very careers depend on inter-denominational and interreligious divisions; and that subtle religious indoctrination facilitates any given church's corporate and political goals. Such ambitious goals require steady support and regular income. This is usually achieved by controlling church membership through the shrewd application of denominational dependency techniques, whilst fuelling factional fear and suspicion of 'the opposition' – such opposition usually comprising other religious or socio-political groups who are *obviously* in league with the devil by virtue of the simple fact that they are *not* 'with us'!

Needing at all costs to protect their power, prestige, and possessions (the three pernicious 'Ps'); the leaders of these groups are totally dependant upon either a well-pandered membership (B facile intemperates), or more

29

commonly a subtly-exploited, credulous and suppressed membership that comprises well-intentioned but theologically unsophisticated and/or idealistic individuals (A injudicious idealists). Hence the greater part of this (C) group's 'vocations' are spent not in areas of true ministry, but instead, ensuring the continued loyalty of the membership and the defense of the institution that provides them a comfortable and prestigious career.

In contrast to certain fundamentalist clerics who may in fact be acting out of a sincere but misguided ideology, these ego-materialists ('C') are fully aware that they are deceiving and manipulating their wards. Without doubt, the primary blame for the proliferation of sectarian religion lies squarely and accusingly at their feet. Because these ambitious clerics and their associates, (i) manage their churches, temples, mosques and synagogues more as sovereign businesses than as social ministries; and (ii) because they place their own selfish and material concerns before ethical, moral, or even 'spiritual' issues – this third category may justly be labeled *'corporate ego-materialists'*.

In summary, and remembering that we are specifically concerned with distinguishing the root *causes* of psychopathic sectarianism, we can now identify three hypothetical personality-groupings associated with the growth of sectarianism in religious circles. Loosely defined as 'the credulous' (A), 'the apathetic' (B), and 'the exploiters' (C) respectively. Remembering that we are dealing specifically with the causes of religious sectarianism as opposed to simple demographic variances, we should perhaps acknowledge that there are of course many good and noble reasons for discrete religious communities to develop independently and sustain themselves emotionally and materially, which are *not* necessarily part of this greater sectarian problem. For instance, simple ethnic, cultural or traditional loyalties, or geographic or other demographic influences, or even the magnetic draw of a genuinely inspired pastor.

We should also be aware that individuals in any given religious community might harbor or display any combination of the aforementioned features (A, B, or C) at different levels and intensities of expression that may, or may not be characterized by the same excesses or deficiencies in the community as a whole. Except in extremely rare cases – such as in obscure or radical cults – it is highly unlikely that any given religious community could be described in such general, but definitive terms. As always, there is a great danger in making generalizations, but in this case perhaps there is an even greater danger in avoiding making them? Apathy, as much as immoral activity is responsible for the presence of evil in our world. As the old saying goes, "All it takes for evil to prevail is for good men to do nothing."

The issue of sincerity should also be reemphasized, for indeed there are many religionists (both clergy and laity alike) who serve as unwitting promoters of sectarianism in the sincere belief that they are truly serving God. But as mentioned in Chapter One, in such cases it is their wisdom and judgment, and not their sincerity that is under question. But sincere errors are still errors all the same. Exclusive religious attitudes in any shape or form contradict the universal, and therefore all-inclusive 'love-thy-neighbor' ethic which is – and according to the major faith traditions always will be – at the root of true spirituality. Therefore any religious institution, group, or individual who does not advocate and actively pursue a truly universal quest for an all-inclusive global spirituality can be declared fundamentally deficient. One could even argue that because of their sectarian leanings any such religious agents or agencies are in fact *inimical* *of true religion.

To summarize: Our observations so far have presented us with three broad, overlapping and interconnected explanations for the existence of sectarian-based problems in religion today that by and large equate to; (i) environmental causes; (ii) personal motivations; and (iii) material or corporate objectives, that in turn equate respectively to: (A) *well-intentioned ignorance*; (B) *selfish convenience*, and; (C) *materialistic motivations....* hardly the most noble of foundations for any religious ideology. Consider for instance if someone were to register these character traits on a vocational resume, one wonders indeed how many job offers they would receive? Which in turn begs the question: How then do institutions that foster these vices grow to positions of such public importance and popularity – especially in modern, supposedly-enlightened, and even democratic nations?

Authoritarian and Humanistic Religion
One reason given by psychologist Erich Fromm draws an interesting distinction between those whose psychological makeup inclines them towards disempowerment vs. those on the true journey to self-actualization. Introducing us to the 'authoritarian' and 'humanistic' approaches to religion, Fromm argues very convincingly that the surrender of ones (God-given?) individuality in return for a sense of dependent, albeit disabling security, is commonplace amongst religious adherents. Worthy of particular attention perhaps is his observation that despite their modern authoritative structures, most of the world's religions actually originated in humanistic principles.

In this first quote, we can see that authoritarian religions are fundamentally compatible with the sectarian mindset:

---

* Inimical; injurious or harmful to; adverse; hostile

31

The essential element in authoritarian religion and in the authoritarian religious experience is the surrender to a power transcending man. The main virtue of this type of religion is obedience; its cardinal sin is disobedience. Just as the deity is conceived as omnipotent or omniscient, man is conceived as being powerless and insignificant. Only as he can gain grace or help from the deity by complete surrender can he feel strength. Submission to a powerful authority is one of the avenues by which man escapes from his feeling of aloneness and limitation. In the act of surrender he loses his independence and integrity as an individual but he gains the feeling of being protected by an awe-inspiring power of which, as it were, he becomes a part.

Speaking of the humanistic approach, Fromm compares it to "early Buddhism, Taoism, the teachings of Isaiah, Jesus, Socrates, Spinoza, certain trends in the Jewish and Christian religions (particularly mysticism), and the religion of Reason of the French Revolution." Fromm summarizes the humanistic religious approach as follows:

(Humanistic religion)…is centered around man and his strength. Man must develop his power of reason in order to understand himself, his relationship to his fellow men and his position in the universe. He must recognize the truth, both with regard to his limitations and his potentialities. He must develop his powers of love for others as well as for himself and experience the solidarity of all living beings. He must have principles and norms to guide him in this aim. Religious experience in this kind of religion is the experience of the All, based on one's relatedness to the world as it is grasped with thought and with love. Man's aim in humanistic religion is to achieve the greatest strength, not the greatest powerlessness; virtue is self-realization, not obedience. Faith is certainty of conviction based upon one's experience of thought and feeling, not assent to propositions on credit of the proposer. The prevailing mood is that of joy, while the prevailing mood in authoritarian religion is that of sorrow and of guilt. Inasmuch as humanistic religions are theistic, God is a symbol of *man's own powers* which he tries to realize in his life, and is not a symbol of force and domination, having *power over man*.

Based upon this informed comparison, it is intriguing to note that Christ himself would apparently have been more at home with the Renaissance humanists that with those ignominious religious institutions that even today, continue to propagate authoritarian traditions so audaciously in his name. When considered in context of the modern sectarian dynamic, we can see that all those environmental aspects of religion that foster and reinforce a neurotic ego are present in the authoritarian model. Whilst to the contrary, the humanistic ethic (as here defined) encourages a bold (God-centered?) individuality that by its very existence, challenges the authoritarian principle of abject surrender. It is not mere coincidence that the two most enthusiastic progenitors of authoritarianism in religion – namely Roman Catholicism and Islam – maintain an aggressive 'Index' of prohibited works on the basis of orthodoxy whilst at the same time proselytizing their own often-unqualified views indiscriminately.[*] Historical manuscripts that allude unfavorably to the convoluted fabrications of dogmatic religionists have thus been denied to those who probably most needed to read them – a trend that continues today amongst Protestant Fundamentalists and other literalist traditions, whose fear of scientific criticism or exposure apparently outweighs their collective confidence in their own declared religious 'truths'.

This suppression of scientific scholarship reflects a tradition of gross denial insidiously masquerading as moral censorship and so-called 'religious education'. Consequently the tragic irony manifested in so many contemporary religious institutions; that of nullifying the foundational principles of their very own founders who, despite their perception as 'religious' characters were indisputably enlightened humanists all.

We are left with the disturbing realization that contemporary religions have by-and-large actually re-sacrificed their respective deities (or messiahs, or prophets, or principles) for the comfort and security of authoritarian compliance, along with the many associated prejudices. For the loyal adherent, the security of conforming to the popular norm (at the local level) eventually becomes more important than observing (or even understanding) the original universal principles of the respective founder(s). For why bother seeking for oneself when "they" (the religious authorities) already have all the answers? Indeed, why bother seeking at all if it will result in anxiety of any sort! When we further consider that authoritarian, and/or autocratic religious institutions such as Roman Catholicism, Protestant Fundamentalism, Orthodox Judaism, or radical Islam for

---

[*] Roman Catholicism is effectively a continuation of pre-Reformation Western Christianity which conducted mass suppression and censorship of competing ideologies for centuries

example, constitute the vast majority of the religious organizations in the world, with (for instance) "well over 90% of the U.S. population"[5] claiming membership of said organizations (albeit with fluctuating attendance) – this surely begs the question of whether such indulgent environments are morally or psychologically healthy for the country – or for the world at large for that matter... and if not, then what are we going to do about it?

Education or Indoctrination?

Well, education is one answer of course. But unfortunately a true, universal, and educational approach to religion is precluded at present by the fact that any internally-orchestrated educational approach to religion in the major denominations requires the active participation of the existing high-ranking clergy – ecclesiasts for the most part already long-ensconced in partisan-based authoritarian traditions, and who have a vested interest in maintaining the sectarian status quo.

Furthermore, true education (vs. indoctrination) promotes the development of independent (and therefore non-dependent) thinking, which weak, controlling, authoritarian, or corrupt leadership in any sphere has always viewed as directly threatening. In an ironic denial of the aforementioned personal characteristics and driving principles of the founders of the major religions whose urgings to "seek and find" are remarkably consistent across the board – the pioneering or heroic spirit in the contemporary religious setting is often purposefully and callously suppressed by the sectarian ethic – albeit by shrewd and subtle means. Seeking the unique experience of 'The Divine' or 'The Truth' or 'The Way,' as did Confucius, Socrates, Buddha, Isaiah, Jesus, Mohammad, Luther, and Spinoza (amongst many others); the ardent believer soon discovers to his or her cost that such independence of spirit is not at all welcomed in the denominational realm. Sooner or later, he or she will have to choose between the traditional comforts, convenience, and pseudo-certainty of mass-produced and spoon-fed religion or, risk the emotional and spiritual challenges of stepping out boldly upon the personal quest for truth. This is plainly and simply because the primary instruction mode of any partisan institution whose teachings are *not* self-evident *must* of necessity be orthodox and authoritative, and thus may be termed 'indoctrination'. It is a miserable coincidence that the teaching system best suited to religious instruction so readily lends itself to sectarian manipulations. Consequently, unscrupulous instructors operating under the guise of piety frequently abuse it. And although certain teaching environments may legitimately require such a proselytizing approach (e.g. when being trained in vehicle mechanics, or languages), the core subject material of genuine religion is rarely well disposed to systematic, methodical delivery. Nevertheless, religious 'education' is cleverly termed such by would-be evangelists precisely because (as they well know) there is a subtle difference between learning by direct instruction (indoctrination), and learning through the combined educational process of guidance, investigation, discovery, *and* instruction. One system *tells* you what you need to know, whilst the other leads you into discovery. One instructs and informs the brain, whilst the other employs and enlightens the mind. The first is essentially rote training as in obedience training for dogs for example, whilst the latter allows for one's full and cogent inclusion in the discovery and learning process as a unique and intelligent human being – even to the point of encouraging dissenting perspectives. Both techniques have their merits of course, and are often fruitfully combined in teaching environments. But like all tools each has a specific purpose, and there are always some activities that certain tools should simply *not* be used for. When presenting technical facts and systematic data for example, indoctrination is appropriate because indoctrination, whilst informing, also serves to inoculate against erroneous procedures in the same genre. This is fine and dandy when there is only *one* right way to do something. Putting the wheel on your car the wrong way for instance may ultimately be very 'educational' but the price of that discovery may very well be your life. It would be better to first be indoctrinated in the correct mechanical procedures and avoid unnecessarily dangerous learning situations.

When dealing with philosophical, abstract, or *metaphysical*[*] concepts however, indoctrination may be expedient but it is rarely ethical. The true and sincere study of religion requires an educational approach. When dealing with such topics the *process* of education is as least as important, if not more so, than the conclusions reached. Otherwise, how indeed do we guarantee the integrity of any of those conclusions? But instead, indoctrination side-steps the true education process and attempts to deliver absolute conclusions that cannot be challenged. And here we see the reason for the career religionist's preference for indoctrination over true education and, for labeling what is actually religious indoctrination with the title 'religious education'.

Obviously, those who label themselves religious *educators* are going to be more warmly received than those who may more honestly declare themselves *religious indoctrinators*. But why complicate the

---

[*] Metaphysical; immaterial; incorporeal; highly abstract; beyond the physical

religious question any more with belated concerns about honesty? The subtleties between the two teaching approaches are rarely discussed publicly for obvious reasons. Consequently, the ratio of indoctrinators vs. genuine educators within traditional schools of religion remains sadly disproportionate in favor of the dogmatists. It is not happenstance for example that the academic recruitment slogan of the Roman Catholic Christian Brothers for many years was "give us a child before the age of seven, and we'll give you a good Catholic"[*] Shouted all across the European continent with hardly a trace of ignominy, such a slogan could equally be applied to a wide assortment of modern, corporate, religious education policies, most notably those employed in the Muslim schools of indoctrination known as Madrasas; where young students are drilled persistently in Islamic ideology often as interpreted by fundamentalists and extremists. But the Muslims have other competition too.

Ignatius of Loyola, the founder of the scholarly Jesuit Order – the great teachers of the Roman Catholic Church since the Protestant Reformation – made the following founding statement: "We should always be prepared so as never to err to believe that what I see as white is black, if the hierarchic Church defines it thus." [6] The influence of the Jesuits in terms of their shaping of the modern Catholic paradigm is incalculable, but the question is, should Catholics really be entrusting their spiritual education to those who, against all the evidence, will swear that black is white if so directed by their superiors? Thankfully the Jesuit Order, being comprised as it is of men of intellect and learning has found itself in recent years increasingly opposed to conservative church policies, and has even gone so far as to champion the cause of 'Liberation Theology' in direct opposition to papal authority.[†] Although the Jesuits' militant actions in South America can hardly be discussed in context of their priestly vocations; their accumulated education in history, the arts, the sciences, and in philosophy has it seems finally borne its humanitarian fruit. That is, freedom from dogmatic constraint and the humanitarian courage to respond to their consciences first and foremost.

The initial command by Ignatius to his followers to place absolute confidence in the office of the papacy is an example of the historical collaboration between injudicious idealists ('A') and corporate religious institutions ('C'). But such a union presumes upon a condition of relative

---

[*] The Christian Brothers; founded in France in 1684 as a lay-Catholic educational order, have recently been vilified in the international press for decades of abuse of minors in their care
[†] Jesuit priests have actively supported armed rebellion in the cause of humanitarian justice

ignorance and naïveté. Nearly five hundred years on, one would be hard pressed to find a Jesuit priest who still fits the profile of an 'injudicious idealist'. Ignatius' incongruous instruction to 'blind obedience' has at last finally and rightfully succumbed to the ethics of the well-informed conscience when facing issues of moral gravity and social concern.

We can see therefore that the term 'religious education', when applied in the context of sectarian religious institutions is at best a misnomer; at worst a deliberate deception; and in any case is erroneous and *solecistic.** Even in those cases where there is no *deliberate* misuse of religious propaganda for materialistic reasons, the erosion of religion's noble founding principles is compounded by the posting of poorly educated (or selectively educated) and marginally-trained religious officers – yet another hallmark of authoritarianism. Because of dwindling vocations, this disturbing trend has increased rather than decreased in recent decades as religious corporations struggle to staff their organizations. Such 'ministers' frequently have little or no idea of the psychological impact of religion on their wards, neither of the spiritual (or psychological) needs of their community; nor of their own responsibilities thereof; and indeed, may not even have had a genuine personal religious experience themselves.

Drawn to positions of ministry for many 'less-than-saintly' motivations (to be reviewed shortly) many such ministers are intellectually and psychologically ill-equipped for any position of leadership – whether secular or religious. But because the recruitment process is generally geared towards identifying credulous-submissive 'A'-type prospects, many are 'chosen' simply because of their acquiescence or obedience or, for their PR or fundraising skills, and therefore function as little more than passive and compliant low-level administrators or salesmen: Obsequious *sycophants*[†] in the service of multilevel religious corporations in other words. As a result, public access to the essential core values of the religious life is further obscured not only by these arguably 'unqualified' clerics, but also because of the aforementioned underlying impulses of so many high-ranking ecclesiasts towards materialistic and selfish ends – not so surprising in what has surely become one of the world's largest (if not *the* largest) most influential, and profitable business.

Considering then the requisite orthodox conservatism of existing religious leaders; expecting them to adopt a truly educational approach to their ministries is doubtless an over-ambitious expectation. Indeed, one may

---

* Solecistic; an impropriety, a mistake, a misnomer
[†] Sycophant; a toady; a flatterer; one who grovels, or butters-up to their superiors

solidly conclude that those who achieve high positions of authority in sectarian religious institutions have done so precisely *because of* their blind orthodoxy and corporate obedience. And whilst we may honor the implied virtues of submission and conformity to an established tradition – we must also candidly acknowledge that neither of these traits (when expressed in a denominational setting) has ever featured amongst the founding principles of a true and objective education.

It has always been pioneering enquiries rather than orthodox conservatism that has facilitated true human enlightenment and growth. But as we have seen, pioneering enquiries are simply not part of the authoritarian agenda. Based upon personal experiences or revelation, many sincere scholars of the various religions who were gifted with great insight and spiritual tenacity have been censured, discredited, excommunicated and even put to death for assuming the inspired roles of prophets, sages, and spiritual leaders. From the mystic sects of early Christianity to visionaries like Joan of Arc; or from Nicolai Copernicus, Jan Hus, Galileo, and Martin Luther of Reformation times; to modern Catholic theologians and scholars such as Dr. Matthew Fox, Father Tissa Balasuriya of Sri Lanka, or famed Jesuit mystic and philosopher Anthony de Mello whose popular books were recently banned by the Vatican.[7] Each in turn followed the dictates of their consciences no doubt expecting their sincerity to be ratified by the institution to which they had so loyally given their all. Unfortunately, each would find to their cost that true enlightenment, whether secular or spiritual, is the nemesis of suppressive religious authoritarianism.

Of course, the same dynamics are at play in the world's other authoritarian religions, most notably amongst the aforementioned 'big three' monotheistic traditions; Judaism, Christianity, and Islam. But the problems don't stop with mere censorship. I would argue that the single greatest problem that fuels sectarian thinking within these particular religions is their shared, psychologically-divisive theologies. We cannot go into too much detail here today, but the final chapter of *The Color of Truth Volume I* exposes the historical problem of dualistic thinking that centers on a 'good vs. evil', 'God vs. Satan', and 'secular vs. the sacred' model, as being a major cause for psychopathic sectarianism amongst religionists today. In brief, this is the mindset that allows any particular group to align themselves with the 'good' side in order to project absolute evil onto the 'bad' side – which of course, then justifies destroying them! In the case of religious communities the 'bad' side is usually any other religion, ideology or scientific theory that challenges the orthodoxy of the group. Whenever inspired individuals rise to challenge the host group's authority (such as the

Reformation's Martin Luther for instance), they have usually found themselves demonized and castigated – in spite of the objective quality of their arguments, their previous service to the group, or their own personal integrity. Many good and wise souls have thus suffered terrible injustices at the hands of their own religious leaders, simply, sadly, and ironically because they were invested with the very same 'universal spirit' that drove the founders of the various faiths to seek a higher level of truth in the first place. More understandable when the competing arguments are purely theoretical, this retentive 'closing of the ranks' when challenged by outside thought still prevails amongst more dogmatic traditions today.

This troubling 'secular vs. the sacred' and 'evil vs. good' *dichotomy* *surfaced in medieval Europe in the debate between Church-sanctioned *scholasticism*[†] and the secular philosophy known as *rational humanism*[‡] that in large part gave birth to Renaissance thinking and the eventual rejection of much suppressive religious orthodoxy. The prevailing scholastic view presupposed that Aristotelian thought, and St. Augustine's theology could be aligned with the Bible and contemporary church teachings. However, whenever there was a conflict between reason and 'revelation' the theologian always overruled the philosopher-scientist. In short, religious beliefs trumped cold logic. Eventually scholasticism foundered when the Christian Church could no longer suppress scientific truths that challenged orthodox thinking.

Sadly however scholasticism's legacy continues. Many of the catechistic tactics of medieval 'religious instruction' transmigrated to the new Christian denominations after the Protestant Reformation, and resulted in the disturbing continuance of religion's most endemic problem, namely; the process of allocating the most important and influential teaching-and-guidance posts to the very people most unsuited to be true educators, that is; the indoctrinators – the ecclesiastical company men. Nearly five centuries later, selective or exclusive systems of religious indoctrination complete with their associated manipulative psychologies and suppression of 'unorthodox' or 'heretical' truths, remain not only the central defining features of denominational thinking, but are the chief instruments for the proliferation of sectarian attitudes in our world today.

---

* Dichotomy; division into two usually-contradictory parts
† Scholasticism; Christian philosophy of the Middle Ages that was based on the authority of Aristotle, the Bible, and the Latin Church Fathers
‡ Rational humanism; as the name suggests – a rational philosophy based on the humanistic belief in the innate dignity and worth of the individual

In a telling report following the pedophile scandals of the 1990s, Pope John Paul II noted the urgent need for reform in the formation of priestly vocations. Whilst his urgings to "selfless, loving service" are obviously to be commended, more noteworthy perhaps is his insistence that:

> Future priests need intellectual formation, which emphasizes an in-depth study of philosophy and theology, at all times maintaining fidelity to the teachings of the magisterium.[8]

Clearly, the preeminent concern is adherence to tradition. His statement is a definition of indoctrination, not true education. But then again, given the history of Christian dogmatics how could it be anything else? Vain theological attempts to rationalize mythic beliefs will continue until truth eventually bears witness unto herself – until which time – religious institutions must of necessity vigorously employ 'blind faith' and indoctrination as their *Machiavellian*[*] pillars of survival. The required unquestioning obedience to literalist traditions based upon inflated presumptions of divine authority is tantamount to spiritual censorship. For not only is religious indoctrination *not* education, it actively *blocks* the natural learning process by forcefully engraving the mind with defensive, (and as far as other faith communities goes) – often hostile presuppositions. As such, religious indoctrination is fundamentally anti-truthful inasmuch as it attempts to harness the natural idealism and virtuous curiosity of the young and, through subtle intimidations and other psychological manipulations, deceptively convert those energies into that which will primarily benefit the organization and her officers. Amounting to little more than intellectual and emotional slavery, religious indoctrination thus starves the mind of true knowledge, and in doing so condemns its victims to live either in an emotional fantasyland or, to live vicariously through the religious role models provided. By identifying with *their* chosen perception of God, Allah, Jehovah, Yahweh, Ultimate Reality (or whatever the case may be), and infused with supreme confidence in the exclusive authority of their own clergy, well-indoctrinated adherents are capable of the most illogical and socially-destructive psychoses.

The same results occur when the absolute object of faith is the Torah, the Bible, or the Qur'an; or any similar utter belief in any particular person, doctrine, creed or article of faith. Associated religious habits,

---

[*] Machiavellian; suggestive of political expediency, deceit, moral indifference, or cunning. Named for the political writings of Niccoló Machiavelli (1469-1527), esp. *The Prince* (1514)

traditions, beliefs and addictions, soon fuse into a highly emotive 'life-of-faith' that possesses the individual mind permeating family, society and culture. Sometimes unwittingly perhaps the blind thus baptize the blind, and the collective psychosis multiplies. The more absolute and fundamental the belief the more likelihood that; (i) personal education has been arrested; (ii) delusional thinking is present; (iii) addictive tendencies are developing; and (iv) that a preponderance to extreme or fanatical behavior will emerge. None of which have ever been remotely associated with true spiritual growth.

In Conclusion...

Thus we observe several ways in which any given religious institution suffers ethical and moral compromises in direct proportion to its collaborative advance into 'worldliness' or authoritarianism; adopting political, economic, educational or social policies that run contrary to the original spiritual-humanistic principles upon which it was, in most cases, founded. Healthy growth in any family – even the historical family of man – is a process that *encourages* development of individual wisdom and personal fulfillment to better serve the *universal,* and therefore *not* partisan, whole. On the other hand, disempowering individuals through subtle authoritarian indoctrinations may be very profitable for the organization, but is not by any definition either moral or spiritual, and only serves to reinforce a debilitating dependency upon sectarian institutions and authority figures.

Such callous subjugation, usually achieved in the first place by a selective suppression of (universal) truths, constitutes no less than an insidious attempt to deny the rights of the individual spirit. But the spirit (or psyche) as the essential core of the human experience simply cannot be denied. As an essential aspect of the human character, the psyche simply *must* have expression. The key issue of course is whether or not those forms of expression are ultimately actually healthy or unhealthy – either for the individual or for the community at large?

Attempts at suppression whether subtle or brutal, whether recognized or not, invariably result in psychological alienation or, the manifestation of a wide variety of individual and collective neuroses. In short; a mentally disturbed religious population. Yet despite all the warning signs and expert opinions; just like co-dependants in an abusive relationship we persist in making excuses for our dubious religious allegiances and return time and time again to the serpentine embrace of these Machiavellian institutions, believing somewhere deep down that we somehow actually 'need' their security and familiarity. Unfortunately, the pernicious roots of religious indoctrination are so intertwined into social history that few can any longer discern the wheat from the weeds so-to-speak. Inasmuch as people continue to seek solace in faith and fantasy vs. knowledge and truth, that state of social confusion will continue. Whilst integration, conversion, and/or 'rehabilitation' into any sectarian group may indeed offer the individual a passing sense of security and belonging, the plain fact is that the operational norms of such groups remain in basic denial of key universal principles and are therefore fundamentally counterfeit.

We may then summarize that the major cause of pathological sectarianism within religion is a collective ignorance (in the form of misplaced idealism), fuelled by selfish or fear-based motivations, and then sanctified by religious indoctrination in an authoritarian atmosphere. No longer able to depend on a compromised clergy to tackle these issues with forthright confidence – especially without the support of their supervisors – the task of replacing ignorance with knowledge; division with unity; and pathological sectarianism with a universal confidence in the founding principles of brotherly love, falls as always to persons of integrity, courage, wisdom and conviction, who (thank God) continue to place universal values above their own selfish concerns. A case of religious humanitarianism vs. inhumane religionism perhaps? Whatever the labels, like the great and true leaders of history, such men and women of courage and vision will invariably be altruistic-and-humanistic vs. authoritarian-and-elitist, both in their principles and in practice.

In an enlightening but surely not altogether unexpected irony, we conclude by noting that in contrast to the great majority of career religionists in established institutions, the devoted social scientists of today, with their emphasis on vocational discipline, academic knowledge, and professional integrity, more substantially reflect the founding virtues of the true (and invariably humanistic) saints, sages, and prophets of history.

With this very important point in mind, let us now take a closer look at the specific characteristics that either draw out or shape the personalities of those individuals whom we have identified as being at the heart of society's most enduring religious problems.

CHAPTER THREE

THE SACRED AND THE PROFANE

Taking a closer look at the phenomenon we call religion – specifically the difference between 'true' and 'false' religion, and the personal motivations for any given individual to become entrenched in one tradition or another

Considering the evidence so far, it seems clear that there are two very different types of religion active in our world today: Firstly, we have what I term 'true' religion that serves universal needs, principles, and purposes. Secondly, there is religion that caters to selfish human desires. At its very best, religion would be comprised only of the former but sadly, religious beliefs are – more often than not – shaped and formed out of the fears, superstitions, hopes, and desires of the narcissistic mindset. In such cases 'God' or 'Allah' or 'Ultimate Reality' – or whatever the preferred title – are simply the token names that sanctify the development of a collective egoism, resulting in the creation of self-serving, sectarian social clubs which we audaciously call 'church.' Having long since sacrificed the integrity of inspired founders for political, social, and corporate security, such religions present the potential member with an apparently 'divinely-sanctioned' environment wherein he or she may exercise the most primal form of idolatry. Namely, self-worship – albeit in a projected form. Consequently, we have an array of prominent religious institutions whose most outstanding achievement to humanity is in their ability to perpetuate systematic mass-neurosis, sophistry and self-deception on a historical scale.

Subtly couched in pious rhetoric, the ultimate goals of such religious groups are no different from their ambitious political or commercial counterparts. Contrary to religious creed or catechism, the primary objective is neither the search for truth nor even the spiritual development of the individual. It is simply to ensure the survival and proliferation of the group, church or institution. If that objective must be achieved at the expense of 'competitors' then so be it. The fact that one's competitors in the field of religion are technically also supposed to be one's 'neighbors' whom one is also divinely directed to "love unconditionally"... hasn't substantially interfered in the relentless pursuit of self-serving *geopolitical* *goals – with all the associated untenable overtones. "We are right, therefore you must be wrong. God is on our side, therefore we have the divine right to denounce, deny, or destroy you.. (brother)." Obviously, such religion is of little use to God – especially a Universal God of True Love. Although they may offer some emotional solace to neurotic or narrow-minded adherents in the short term, and feather the materialistic nests of its clergy, the eventually destiny of such religious institutions is to be dammed by wiser generations. But that will be then, and this is now.

Because we humans are *credulous*† beings, it is natural for religious and mystical traditions to flourish most pervasively amongst those communities whose scientific knowledge or socio-political awareness is either limited or suppressed. Accordingly in the centuries leading up to our modern age of high-tech communication – and especially as knowledge of the natural world increased – the level of society's psychological dependence upon religion and myth has tended to decrease in equal measure. However, from Renaissance times onwards and particularly in recent years scientific research has (perhaps inadvertently) served the dual purposes of both eliminating *and* confirming certain religious precepts. Many erroneous teachings have thankfully been exposed, but other religion-related phenomena like certain types of personal religious experiences have now been recognized by science as 'real' occurrences. The authenticity of certain mystical experiences – at least in the direct experience of the subject – is no longer being denounced by strict empiricists as 'mere superstition'. Reported in diverse religious traditions beyond social or geographical boundaries, there are simply too many parallels, and too many enormously changed lives to discount this phenomenon as anything but 'real' – at least in the radically-empirical sense as defined in the introduction, (see p ix).

---

* Geopolitical; to do with geographics, politics, demographics, and economics
† Credulous; having the capacity to believe; (and/or) disposed to believe too readily; gullible

Despite this tacit recognition by science however, these phenomena continue to defy full and rational classification. The fact that neither religion nor science respectively can fully explain, nor completely dismiss these 'real' albeit paranormal events furnishes us with a prime opportunity to establish some common ground between these traditionally-differing schools of thought. Psychology in particular, and especially those areas that deal with religion-related phenomena shows the greatest promise in bridging what has traditionally been seen as an unapproachable objective – the eventual fusion of science and religion in a shared *ontology.** If only we can separate that which is 'true' in religion from that which is not, then perhaps the world's faith traditions can yet reform their institutions to reflect once again, those original and universal truths that each was founded upon.

Our focus in this chapter then will be on identifying what I term the True religious experience (with a capital 'T') as distinct from false, pseudo, self-induced, psychotic, quasi or *psychotomimetic†* religious experiences. This will involve cataloging the virtuous features indicative of affiliation with True religious experiences (soon to be explained), as well as listing other 'less-than-virtuous' personality traits and behavior types all-too-commonly associated with religious affiliation. Hopefully, this will help clear the way for our subsequent discussion concerning religion's productive essentials.

But before we move on, perhaps it should be reemphasized once again that the express purpose of this book is to *tackle* religious dysfunction – not to pander to it. Specifically, we will emphasize those features and traits that continue to contribute to the collective geopolitical problems discussed in Chapter Two; moral corruption; corporate primacy; murderous fanaticism; immoral exploitations; radical fundamentalism; well-intentioned ignorance; selfish convenience; materialistic motivations; pseudo-religion; prejudice and bigotry; hypocrisy; and finally – psychopathic sectarianism.

Social Benefits of Religion

Having already expounded at some length upon the collective evils of religion, and in order to help avert the inevitable accusations of anti-religious bias in this work, let us begin our discussion by counterbalancing the books somewhat with a brief summary of those features of religious institutions and thought that have generally been recognized as productive and fruitful contributions to society – even by the critics. These points are

---

* Ontology; the branch of metaphysics that deals with the nature of being
† Psychotomimetic; tending to induce hallucinations, delusions, or other psychotic symptoms

made in respectful acknowledgement not only of the historical good that the various religions have achieved, but also in recognition of the continuing potential of religion – when functioning virtuously of course – to play a central role in the remedial cleansing of social pathologies.

Traditionally, religious institutions have:

- Provided a place of hope
- Supported altruistic enterprises
- Accommodated idealistic theories
- Balanced secular and political excesses
- Helped the poor, the needy, the destitute
- Fostered community growth and stability
- Provided answers to "The Great Unknown"
- Traditionally championed social and moral values
- Provided role models and heroes such as saints etc.
- Been an expression of family and cultural tradition
- Provided a sense of security in fearful circumstances
- Been a major center and instrument of classical education
- Provided a locus where one may develop a sense of 'the sacred'

In addition to these generally positive functions of religious institutions, religion nurtures, accommodates, and supports the whole gamut of humanity's needs, wants and desires in many ways. Although this may have both positive and negative implications (as we have seen), the historical importance of religion to society cannot, and should not be underrated. Not unlike a massive extended family, religion links cultures and civilizations – a living organism if you like, that stretches not only into the past and the future, but equally from the known to the unknown; from fear to expectation; from insecurity to security; and from despair to hope. Thus, religion has undoubtedly served a crucially important sociological and psychological purpose. But aside from religious teachers offering moral and ethical guidance, and religious organizations being a locus for charitable enterprises, religious thought has served perhaps the more important function of filling-in-the-gaps as it were, between that which we know and understand, and that which we do not. For whenever we are faced with the unknown we invariably project either our hopes, or our fears into that void. Understandably religion, like many other human institutions is often a mix of the two (both fear and hope), but at the end of the day religion, probably more than any other social institution still offers a widespread hope in the face of the unknown. As such religion has always, even in its most primitive or barbaric forms, furnished human beings with some of the most essential psychological tools to cope with the unpredictable challenges of life.

But these listed attributes only speak to religion as an inevitable social development that serves the communal needs of individuals and communities alike, and does not therefore account for the numerous specific instances of paranormal happenings that often drive individual religious beliefs in the first place – yet are so difficult to explain scientifically. As a pragmatic work, we will not be descending into the convoluted arena of religious beliefs and subjective opinions other than to disambiguate certain religious claims. Nor indeed can we afford to give credence to unverifiable claims of paranormal happenings. But as we continue our search for whatever 'trueness' exists beneath the social ills that infect religious institutions, we would be remiss if we did not thoroughly evaluate the phenomena of the 'genuine,' or 'mystical' religious experience encountered by so many in a personal, intimate, and life-changing manner.

In his work entitled *Mysticism and Philosophy (1960)* W.T. Stace neatly describes this phenomenon as;

> ..a universal experience that is essentially identical in phenomenological terms, despite wide variations in ideological interpretation of the experience.[1]

In other words a metaphysical, personal experience common to all religions and cultures throughout history, even to be found in many non-religious settings; only interpreted in different ways. Experiences that not only transform the lives of affected individuals but, through their effects, can also change the course of history. Where does *that* experience come from – and why? What is the origin, purpose, or cause of these incidences of so-called 'spiritual enlightenment'? What exactly are these apparently *extraneous*[*] manifestations whose power and effect is such that even second-or-third-hand accounts can elicit religious conversions from the uninitiated?

The True Religious Experience

Well, contrary to the views of many pragmatists who are understandably very frustrated with the many, varied, and often contradictory claims of the religious world, this writer agrees with scholars such as Carl Gustav Jung, William James, Erich Fromm, Carl Rogers, and Abraham Maslow amongst many others, who recognize that bona fide life-altering religious experiences

---

[*] Extraneous; (in context here) coming from the outside; extrinsic

have occurred, and continue to occur to many individuals, and remain at the true heart of man's historical preoccupation with religion. The real difficulty of course comes when we try to explain them.

Like W.T. Stace, the Tantric scholar Blofeld noted in the 70s that although often interpreted subjectively, "Confirmation of the genuineness of mystical experience is to be found in the high degree of unanimity observable in the attempts to describe its nature." [2] Indeed, speaking from firsthand experience this author can confirm the existence of the True religious experience as a phenomenon that; (i) originates in an 'other-than-conscious' place; (ii) arrives (in the first instance at least) as an 'unanticipated arousal of the emotions', and (iii), has measurable long-term effects, either physiological or psychological (or both) upon the visited subject. Sometimes described as 'an epiphany' or a 'peak experience' that can occur apart from the formal religious environment, the interpretation by the visited subject that something 'external' or extraneous to their consciousness has been accessed is commonplace. This sense of 'external visitation' separates the True religious experience (in the context of this work) from a wide range of *endogenous*[*] happenings that could loosely be called 'religious' but which in fact (as the term endogenous implies), are more likely a product of an overactive imagination or religious hysteria in some form or other. Indeed, unscrupulous religionists are not beyond claiming mystical visitations in an attempt to validate their own beliefs or excesses – or to achieve some measure of notoriety. But this is where we find what separates what I term the True religious experience (with a capital 'T') from all other religion-related experiences or manifestations. For although the enigmatic True religious experience as here defined remains a compelling, if yet mystical testament to the virtuous potential of religious practice – the most common unifying feature throughout is its extraneousness. It happens *to* the subject. It is not something that can be conjured up at will. For this reason, the central defining feature of the True (or genuine) religious experience as referred to in this work will be the proof (or at least the indication) of an 'other-than-conscious' or extraneous origin.

Extraneous Origins

Sometimes referred to as an encounter with the Divine or 'the call', the True or genuine religious experience (TRE) has the uniformed effect of profound and positive changes in the life of the subject – although not necessarily permanent ones. Originating 'outside' of the subject's consciousness, but

---

[*] Endogenous; originating, produced or growing from within

accessed by, or penetrating into, or intruding upon it in some form or other, the genuine religious experience is first *consciously* manifested in the subject as a reaction or response to unknown and/or unanticipated stimuli. Often accompanied by; (a) sensations of bliss and fearlessness, (b) the inexplicable presence of previously un-displayed wisdom, and/or (c) other 'spiritual' gifts such as healing or clairvoyance, the results of such visitations bear testament to the reality of something *real and substantial* happening during these encounters that is outside of normal parameters. Although often (but not always) escaping the exacting empirical standards of definitive science, simple observation of the consequences of these apparent 'visitations' upon subjects including the immediate resolution of neuroses and other personality disorders, supplies sufficient proof for the acceptance of these events by most social scientists.

Arguably related to more common emotions such as falling in love, or other obsessive preoccupations of one sort or another, TRE's as defined in this work may indeed contain similar joyful symptoms. But in the case of the True religious experience the associated joyful feelings are symptoms that have unexpectedly 'arrived' – unattached to any conscious object – rather than being generated from within the individual by a conscious ego-based fixation with another person, thing, idea or religious belief. But of course, this does not prevent the later interpretation (or misinterpretation) of the event by the individual through their own particular religious paradigms.

Identifying the Origin
Considerable scientific effort has already gone into differentiating between those religious experiences that range at one end of the ego-continuum, including simple emotions, sensations, and sentiments associated with normal religious practice; to reports of paranormal visitations whilst the subject is in an apparently semi-conscious state. Cases such as the miraculous apparitions of the Holy Virgin at Lourdes, France in 1858; or at Fatima in Portugal in 1917 for instance.

In attempting to identify the locus of these happenings in the human subject, science has tentatively linked the religious notions of spirit and soul, to Freudian 'superego' and 'psyche' concepts, as well as incorporating Carl Gustav Jung's findings on the *collective unconscious** (see ♣ 1). This has provided science with a more familiar environment from where to explore

---

* Collective unconscious; in Jungian psychology, a part of the unconscious mind, shared by a society, a people, or all humankind. The product of ancestral experience, it contains concepts of science, religion, and morality, for example

49

religious phenomena. As a result, and based upon these more pragmatic interpretations of 'the spirit' or 'the soul' psychological research has since confirmed the veracity of the more private 'mystical' or 'peak experience' as a real, albeit still technically-indefinable phenomenon associated both with the religious environment and with supra, or sub-consciousness. But the debate continues as to the true origin or cause of these phenomena. For example; are these events caused by biophysical occurrences such as chemical reactions in the brain, a stimulus from the realm of the deep unconscious or, some other completely external, metaphysical, or supernatural cause (such as God, the spirit world etc)?

In the meantime, whilst science continues to search for an answer, those who have had the experience themselves remain in no doubt whatsoever that they have been 'touched from beyond' as-it-were. Indeed, it is the inexplicable results of such experiences upon the subject that prompts the continued efforts of science to unravel the mystery. Rather disturbingly however, religious theorists remain content in most cases to simply declare these happenings "mysteries of faith." Ambiguous, non-empirical terms such as 'grace' and 'heavenly visitations' abound, and the debate is thus drawn into the emotive labyrinth of subjective beliefs and opinions.

Considering the traditional difficulties of carrying out physical research upon metaphysical subject material, perhaps a better approach to identifying the true nature of TRE's is to use science and psychology to eliminate those aspects of modern religion that we can clearly identify as pathological; as well as any social and geopolitical aspects. Let's first get rid of the stuff that we know isn't truly 'holy' in other words. Then, as we advance along the process of elimination drawing ever closer to the psycho-social kernel of religious practice as-it-were, we should predictably approach what is indeed truly 'spiritual' – at least in the context of our definition of TRE's. Hopefully, this is how we will draw closer to isolating and identifying the origins, meanings, and purpose(s) of True religious experiences, and how they fit into our modern societies.

Synthetic Religious Experiences
Whilst acknowledging that any encounter or occurrence in life could be subjectively interpreted as 'a religious experience' depending purely upon one's faith perspective and personal opinions, naturally we must draw a definitive line somewhere in the interests of clarity. Therefore, in contrast to the aforementioned True religious experience, whose central identifying feature is its origins in an 'other-than-conscious' place, we will now identify a broad band of endogenous religious episodes that we term 'synthetic'; not

necessarily because they are artificial or contrived, although that may indeed be the case, but we use the term 'synthetic' in order to draw a sharp contrast between TREs and those many other religion-related happenings that can be shown to originate in the constructs of the active consciousness. In this sense therefore, the term 'synthetic' does not *necessarily* imply a value judgment of those whose lives of faith include these types of experiences, but it does recognize the superior qualities associated with TRE's. In short, it is a relative comparison: TRE's are consistently beneficial, whilst many other religion-related events and beliefs that can be traced to subjective human origins are often counterfeit and/or harmful – either to the individual or to society at large. In short, TRE's when properly identified, have a universal consistency and integrity that can be relied upon. Endogenous religious experiences on the other hand, whilst occasionally producing positive results cannot by definition, claim *transcendental** status. The latter can be accounted for either as phenomena or non-phenomena (as the case may be) that stem from either; (a) personal-subjective causes, (b) environmental influences, or (c) any of a range of psychologically-based religious expressions that may be considered either healthy or unhealthy.

Environmental and Subjective Causes

Human personalities can be said to be formed by the amalgamation of three main forces; (i) our psychobiological genes, (ii) the environment(s) in which we were raised, and (iii) the personal choices we make throughout life. In other words each of us are the psychobiological product of our ancestral genetics (i), who then grows up in some sort of community (ii), and is constantly affected by whatever personal choices we make throughout life (iii). We will deal with this topic in more detail in Chapter Thirteen, but enough for now to use these admittedly general categories to center our discussion around the main causes of endogenous (or 'synthetic') religious experiences.

With the understanding that none of us are born with 'perfect' genes (i), and are therefore prone to all manner of physical and emotional stresses – especially in a social environment that is equally imperfect – let us begin with the environmental causes (ii). Environmental influences on religious experiences occur when the religious adherent interprets personal feelings or sensations experienced from their socio-cultural surroundings as being 'mystical' 'religious' or 'spiritual'. This is often because he or she is in an external environment such as a church or a meditation group and therefore

---

* Transcendental; (in context here) supernatural-extraneous; not endogenous

associates what may be otherwise considered normal *psychobiological*[*] sensations to religion or spirituality. One example of this is the physiological and emotional arousal that many churchgoers experience when participating in sacraments or rituals believed to bestow special graces.[3] Because of the religious location and activity these sensations are naturally interpreted by the individual as 'an experience of the Divine'. The question remains though; is the Divine actually present – or is this just another case of environmentally-induced religious hysteria?

Another psychobiological cause of endogenous (or 'synthetic') religious experiences is more difficult to evaluate because it includes those purely 'subjective' and very conscious experiences that may indeed carry all the outward hallmarks of piety or spirituality, but that actually originate in the subject as self-induced happenings. For example, various levels of religious hysteria can and do arise from ritualistic chanting, singing and praying, as well as from other austerities such as fasting, flagellation and asceticism. Although generating genuine feelings of well-being and pious euphoria in the subject, such happenings are clearly psychobiological in origin. Furthermore, these experiences invariably occur *without* the associated life-changing consequences or substantial manifestations as listed for TRE's and may also include; (i) unsubstantiated claims of religious experiences; (ii) self-induced trances; (iii) *glossolalia* (speaking in tongues); (iv) religious hysteria; (v) arbitrary hallucinations, and (vi) unverifiable claims of communication with the dead – to name but a few.

Perhaps we should reiterate again that our attempts to theoretically separate TRE's from so-called 'synthetic' or endogenous religious experiences is not an attack on the sincerity of the adherent, nor even of the authenticity of the experience *to* the subject – for indeed, we need only look to the reactions of football supporters vs. those who have no interest in the game to see 'authentic' and undoubtedly sincere emotions on display. Using this example as a parallel, I would argue that such emotions – although very real indeed to the sports fan – have only come about because of the subject's personal devotion to the object of worship; in this case 'the team'. The proof that it is essentially a subjective, or endogenous experience is shown in the lack of a similar reaction from non-fans – or even of the opposing fans for that matter. What is also very important to note is the ease with which one could feign excitement or enthusiasm for 'the team' if so inclined. Not wanting to feel ostracized, or just wanting to feel safe and secure within the

---

[*] Psychobiology; (or biopsychology) study of the biological functions of the mind, emotions, and mental processes

animated throngs are often reasons enough. Therefore, whilst allowing for the possibility of 'genuineness' in some of these abovementioned endogenous religious occurrences, the high likelihood of artificiality, psychobiological misinterpretations, or even fraud must also be recognized. Consequently, the aforesaid instances of the previous paragraph (i)-(vi) cannot be included as a source of data in our empirical observations.

To the unschooled subject or trusting observer on the other hand, many such questionable religious experiences can appear credible and authentic and can quickly take on a life and history of their own. Indeed, many such endogenous incidences or associated religious claims have launched would-be prophets onto the stage of public acclaim; only to result in an overall weakening of that which is authentic and productive in religion. The fact alone that any given individual may *believe* in the validity of such experiences in any particular case is unfortunately of little value in a scientific discussion – unless of course that discussion is specifically about the dynamics of subjective beliefs. Just like synthetic religious experiences, subjective religious beliefs also originate (or take form) in the human mind, and therefore usually lack the essential objective dimension necessary for empirical discussion. After all, when it comes to religion anyone can believe anything they like. Or for that matter, can claim anything they wish regardless of scientific verification. It must therefore be left to the common sense of the reader to apply the mathematics of logic to any given instance of claimed religious experience.

For example; if an individual who craves attention and recognition, or has other overt or covert egocentric, materialistic or political motivations suddenly claims to be receiving "messages from God" without any of the supporting signs as illustrated in the aforementioned TREs, then we must of course consider the very real possibility that this person is either faking or delusional. Any other interpretation would be naive and open to suspicion. As previously implied however this does not in any way discount the normal religious experiences of millions who subjectively experience 'something benign and good' during the observance of rituals or sacraments, or resulting from prayer or meditations. In the context of this work, it is understood that these may very well constitute 'mini-doses' of the True religious experience so-to-speak – only in a milder, more subjective, and less dramatically-impacting form. But because of their personal, intimate and *possibly* subjective natures, and because of the *possibility* of fabrication or fakery; we cannot, for the sake of transparency include them in our discussion further.

Psychosis and Psychomancy

At the complete opposite end of the spectrum from the True religious experience are other very 'real' phenomena that occur within religious settings that constitute clinical or severe mental illness and have generally negative, or destructive symptoms and effects. Persons committing murders or mass suicides for example, after "hearing voices" or believing they are following God's will, or other less obvious perversions of religious teachings that lead to extreme or fanatical actions on the part of the religious adherent. Whether conscious or unconscious in origin, or whether caused by environmental, 'spiritual,' or subjective influences, these equally 'real' but not 'True' (with a capital 'T') incidents constitute a separate classification which can be attributed either to psychotic disturbance or *psychomancy.*[*] Whether or not such concepts as 'evil spirits' can be accurately assessed by science is beyond the reach of our discussion today. So, other than acknowledging the existence of that seriously disturbed mental condition that may be attributable either to psychomantic or psychotic sources, we must be temporarily satisfied with listing its symptoms and recognizing that those who display such symptoms are definitely *not* in the 'True religious experiences' class as here defined, which has distinctly positive effects as a central feature. These other experiences may indeed be very 'real' as psychological, emotional, or even spiritual events that affect the visited subject, but are not in this case 'True' with a capital 'T'.

Thus we establish a differentiation between (I) the True religious experience that arrives unexpectedly, has profound, life-altering positive changes in the individual and originates in an 'other-than-conscious' or extraneous place, and (II) 'other' types of experiences within the religious setting that comprise the groupings 'synthetic', 'endogenous', 'subjective', 'psychotic' or 'psychomantic' as defined above. Keeping these categories in mind, let us now review some of the most common reasons for pursuing religious affiliation at the personal, collective, and environmental levels of religious society.

Individual Features of Collective Problems

Presupposing that there are indeed hidden truths within religion that still await discovery and interpretation; and using the logic that if we identify, classify, and separate the identifiably-dysfunctional, sociological and psychological forms of religious behaviors against the backdrop of religion in general – then whatever we are left with will hopefully reflect the

---

[*] Psychomancy; associated with occultism, the raising of spirits, sorcery etc

essential core values and attributes of authentic religion… let us now list that colorful selection of often less-than-perfect human motivations for religious involvement in the form of hypothetical character definitions, divided into the two main classes of, (A) ecclesiastics and (B) laity.

(A) Ecclesiastics – Vocational Motivations: Under this classification we consider that wide category of persons employed in religious work in some form or another in an official capacity. Ranging from formally ordained clerics through any number of affiliated church positions including associate or lay-ministers; parsons, vicars and reverends; priests and nuns; rabbis and muftis, and on up the scale to Bishops, Cardinals, Patriarchs, Imams and the like; this category overlaps the laypersons category (B) in several definitions especially in those cases where laypersons aspire to church office. Remembering again that we are seeking to separate the True (with a capital 'T') in religion from the false, this incomplete list should be read in conjunction with the previously discussed 'intrinsic, extrinsic, and quest' behavior types, and against the data on collective religious problems already discussed. As a historical reference, positive role models in this category in the Christian tradition might include St. Paul, St. Augustine, St. Francis of Assisi, St. Clare, Martin Luther, or Mother Theresa. For such ecclesiasts vocational motives may include (in a generally-descending order of virtue):

- *Responding to 'The Call'* – those who enter ministry in direct response to a personal spiritual or mystical experience
- *Searching for the Sacred* – those who approach ministry as genuine seekers, believing the religious life to be the most virtuous route
- *Genuine Altruism* – those humanitarians who join the clergy to be effective by supporting and administering social and charity work
- *Missionaries and Evangelists* – enterprising romantics who see themselves as 'ambassadors for God' or recruiters for God's army
- *To be an Educator* – those who want to be teachers in the service of God, spreading whatever brand of 'good news' they believe in
- *To be a Counselor* – those who have gifts of compassion and understanding, and wish to genuinely serve others
- *Institutionalized Believers* – those strictly conditioned to loyal, obedient, and unconditional support of their church
- *Conformers and Reformers* – those who see religious ministry as a means to affect local / regional social development
- *Romantic Notions* – those who are emotionally and psychologically inclined to quixotic idealism

- *Political Goals* – those who see ministry in a religious institution as a short cut to political influence
- *Bureaucrat* – those who simply want to be involved with a global organization that has well-established traditions and processes
- *Parent Pleasers* – those who choose religious ministry because of parental or peer pressure
- *Security* – those whose motivations hinge upon job security, pay, and conditions that guarantee a prestigious job for life
- *Father Complex* – those who need to play the role of 'daddy' on a grand scale – using the church as a platform for a resolution
- *Megalomaniac / Authoritarian* – those who crave power and control over others, and once again, use the church as a platform
- *Actors and Actresses* – those who love the limelight and revel in public attention – what better stage than a popular modern church
- *Socially Inept* – those whose limited social skills leave them unsuitable for a more technically or socially demanding secular field
- *Gynophobics, Misogamists and Homosexuals* – joining "the club" [*]
- *Bullies and Abusers* – those who would use their authority to inflict physical, emotional, and psychological abuses on minors
- *Borderline Psychotics* – those who would escape into their own subjective worlds using the veil of assumed piety to sanctify it
- *Paedophiles and other Sex Criminals* – those who see religious ministry as the perfect camouflage for predatory sexual activity

(B) The Laity – Personal Religious Motivations: Of course, laypersons will also have motivations that encroach upon these definitions, as do some of the following listings apply to ecclesiasts. In institutions with distinct clergy-laity boundaries however, the political environment does not usually facilitate laypersons rising to authoritative positions. Hence there are fewer circumstantial opportunities for vocational influence or abuse. On the other hand – and with respect to the necessary generality of these findings – there are far more slots as-it-were for the credulous, the naïve, and the apathetic as discussed in Chapter One. As before, this provisional category should be read in observational (vs. judgmental) mode, and with reference to the aforementioned personality classifications and collective problems within religion. Positive role models in this sphere might include Florence Nightingale, Mohandas Gandhi, Albert Schweitzer, and Frank Duff.[4]

---

[*] (i) Gynophobia; fear of women. (ii) Misogamy; hatred of marriage. (iii) Within Roman Catholicism in particular the existence of a long established "fraternity of homosexuals" comprising as much as 70% of the priesthood has been confirmed

- *Seekers, Altruists, Spiritually Motivated, and Loyal Faithful* – as described in (A)
- *Aspirations / Pretensions to Sainthood* – usually harmless do-gooders with an idealistic and romantic mindset
- *Habitual Traditionalist* – those following a lifelong habit
- *Sentimentalist / Emotionalist* – those hooked on the emotive ceremonies and paraphernalia of religious tradition; rituals, hymns, ceremonies, sacraments etc
- *Promise to God – "I'll go to church if..."* – those who see religion as meeting the demands of a very conditional, and rather naïve God
- *Aspirations to Ecclesiastic Office* – often motivated by the same urges as ecclesiasts (A)
- *Obsequious Sycophants* – those who think they're impressing (or fooling) God, or their own local ministers, whilst simultaneously accumulating 'good' points for heaven
- *Theophobiacs and Poinephobiacs* – those who fear an awesome God – or the prospect of eternal punishment
- *Hadephobiacs and Satanophobiacs* – those who fear the devil and eternal hellfire
- *Ignorant / Confused* – hoping to find the answer to the 'meaning of life' and other profound questions
- *Guilty* – those who see strident religious practice as recompense for past or present sins
- *Superstitious* – those who use religion to accommodate and/or justify a host of illogical beliefs
- *Social Outcast* – Lonely or socially inept persons who seek community through religious affiliation
- *Occasionals* – churchgoers only for social events or local customs such as weddings, funerals, Christmas etc
- *Deprived of Parental Love* – seeking substitute father-figures in ecclesiastical or supernatural role models
- *Customer / Audience* – seeking entertainment – sees the minister as the 'MC' and is disappointed if/when he doesn't perform adequately
- *Chronic Religionists / Religious Addicts* – those that simply *cannot* stay away
- *Business Opportunist* – sees opportunities for business contacts
- *Socialite* – sees church community as a social club or dating service
- *Emotional Juveniles* – those who never want to grow up and take responsibility for their own spiritual education

- *Obsessive neurotics* – (take your pick...)
- *Psychotics and Sociopaths* – those who would use twisted religious logic to sanctify antisocial or criminal behavior, including terrorism
- *Paedophiles and other Sex Criminals* – those who see religious ministry as the perfect camouflage for predatory sexual activity

It is unfortunate that accurate numerical data cannot be presented in support of these first-hand findings of the author; a task that may be difficult to achieve given the judgmental overtones of some of the listings. It would be interesting for instance, to see how each of these listed traits or motivations apply to the average churchgoer or cleric, and to what proportions in regard to different denominations. Perhaps one day we will find enough forthright interviewees to compile such data.

For the time being however, the reader can see by these commonsense examples of motivations for religious vocations or affiliations that much that has been traditionally labeled as 'spiritual,' 'holy,' or 'religious' behavior might be better classified under the sociological and psychological terms of remedial psychology. In other words, chiefly because of the social and corporate demands for institutional survival in today's world, there is no longer any morally-distinguishable difference between large authoritarian religious institutions and secular organizations – if ever indeed there was. Indeed, if there is any noticeable disparity in morality between secular and religious organizations it is to religion's ultimate demerit; inasmuch as religious institutions are *supposed* to be holding the higher moral territory. But as we have clearly seen, they are instead evading public and legal accountability for criminal transgressions, whilst simultaneously promoting an unprincipled sectarianism as a corporate goal. In contrast, most secular professions must hold themselves to stringent ethical, legal and moral standards, and do not as a rule presume upon the naiveté of a trusting public to escape accountability for their sins: If and when they commit crimes, they generally get caught and pay the price by law. In comparison to the circuitous evasions of certain career religionists, secular abuses appear comparatively straightforward.

Despite the good work done by so many, churches have, for far too long masked, camouflaged, or justified behaviors and attitudes that at best can be described as inappropriate, and more often as morally bankrupt. Presenting themselves as agents of moral guidance, emotional support, and spiritual instruction, authoritarian religionists have systematically encroached upon social, political, educational, and scientific territory, corrupting both the trusting communities *and* the social systems they invade with a disarming, but *ectopic*[*] piety. Whether applied by the point of a sword or the point of a pen the results are the same. Authoritarian religious institutions can only thrive on the fears of disempowered members who, as long as they remain under denominational constraints, cannot possibly develop the emotional depth nor intellectual capacity to challenge those authorities; let alone achieve a truly enlightened understanding of Divine love. Nor can such methodical repression ever benefit the fruitful advance of human society, or of individual human spirituality. Obviously, something urgently needs to be done.

---

[*] Ectopic; abnormally positioned, deformed – a violation of the norm

PART TWO

THERAPEUTIC FOUNDATIONS

Looking at human classification and categorization systems, especially how we organize information and how we discern 'truth.' Evaluating the role of psychology in relation to solving religious-based problems in society, and reviewing Freudian, Jungian, and religious theories that address the psychological / noumenal realms

CHAPTER FOUR

CATEGORIES AND CLASSIFICATIONS

Taking a closer look at the manner in which we process information, with a view to discerning what exactly we mean by 'true' or 'truth' in context of an increasingly integrated multicultural world

Recognizing that most if not all of the aforementioned individual and collective problems within religion incorporate some aspect of human cognition; then a general understanding of the processes of (a) appraisal and (b) dissemination of information is vital to the diagnostic, prognostic, and remedial procedures that may be employed in resolving those problems. Hence we open part two of this book with a clarifying exploration of the *taxonomies*[*] employed in the information-gathering processes common to the human mind; the personal, religious, academic, and/or scientific quests for 'absolute truth'; the systematic classification systems used everywhere in research, education, and religious pursuits at both the individual and the institutionalized level.

This brief exploration is undertaken partly to help us understand the intrinsic origins of sectarian thinking, and partly to highlight both the necessity for, yet the profound limitations of human classification systems in the face of universal, or truly objective reality. With a clearer understanding of the highly subjective manner in which we assimilate information we may, it is hoped, begin to move beyond mere subjective thinking and into the bridging realm of true objectivity. Accordingly, the conclusions of this chapter will pave the way for the introduction of a new and more inclusive classification system that incorporates both the scientific and the religious understandings of the structure and functions of the human mind and spirit.

---

[*] Taxonomy; a systematic classification system

Subjectivity, Objectivity, and Taxonomies

As evidenced by the resolute albeit often contradictory convictions of various philosophical schools, the cognitive education process – most especially in partisan or religious circles – remains plagued by problems that continue to obstruct the objectives of true erudition. Since the human mind is at the center of any such process inasmuch as the faculties of observation, perception, understanding, discernment, interpretation and judgment are cognitive features of an active mind; then the religious education process and any irregularities associated with it are very much psychological concerns. This fact alone surely qualifies psychologists to tackle the two main problems associated with traditional religious instruction namely, (a) suppressive indoctrinations, and (b) elitist thinking – wherein lie the toxic roots of pathological sectarianism.

Having already briefly discussed the issue of indoctrination, let us now review the closely-related problem of elitist thinking; that rather proud tendency of humans to think subjectively-and-exclusively vs. objectively-and-inclusively; the latter being the truer definition of the authentic educational mindset. Although deliberately advanced by many false teachings, the exclusive-elitist mindset (in opposition to the inclusive-collective mindset) is inadvertently fostered by two other factors common to all spheres of learning and instruction. Those factors are (i) subjectivity, and (ii) inadequate taxonomies. Insofar as these are present in the learning process they often obstruct the accumulation of consensual or universal knowledge. To put it another way; we differ and argue about various 'truths' chiefly because of the existence of (i) personal perspectives and (ii) 'artificial' classification systems.

Firstly let's revisit the matter of subjectivity: Since all human beings are both unique and subjective, information is understandably processed in a unique and generally subjective way. Thus, different opinions are not only unavoidable but are arguably the very essence of collective truth (but only when viewed objectively of course). As Oscar Wilde astutely put it, "A truth ceases to be true when more than one person believes in it."[1] By this we may assume he was referring to the deeply personal and uniquely subjective aspect of each human mind as it accepts or rejects 'truths' in life. He may also of course have been alluding to the vast difference between a personally-*experienced* truth and a second-hand *belief* – the profound difference between knowledge and faith that very few dogmatists have ever given serious thought to. Perhaps Wilde should have said that any truth ceases to be true precisely *because* a person *believes in it* – rather than actually *knowing* it to be true – in which case even one person simply *believing* in any given truth is reason enough to question its validity. The act of believing is itself the main issue of concern; not just the object or idea that it refers to. The greater danger then arises when we allow our personal subjective beliefs to coagulate into elitist social structures (usually in the form of religious institutions), thus giving a false sense of reality and substance to unverified opinions that rightly still belong on the philosophers desk. And although faith is arguably a great human virtue under certain circumstances; solidifying our religious or philosophical hypotheses with traditions and rituals serves chiefly to justify, fuel, and even sanctify our ignorance and our arrogance. (Please excuse the clumsy generalizations). In the absence of a greater personal knowledge or experience we tend to use religious rituals and creeds to substantiate our beliefs, and then somehow try to force the universe to defer to our viewpoint. And if the universe stubbornly resists, well, we still have 'our faith' to comfort us. But as we mentioned before; although we are each at liberty to believe anything we wish, such beliefs may be – and very often are – far, far removed from the truth. Sadly and inevitably, someone somewhere will pay the price for our ignorance and our intransigence.

Secondly, and compounding this first subjective factor are those myriad complications arising out of the inexact nature of the *etymological* [*] classification systems common to the sciences and religions, as well as our individual usage and understanding of them. In other words, the incompleteness and artificiality of academic categories. This not only includes standard scientific taxonomies such as the labels 'mathematics, biology, chemistry, geography' etc., but also the verbal gymnastics associated with various hypotheses, theories, doctrines, dogmas, opinions, and beliefs, as well as other *semantic* [†] complications.

For instance, what I may perceive as 'true' or 'real' or 'scientific' or 'religious' or this-or-that, may very well be different to your perceptions and understandings. This is simply due to the unavoidable inconsistencies that arise out of our differing interpretations of particular words or ideas – from time to time and from culture to culture. Words are only metaphors after all. You say "God" and I say "Ultimate Reality". You say "truth" and I think "sincerity". You see a beautiful fish swimming in an aquarium – and I see lunch. As unique individuals we each have a right to a unique perspective, but there is always a greater reality. This is not a matter of 'right' and 'wrong' per se, but more a matter of seeing the bigger truth above-and-

---

[*] Etymology; a branch of linguistics that deals with the origin and development of words
[†] Semantics; the study of meaning in words and language symbol forms

beyond individual perspectives. That fish may indeed become my lunch later on but right now, it is also your beautiful fish. In either case it is still a fish. It would be pointless to fight about who had the 'truest' perspective. But we usually do, don't we?

Culture, social environment, education, and the accurate use of language – all have their bearing upon our ability to communicate effectively. Naturally, the further apart the perspectives or the less familiar the person, the topic, or the situation, the higher the likelihood of misinterpretations. Even when scholars of the same genre debate misconceptions and misunderstandings are common, although perhaps nominally masked by the requisite diplomacy of civilized discussions. Thankfully however, the rules of the scientific method minimize these misunderstandings. Obviously, at lesser-educated or more superstitious levels of society we may expect more acrimony. The more abstract or complex the topic (such as religion and spirituality for instance), the greater the risk of subjective interpretations, and there is always the added risk of irrational beliefs and opinions further clouding the issue. When such differences of opinion arise they may or may not result in enmity and discord but they do invariably distract from the matter at hand, which *should* be the accurate discovery and efficient accumulation of knowledge and truth. In short, our inherent subjectivity (i), coupled with inadequate taxonomies (ii), as well as poor individual comprehension skills (iii), are the greatest impediments to objective learning. The 'normal' human interpretation process in other words, is fundamentally flawed. But if this is actually the case, then what then is the solution?

Well, what is apparently needed is a comprehensive, universal language that can neither be misquoted nor misunderstood. 'Perfect' communication in other words that only reflects fundamental truths. Instead of using human language to try to convey to others piecemeal what we merely *believe* to be true, perhaps we would have been better advised to first find out what is in fact universally true, and *then* build our language systems around it? Such as with the 'languages' of science and mathematics for example, where errors of understanding are relatively rare even across international boundaries. Instead of limited languages trying to define truth, truth in these cases defines the language. It is a simple case of *not* putting the cart before the horse. Ethical scientists have always followed this rule but many career religionists and pseudo-scientists on the other hand have made a life's work of ignoring it. Indeed, most of religion's historical difficulties can be traced to the proud tendency of religious scholars to presume to put into words that which privately, they knew was beyond their grasp. But whether based in faith or not, longstanding religious institutions are not built upon vague concepts. Just like political ideologies they too must have authority for their existence and justifications for that authority. Rock-solid concrete creeds and doctrines conveniently supply that authority; constructs that in turn give rise to a new type of social parasite; those who (well-intentioned or not) prostitute their intellects building careers out of constructing clever, but ultimately misleading apologetics for speculative dogmas and doctrines. The mountains of such materials gathering dust in the religious archives serves mostly to intimidate would-be searchers-of-truth who, in their admirable but misguided humility and believing in the intellectual greatness of esteemed church scholars, dare not presume to challenge long established creeds, let alone engage the daunting task of unraveling complex and intricate dogmatics. Their understandable mistake of course is in not recognizing the ultimate smallness of such intellectuals, who have in many cases done no less than sell their sycophantic souls. And we, trusting, all too often follow them unwittingly into the abyss.

The reader should understand that these rather challenging and confrontational statements are not being made to arbitrarily attack religion per se, but more to challenge our own personal credulity, our historical gullibility, our disturbing willingness to allow others to do our thinking for us. Surely after so much bloodshed in history, still ongoing today – and mostly carried out by well-intentioned but naive religionists – nobody will argue this point. But shedding light into dark and secretive places can be particularly disquieting, especially for those who have made themselves comfortable there. It has been my experience that True revelation (with a capital 'T') ultimately and eventually bears witness to itself. However it rarely if ever, translates manifestly into absolute dogma.

So, if we are agreed that this particular education vs. indoctrination, and subjectivity vs. objectivity problem arises in the first place out of presumptuous and / or preemptive dogmatics; which in turn are based upon partly-comprehended truths (at best); then we may justly surmise that if we can somehow acquire a universal language-form that parallels universal principles and laws, and *then* apply that language to our existing limited taxonomies and religious-truth claims; then hopefully the final outcome will be the elimination of conceptual errors and the fusing of previously discrete taxonomies into one universal etymology. In short, the materialization of a comprehensive language-of-truth that would simply bear witness to itself. The natural consequences of the emergence of any such comprehensive language would finally mark the end of non-collaborative, or non-interdependent thinking such as exists in sectarian ideologies. Sectarianism in all its destructive forms would then be exposed as the ignorant foolishness it really is and we could all then begin the collective journey of true, whole, and objective education.

Of course, this all sounds wonderful until we realize that in order to get to that place of discernment where we can accurately judge what is and is not 'universally true', and before we can translate such into any new *lexicon*, * we first have to process all manner of information through our faulty, and very subjective human minds... and through equally-limited artificial taxonomies. Understanding this process is obviously crucial to the accurate discernment of truth as and when it emerges, and by consequence is vital to the clear identification of existing errors.

Universal Truth Theory
All human systems of learning that incorporate a subject-and-object, student-and-teacher model require some form of classification system for data. Whether the teacher in the model is a person such as a schoolteacher, parent, cleric, or college professor, or whether the object of instruction is in inanimate form such as an article, book, or media outlet the rule is the same: Information is imparted to the student, reader, or observer through the process of organizing and classifying information into digestible bytes.

For example; at the most preliminary level we have the literary classification of language both written and spoken, beginning with our ABC's and advancing through words, to sentences, to paragraphs. Then we have further classifications such as literature, academics, politics, religion, science, economics and so forth, all of which use common language as a tool wherein we tailor the information to be imparted into further sub-categories again, for ease of understanding and assimilation. This is the traditional way human beings have educated each other since the rise of consciousness. We start with little bytes, to snacks, to huge great mouthfuls of information, but only (if we are wise) moving onto the next greater category once we have digested the previous one(s). If we change the sequence by proffering too large a mouthful before the smaller ones have been fully digested, we will only achieve mental indigestion so-to-speak, resulting in confusion and half-truths. After all, one cannot expect to understand Shakespeare without first learning one's ABC's. Nor can we expect to run before we have crawled.

In this manner human education processes follow the dictates of that cosmic law that states that things *must* occur in sequence one after the other,

* Lexicon; dictionary or stock of terms used for a particular language

67

in the correct order: The concept precedes the plan, which in turn precedes the action. Formation precedes development and growth, which in turn precedes maturity. The seed precedes the sapling that precedes the tree, and so on. We crawl, then we walk, and then we run. In almost any area of life, we can identify such three-stage developments that generally correspond to these principles, and whilst human intelligence obviously introduces a whole new range of complexities the formula remains the same. We observe, we interpret, we comprehend. We feel, we think, we act. We want, we plan, we get, and so on. We may, by force of will try to interfere with these principles, but always ultimately to our cost. When we take action for example without thinking through the project beforehand, we usually (unless we are very fortunate) come to grief. At very least, we cause unnecessary stress either for ourselves or for others through mistakes, delays, inefficiencies etc. Likewise, responding blindly to our passions (or our beliefs) without rational consideration also has its cost.

For now we need but acknowledge the simple and obvious fact that we human beings – both as individuals and in collective groups – are at very best in a constant process of observing, absorbing, and assimilating fragments of information in categorical bytes. What's more, and contrary to the often-asinine intimations of far too many religionists, we undoubtedly still have a great deal to learn before we even dare to approach anything resembling 'absoluteness'. Truly absolute statements should ideally only reflect total, complete, and comprehensive knowledge. Hence, absolutism as a religious tenet is fundamentally contradictory. It is inappropriate, ill conceived, and ultimately born of ignorance and pride. It is no coincidence that both absolutism and sectarianism share these vices, for indeed they are very closely related. Both presuppose the superiority of one's own opinions, or of one's peer group over heathen or enemy 'others' without being in full possession of all the facts. Absolute judgments – just like sectarian judgments – arise from a base of relative ignorance or, from a condescending subjective bias. As seen in the rise of religious terrorism worldwide, ignorance and absolutist thinking – combined with elitism – constitute a very dangerous mix. Humility and dogmatic arrogance cannot coexist; hence the profession of humility as a core spiritual virtue in the founding principles of the major faith traditions. Sadly, it is not practiced with nearly as much vigor as it is advertised. In an ideal world we would make a lifelong habit of rethinking our partisan and absolutist tendencies from this 'humility first' perspective. For as long as we realize and humbly accept that we are 'just learning', most of the attitudes and beliefs that fuel the destructive excesses of sectarianism simply could not develop. One day in the distant future perhaps we might indeed be qualified to claim a comprehensive understanding of cosmic truth. But based upon the improbability of any of us alive today reaching that goal, we may safely surmise that the notion of universal or absolute truth will for the time being remain an objective *concept* as opposed to the partial and subjective *theories* that most of us carry around with us: Theories, (especially when in the form of religious beliefs) that although having no substantial reality we nonetheless confidently declare as "Truth." That which is both subjective and partial however, cannot by any definition be 'complete' in the universal sense – and therefore cannot be defined as 'universally true'. The same rule applies to all areas of human endeavor; whether science, academics, religion or whatever, no isolated agency has the right to declare anything 'absolute' unless it can be unequivocally recognized as such by all other human agencies at face value. Even in the event of such a consensus the wiser ones amongst us would still no doubt caution against presumptuous declarations.

So, whilst rightfully congratulating ourselves upon the great leaps and bounds of learning achieved during recent decades, we must at the same time acknowledge the limitations of the traditional approach to learning that is represented by our piecemeal categories-and-classifications systems and ask the very important question: "What if none of these academic, scientific, and religious categories actually exist in universal reality?"

To understand the correlation between human knowledge and universal reality let us now explore this process of systems-based learning through a simple illustration that clarifies three main points, beginning with point number one; the observation that human beings evaluate and think *phenomenologically*:[*]

Phenomenological Evaluations

Phenomenology is both a philosophy and a psychology that suggests that our perceptions of any given 'thing' at any given time are uniquely flavored by our current tastes, values, and attitudes. For example; to identify any substantial object at the most elementary level we usually employ one or more of the five senses. That is to say that through the primary agents of sight, hearing, taste, smell or touch, we embark upon the often unconscious process of recognizing, classifying, and categorizing any given thing – thus giving it both a value and an identity that our mind can grasp. Indeed, without such discerning activity we couldn't function as intelligent beings. However, such value judgments and interpretations are highly subjective

---

[*] Phenomenological; (in context of this work) – of the senses; tastes, likes-and-dislikes

processes, depending almost completely upon our current phenomenological perspectives. These value judgments (or classifications) fluctuate wildly according to our present tastes, knowledge, accuracy of perception, or prevailing circumstances. For example; when we see ripe golden bananas we recognize them as 'food', 'fruit', and 'bananas' (three classifications) and evaluate them according to our preexistent tastes; 'like' or 'dislike' (two more classifications). However, if we happen to be very hungry then the bananas' perceived value (another classification) becomes amplified in direct proportion to our hunger level. All being equal, if a fruit vendor is auctioning rather than selling the bananas at a set price, the hungrier customers will pay more for their bananas simply because their desire is greater and thus they value the bananas more highly. On the other hand, if we have just departed a banana banquet we may not even wish to acknowledge any additional bananas' existence. So, in this simple example we see that 'value' as a classification system represents a very personal and subjective approach to truth judgments that is limited to, and governed by, one's current needs, wants, desires, and level of universal knowledge. To summarize; we evaluate phenomenologically. This is the first point.

Reductive Classifications

The second point is that we have been trained to classify reductively. In other words, partly because we can digest only so much information at a time (usually the less the better) and partly because we have definitive rather than abstractive thinking, we have learnt to classify everything into single, discrete, identifiable units wherever possible. For example; upon being told to collect "some food" from the banquet table we immediately enquire about what *sort* of food to collect. In reply, we are told "some fruit." To which we naturally respond "what *type* of fruit?"… and so on. Obviously, the more specific the definition at the outset, the less potential for confusion. If we are specifically directed to collect "five large golden bananas.." at the outset, then our mind is satisfied, we can embark on our task and life can go on. Such specificity not only minimizes unnecessary confusions, but also saves precious time that can then be used for more important things – such as eating bananas of course. Very rarely is our mind satisfied with blanket categorizations such as 'food' when there is a more specific definition at hand. When it comes to matters of personal importance in any sphere we simply don't handle generalizations very well. We invariably tend to seek more specific descriptions, definitions, and classifications. We just want that added detail. Hence we may conclude that we classify reductively, and specifically. This is the second point.

Universality

The third point is both immeasurably complex in its ontology, yet absolutely simple in its *teleology* [*] and is plainly this: That everything in the known and unknown universe both tangible and intangible, noumenal and phenomenal, is inescapably interconnected at some, several, or possibly all levels of existence – past, present, and future. In simpler language; everything and every non-thing is connected.

This all-inclusive *monistic*[†] principle includes such abstracts as thoughts, concepts, and beliefs – even erroneous ones – as well as the whole physical realm of existence, and thus establishes a theoretical connection between all aspects and features of life. In other words, no matter how advanced we become at identifying apparently discrete specifics, whether it be atoms, ideas, planets, beliefs, or bananas; from a universal perspective all we are managing to do (at best) is identify a fragmentary piece of 'life' in one form or another in temporary, and artificial separation from the cosmically-unified macro-organism we call the universe. Or, in metaphysical terms perhaps we might say 'Ultimate Reality' 'God' or 'Truth' with a capital 'T'. This latest principle is of special import when considering the proliferation of absolute, all-encompassing, or dogmatic statements churned out by adamant religionists who most assuredly have not yet grasped a full and complete understanding of the universe and all that it contains – in which case we may safely declare that any such absolute or dogmatic statements concerning 'universal truth' are either bred of folly or arrogance or both.

If on the other hand we were able to live either long enough, or intelligently enough to fully digest all of the knowledge of the universe, we could (hypothetically) do away with all of the arguments and deliberations that circulate within man-made classification systems, especially within religion. Under such (ideal) circumstances Truth would appear as a unified whole rather than as an overlapping confederation of discrete groupings of knowledge that invariably contain gaps, omissions, and errors. And of course it is due to these very gaps, omissions, and errors, and our associated beliefs and presumptions that we have so much acrimony and confusion in the first place. The solution obviously lies in somehow 'filling-in' the blank spots, but as we said before most importantly; filling-in the blank spots with self-evident truths and *not* the traditional nebulous beliefs or hypotheses of either pseudo-religion or pseudoscience.

---

[*] Teleology; the study of design or purpose in natural phenomena – towards some objective
[†] Monism; the view in metaphysics that reality is a unified whole

But as we have just demonstrated humans tend to process information reductively (i), specifically (ii), and phenomenologically (iii). Yet paradoxically we are also predisposed to holistic, or comprehensive thinking. In other words, we just don't like empty spaces in our theories. When such 'gaps in understanding' present themselves we invariably plug the hole with the nearest available hypothesis or belief. There is barely enough time to think, let alone consider the possibility that the Cosmic Divine might yet try to squeeze through that particular gap.

So few have yet to understand that genuine faith means living with uncertainty, not certainty. And although religious fundamentalists might argue that their lives are indeed based in faith, it might be more accurate to define this type of faith-position as credulous or naive. Certainly most such beliefs cannot be described as either sophisticated or scientifically credible. Complicated perhaps, even clever and complex, but ultimately incredible from a scientific perspective. As previously explained faith is only supposed to be a transitory state where we dwell in temporary uncertainty whilst pursuing knowledge or direct experience, and was never supposed to be an objective in-and-of itself. But regrettably this hasn't stopped the evangelists, the proselytizers, or the indoctrinators from pressing their case. The resulting dogmatic 'faith' rooted in absolute convictions leaves little room for uncertainty or doubt, and therefore little or no room for questions or further learning. Arguably, this isn't really faith at all, but a psychological escape from it – into an imagined world of self-created absolutes. Although this type of faith may bring solace and comfort to the believer, surely any person of principle will endeavor to put reality first? As the famous Anglo-Irish playwright George Bernard Shaw put it:

> The fact that a believer is happier than a skeptic is no more to the point than the fact that a drunken man is happier than a sober one. The happiness of credulity is a cheap and dangerous quality.[2]

Thus the true objective of faith (further learning and knowledge) is inadvertently forestalled. Accordingly, instead of being innately aware of our ignorance and of all the gaps, omissions, and errors in our knowledge, we tend to be blissfully unaware of them. For obviously, we cannot be both "absolutely sure" and consciously aware of our ignorance at the same time can we? Whether scholar or fool, genius or gullible, critical or credulous; under normal circumstances the only time that we experience a (usually very temporary) sense of our own ignorance is when we have a fleeting moment of rational enlightenment, unexpectedly declaring to ourselves "Mmm, I didn't realize I didn't know that!" For a brief second, the ego is made aware of the fact that it still has more to learn, but that moment soon passes and before long we return to our normal presumptuous condition of believing that we already know just about everything we really need to know, and that whatever other knowledge is still 'out there' is just proverbial icing on the cake. This is the troubling human condition that gave rise to the maxim "ignorance is bliss" but with the recent upsurge of so many appalling crimes of 'selective ignorance' on the international front – especially those based on improvable religious beliefs – we are only now beginning to realize the awful price for such historic bliss.

The reality of an *anastomotic** universe of united and indivisible truth will remain difficult for most to accept because it first of all involves contemplating our own relative insignificance as 'just another cosmic fraction of existence' (although that need not necessarily be the case), and because such a belief also presupposes an existing state of profound human ignorance. Despite colorful and *loquacious*† declarations of belief in a transcendent realm and the imperfection of man; for those religious absolutists who "already have all the answers" or for those – secular or religious – whose neuroses are camouflaged by sectarian affiliations, these humbling hypotheses are fundamentally untenable. For to concur with the concept of universalness is to automatically discredit exclusivist paradigms. This in turn exposes the relative ignorance, inadequacies, and insignificance of separatist thinking and the irrelevance of sectarian agencies. This includes all forms of partisan thought, both secular-political and religious. Whether in the form of radical nationalism or religious extremism, perhaps best exemplified in the totalitarian regimes of the twentieth century, and in the fundamentalist religious States of today; the presumption of ascendancy over others, and the willingness to enforce that presumed authority by any means necessary remains the same. Hence those whose identities, careers, neuroses or psychoses are intertwined with sectarian philosophies face the unsettling reality that they are living in a myopia; a myopia what's more that is ultimately a contradiction, an oxymoron in-and-of itself. Those with staunch denominational religious beliefs will sooner or later find themselves living the ultimate paradox; tacitly denying the existence of Universal Truth through the strident practice of prejudicial religion. Or, denying hard-core realities in favor of dearly-held beliefs. This obvious, yet mostly unobserved

---

* Anastomotic; an integrated network of systems such as blood vessels
† Loquacious; very talkative; garrulous; repetitive

fact is affirmed in the many fixed doctrinal statements of the major orthodoxies that effectively prohibited discovery or revelation – whether scientific or religious. Meanwhile, the silent miracle of creation bears daily testament to the cosmic values of change, growth and discovery:

> For the invisible things of Him from the creation of the world are clearly seen, being understood by the things that are made, even his eternal power and Godhead; so that they are without excuse. (Romans 1:20).

In colloquial terms 'God' continuously reveals Himself through the agency of natural law, yet dogmatic religionists often stubbornly refuse to hear Him. How tragically ironic. In the face of so much evidence to the contrary it is painful to listen to increasingly absurd theories as fundamentalists refute cold hard facts in favor of fantastic and ultimately incredible declarations of faith. Not surprisingly, this continued state of denial also accounts for the marked absence of what may be described as 'true' (or natural) spirituality amongst staunch denominationalists. For as long as they remain immersed in delusion and fantasy – especially dogmatic delusions – they can never encounter the living truth.

On the other hand, for scholars and scientists who are still eagerly seeking greater truths, the belief in the existence of progressively higher states of knowledge and awareness remains fundamental to the quest. Set against institutionalized religion's unpardonable record of selective suppression of scientific facts, we can only conclude that if God is planning any future revelations – whether scientific *or* religious – then He will most assuredly be choosing scientists as His prophets. Certainly, if He is paying any attention at all to the news of late, he will not be relying upon career religionists for very much longer. At the very least, those religionists He chooses will be creatures of virtue, learning, and courage rather than those of blind faith and ambition. In this sense, and presuming that there is indeed some profound 'religious' activity operating in yet-unknown realms, it is amongst the ranks of active scientists, and *not* within the ranks of closed-minded clerics where we may expect to find what may technically be termed 'true spirituality'. This is yet another compelling reason for social scientists of courage and integrity to (lovingly) invade traditional religious territory both on humanitarian as well as ethical grounds, so as to facilitate the development of genuine religious virtues. For it is only through strict and consistent adherence to such founding principles as truth, love, and human dignity that any humanitarian organization, whether religious or secular, secures and maintains its essential authority and meaning.

So as we observe the endemically 'worldly' character of the aforementioned personal and collective problems within religion, we may surely conclude that the original 'spiritual' principles – that is, the very same energy that has been the guiding foundation for religious ethics and morals, and the source of each church's claimed authority – has surely been fundamentally compromised and undermined at its very roots. Given religion's supposed role as the purveyor and protector of virtues, ideals, and noble principles, this blatant descent of so many of her officers into hypocritical and ignoble pursuits and the subsequent and justified erosion of public faith in religious authority figures presses the question of where indeed we are now to turn for moral, ethical, and 'spiritual' guidance?

My answer to that question once again, is science: To the study of those rules and principles that underwrite cosmic law, and to the men and women of true faith who have developed the insight and courage to recognize the realities within religion and the sacred potential within science, and who continue daily to build interconnecting bridges. Surely these are the true saints and prophets of today. After all, even by orthodox definitions, God was dabbling in science long before He ever became a religionist – if indeed He ever did!

In conclusion, and serving as the preamble to the following chapters let us again remind ourselves that there is a vast difference between mere beliefs and actual knowledge. Although religious convictions have undoubtedly served many of us meaningfully in times of hope, faith, doubt, uncertainty or despair; and religious institutions themselves have carried out much humanitarian work over the centuries; in these times of great scientific advances in knowledge and understanding, and with so much information at our fingertips, perhaps we might be better employed investing our energies into the activities of discovery rather than continuing to defend or reinforce traditional and often questionable beliefs.

For surely it is in this personal leap of courageous faith, away from the security and safety of doctrine and dogma, and into a place of genuine humility and open-mindedness that we each stand the best chance of truly engaging the truth?

CHAPTER FIVE

DOCTORS OF THE SOUL

Comparing and contrasting the science of psychology with the methods and practices of the religious world in an effort to accurately discern whom indeed best qualifies for the title 'Doctors of the Soul'.

Although it could be argued that the practice or application of psychology has always existed in some form or other in symbiosis with human relationships; historically speaking the science and profession of psychology is barely out of its infancy, with the now-well-recognized discipline of Counseling Psychology for example, only receiving formal recognition in the 1940s. Conversely, institutionalized religion, as an inviolable but changeable component of human culture that has doggedly resisted science's attempts to fully rationalize and categorize it, is as old as human history itself. What then one might ask, gives psychology the mandate to approach the long-established field of religion with anything approaching confidence or authority?

Emphasizing that it is against the backdrop of these aforementioned *problems* in the religious world, and not against the productive aspects of religious practice that we make this assessment; there are at least seven solid answers to this professional-authority question that should be read in context of the findings of previous chapters. In summary, psychology has a mandate to engage religious problems because:

- *Professional Unity and Mutual Respect:* In contrast to religion, science comprises many different disciplines that remain collectively united upon acknowledged principles.
- *Conceptual Discipline and Clarity:* Unlike religion, psychology operates within definable and logical, conceptual boundaries.
- *Youthful Propriety and Transparency:* Psychology is not yet compromised by a "long, dark, and often suspicious" history.
- *Specialization:* Most of religion's functional and social problems can be traced to psychological sources.
- *Professional Integrity:* Psychologists are consistently highly trained in academics, scientific applications, and ethical principles.
- *Chronological Ascendancy:* Religion's traditional dominance in guiding social morality is naturally surrendering to reason and knowledge.
- *Origins:* Psychology's roots also lie in metaphysics.

(1) Professional Unity and Mutual Respect: This qualifier is justified by the aforementioned endemic disunity and partisan conflict within religion. As an incorporated field that is grounded in universally-recognized principles, the science of psychology has a cohesion and stability noticeably absent in any collective overview of the world's religions today. Although differences of opinion and political infighting do abound within the social sciences as much as in any other human institution, there remains an accepted consensus, based upon professional discipline and mutual respect concerning the fundamental ethics, standards, and tenets of scientific operation. This contrasts greatly with the moral and ethical fluctuations of autonomous religious bodies which, by and large, reserve the right to 'alter' their ethics and principles according to the latest (or most convenient) interpretation of their faith. More often than not, those interpretations center upon the glorification of one's own group and the condemnation (however subtle) of outside others. On the other hand, the various sciences freely share information and resources with a view to solid understandings, thereby increasing scientific awareness across the board. This ultimately benefits mankind and is in sharp contrast to the defensive bickering currently present in interdenominational religious wrangling – a state of affairs that does little more than present the spiritual seeker with a medley of either vague, confusing, or absolutist alternatives. The ethic of professional unity and mutual respect seen in the sciences can (we hope) serve as a model to be replicated in collegial form within the religious realm.

(2) Conceptual Discipline and Clarity: Although religion has always been concerned with the supernatural, the mystical, revelation and so forth; such nebulous subject material is obviously prone to many unqualified and/or erroneous interpretations. There is simply no protection against false spirituality being represented as 'genuine' by unqualified or calculating persons. Neither for that matter is there any defense against 'true' spirituality being suppressed or denied either through ignorance or for questionable socio-political reasons. In fact, there is no inherent protection built into the religious system at all to defend even against insanity masquerading as religious piety; with the criterion for official acceptance of any 'spiritual' suppositions or claims appearing to hang heavily, if not exclusively upon their potential to benefit the goals of the host church. In disturbing data collected by psychological researchers Echeverria, Caroll, Warner, and Perry (1996) for example, a direct correlation was found between political objectives and the sanctioning of miraculous apparitions by the Catholic Church.[1]

> Sociological studies have focused upon the factors that influence the Catholic Church to accept only some reported apparitions of Mary as legitimate. For instance, Warner provides critical historical documentation in support of her claim that the sanctioning of the apparitions of the Virgin Mary has often been linked with official support for sexual suppression. Perry and Echeverria argue that apparitions have been used both to facilitate social control on the part of the Catholic Church and to boost national prestige. Their latter claim is congruent with Carroll's claim that even when countries have similar frequencies of reports of Marian apparitions, such as Spain and Italy, social and political factors have led to differential legitimation of the apparitions by central church authorities.[2]

These findings in no way undermine the possible veracity of mystical happenings, but simply point out a direct correlation between political or corporate motivations and the official acceptance of such claims. Science on the other hand is governed by the rules of logic and cognition – and not self-serving politics. We really need to look at the different standards here: In the case of 'big tobacco' using unscrupulous scientists to cover their deceptions for example, the rest of the scientific world denounced such activities as unethical and fraudulent. In contrast, getting to the true motives behind deceptive clerics' actions requires insight into the secretive and convoluted realm of religious politics and the quagmire of religious beliefs, and who – other than career religionists has inside access to those portals?

We now know that pedophilia was a chronic problem for many years, just as we know that big tobacco was deliberately poisoning millions for profit. Some tobacco executives are finally being punished, thanks in large part to the integrity of a few insiders. But who will hold our slippery senior clerics to account? Who out there has both the requisite knowledge and the requisite moral courage? Who, amongst existing ecclesiasts has the integrity to be a true-blue whistle-blower – and has the courage to face the consequences of losing favor with their superiors? Are there really any heroes out there with the intimate knowledge and understanding of the religious world who are not already compromised by denominational affiliations? Indeed, we might justifiably ask how and why so many career religionists who claim to have been in the 'innocent majority' during the recent exposé of widespread abuses, continued to serve superiors whom they knew to be involved in both immoral and illegal activities? Where indeed were their 'spiritual' or moral priorities when the call came? …and what is it exactly that now qualifies them to continue to receive the respect and trust of the community?

Because of its divergence from the religious sphere, science can approach religious problems objectively and professionally, thus avoiding entanglement in mysterious hypotheses and emotional diatribes – a frequent occurrence between competing religious factions. Psychology brings an investigative clarity and discipline to the table, and is therefore particularly well suited to the examination of emotionally-charged moral and ethical issues that religious institutions may have a vested interest in avoiding – or overamplifying. This does not mean to suggest a direct transference of scientific principles to religious thought is the only resolution to denominational infighting – for that would simply fuse religion with science at the cost of religion's essential identity and core spirituality. Rather, that a clear delineation be made between the 'spiritual' and the non-spiritual features of religion, so that tenable regulations can be drawn up to govern the latter to some degree of accountability.

Modern religious bodies are not just 'spiritual' entities. They are also 'big businesses' with requisite secular structures. The enduring problem has been the arbitrary use of nebulous or 'sacred' terms, concepts, and beliefs to license or approve highly questionable corporate actions, or to sanction very dubious motives – both personal and political. Religionists also regularly reject 'outside' investigative efforts on the grounds that scientists (for example) are not properly qualified to evaluate those living the so-called spiritual life. But the real fact of the matter is that scientific investigators need not be qualified to enter the 'spiritual' or sacred sphere wherever it *truly* exists, because any corrective psychology would not engage truly spiritual subject matter directly in any way. The remedial psychologist's concern is primarily with problematic illegal, immoral, neurotic or psychotic behaviors, which I'm sure even the churches will no longer claim are sacrosanct. In fact, under the assumption that 'spiritual truths' do indeed exist as distinct from empirical or psychical truths, then the religious world can only benefit from the exposure of that which can be *proven* untrue, erroneous, or dysfunctional in religious practice and behavior. Indeed, it could be argued that because of psychology's dogged adherence to scientific truths, and because of institutionalized religion's habitual suppression of the same, psychology is technically the more moral, and thus the more 'religious' discipline of the two.

(3) Youthful Propriety and Transparency: Unlike the religious world that today must anxiously concern itself with the political, corporate, and commercial repercussions of airing its more recent 'sins' in public, psychology is not yet compromised by a "long, dark, and suspicious" history. The fact that some of the habitual problems in the religious realm are themselves historically 'older' than the profession of formalized psychology in no way disqualifies psychology from being able for the task of corrective investigation – no more so than young doctors being declared 'unqualified' to treat their cranky grandparents. In fact, although still a relatively young field of endeavor the science of psychology is armed with many insightful tools that were not available in earlier times for application towards the resolution of social or religious issues. The publication in recent years of methodical studies on social psychology, the psychology of religion, and transpersonal psychology for instance, bears testament not only to psychology's suitability for the task, but also to its ability for the same.

(4) Specialization: Psychology is qualified to approach the psychological aspects of religious problems in a diagnostic and therapeutic mode by simple virtue of the fact that it has already established its reputation as a science of the mind. In this case, and considering the psychological nature of many of the aforementioned 'religious problems' the study of both the individual and the collective religious mind would be psychology's cardinal function. In recent years psychology has opened its doors not only to the study of religious behaviors, but also to the study of a wide range of other reported 'religious phenomena' such as altered states of

consciousness (meditation, trances); dreams and apparitions; glossolalia (speaking in tongues); sensory, quasi-sensory, and extrasensory perceptions, and so forth…and their associated causes and effects. In the second edition of *The Psychology of Religion – An Empirical Approach (1996)*[3] no fewer than 2,000 such separate works on religion-related topics are referenced as sources. This shows that psychology as an investigative science, is indeed tackling the subject and problems of religion with increasing enthusiasm and vigor. Whilst recognizing that debates on theology, revelation, worship, and other such religious specialties are not officially psychology's domain, the authors of the above work do clarify that the area of "beliefs, motivations, cognitions, and perceptions are psychological constructs that, when linked to religion, constitute the basis for a psychology of religion." [4]

(5) Professional Integrity: Here we compare professional training for social sciences or vocational services in relation to training for religious ministry. From a purely secular perspective and based upon the author's firsthand experience, it can be plainly stated that the training and education requirements for graduation in the field of psychology at the advanced level are of a significantly higher professional standard than the requirements for those entering into traditional church ministry. Although there may of course be exceptions to this general rule; deserving special mention is the fact that even in those cases where clerics are trained to high academic standards such as with the Roman Catholic Dominican or Jesuit Orders, the foundation and direction of that training is *conterminous*[*] with orthodoxy and is thus primarily designed to reinforce the denominational ethic. Such scholars are required to serve the denomination first and foremost – often at the expense of greater truth. This fact has somehow escaped the scrutiny of the academic accreditors, who apparently choose to see no conflict between the exacting standards required of technical institutions vs. the extremely liberal course guidelines allowed for denominational religious schools.

In many such schools unproven religious theories are often taught 'as fact' whilst competing scientific subjects are delivered through a religiously-distorted model. There is no true objectivity at work in other words – surely a prerequisite of any genuine educational model? Having paid large sums for formal recognition in the academic field, religious schools can now quite openly offer accredited degrees in the 'science' of theology. And although I too actually hold one such degree, I have always been somewhat mystified at the concept of defining any sort of religious theory as 'science'.

---

[*] Conterminous; having boundaries in common; similar in scope

In contrast, whilst perhaps lacking in sacramental mystique, the so-called 'secular sciences' tend to put the pursuit of universal truths first and foremost in their polities and in their schools. Scientific claims must be proven upon merit, and not simply left to intuitive interpretations or the faith of trusting adherents. Still very much aware of her tentative historical foundations, psychology in particular is especially sensitive to her interactions with the public and remains acutely aware of the importance of the highest moral and ethical standards in the purveyance of the vocational aspects of counseling and psychotherapy. That dull complacency typical of institutions that are effectively already a part of the culture has not yet infected the field. Knowing that the future of the profession depends in great part upon the confidence of a trusting public, practitioners are constantly urged to be models of integrity both inside and outside of their work environments. To this end, a reading of the ethical and moral standards expected of a modern psychologist include such specifics as; *"principles, ethics, moral behavior, responsibility, competence, legal standards, confidentiality, welfare of the consumer, professional relationships, nonmaleficence*, beneficence, justice, fidelity, and autonomy,"[5]* ..amongst many more. The preamble to the American Psychological Association's *Ethical Principles of Psychologists* (1990) reads:

> Psychologists respect the dignity and worth of the individual and strive for the preservation and protection of fundamental human rights. They are committed to increasing knowledge of human behavior and of people's understanding of themselves and others and to the utilization of such knowledge for the promotion of human welfare.[6]

So we can see that in the area of ethical and moral norms, the profession of psychology has pledged to implement and enforce the highest standards and consistently recognizes the need to serve and protect the client, and the general public. Thus doctors of psychology, by very nature of their training, their education, and their standards of professional ethics, can approach the problems of religion with the credentials of true healers. If they also study religion as a specialty, they will undoubtedly be more knowledgeable, objective, and effective (in the humanitarian sense) than their compromised religious counterparts.

---

* Nonmaleficence; to do no harm; cause no injury

(6) Chronological Ascendancy: This qualifier rests upon the central principle of the cognitive learning process; namely, that one's beliefs (if they are legitimate) must *precede* any corresponding knowledge. Faith before experience, and hope (or fear) before actualization in other words. In context here 'one's beliefs' equate to religion of course, and 'knowledge' equates to science. For as we all know, faith is the traditional domain of religion(s), whilst actual knowledge (facts and reality) is usually the domain of science. Faith comes first chronologically simply because there is no *need* for explicit faith after one has actually *experienced* a fact or event for oneself. I don't have to *believe* in something if I already *know* it to be true in other words – if I have *experienced* it to be true in a real and tangible manner. Consequently genuine, unproven faith can only exist in the *absence* of corresponding knowledge – right? In the case of religious beliefs, whether we name such knowledge 'Ultimate Reality', 'Truth', 'God' ..or whatever, this 'faith-first' principle still remains at the heart of true religion inasmuch as one is *learning* about a *relationship* (with God); and rests upon the observable fact that one's beliefs should (eventually-and-hopefully) lead to *actual knowledge* (of the Sacred Other). Faith is not the ultimate objective – knowledge of God is. Even the Bible clearly illustrates the point that faith must come first in the sequence: Set against a Judeo-Christian setting, we see the earliest relationships between God and the patriarchs such as Noah and Abraham evolving from a strict philosophy of absolute faith and obedience – into a familial *understanding* of God by Jesus' time – as a Heavenly Parent who wanted actual *relationship* over obedience. "For I desired mercy and not sacrifice; and the knowledge of God more than burnt offerings" (Hosea 6:6). Absolute and unquestioning faith was appropriate in the beginning because God was 'The Great Unknown'. But as the relationship between God and the Israelites developed, the invitation was to advance into *knowledge* and a *living awareness* of their God. Hence "we believe" whilst we don't know for sure... and then we come to know. Once we know however, we no longer need (blind) faith. Accordingly, in observing the historical failure of so many faith-based beliefs to bring lasting harmony amongst men, perhaps it's now time for us to grow out of our dependence upon naive beliefs, and listen instead to the messages of wisdom and truth conveyed to us (by God?) through science.

(7) Origins: Psychology's roots lie in metaphysics; therefore, as is suggested in the following quotes psychology is equally qualified by its origins in metaphysics to apply itself directly to "matters of the soul." In a telling semantical insight, the *American Heritage Dictionary of the English Language* has two listings under the word "psyche":

1. Psyche: The spirit or soul
2. *Psychiatry.* The mind functioning as the center of thought, emotion, and behavior and consciously or unconsciously adjusting or mediating the body's responses to the social and physical environment.[7]

Bearing in mind the popular notion that the human person comprises 'spirit, mind and body' – (to be read correspondingly as 'religion, psychology and science') – forty years ago professor of psychology David Bakan noted the bridging potential of psychology when he wrote:

> Psychology is a possible meeting ground for science and religion, in that both presumably deal with man's mind, or heart, or spirit, in one sense or another.[8]

This statement not only affirms a professional recognition of the connectedness between the concepts of heart, mind, and spirit, (or body, mind, and soul) but also hints at the reality that psychology – although technically a science and recognized as such in today's world – has its origins in ancient metaphysics. Indeed, it was only during the relatively recent wave of academic classifications that defined and separated the various forms of art and sciences in the seventeenth to nineteenth centuries, that psychology gradually adopted the definitive obligations of 'pure' science, moving away from the phenomenological philosophies of social psychology to the empirical 'observation, measurement, and experimentation' approach of the secular sciences today. This academic separation between science and religion became so entrenched by the late 1900s, that it wasn't until Sigmund Freud approached the topic of religion in some of his theories at the turn of the twentieth century that any self-respecting scientist suffered to even mention the word. Even then, it would take another fifty years of cautious dithering before natural psychology mustered the professional poise to address religious matters with confidence. This point is emphasized to remind the reader that the conceptual divide between religion and psychology is a relatively recent one, and that there once was a time in human philosophy when 'truth' did not suffer the ignominy of being dissected and partitioned into artificial semantic categories for human digestion.

As far as we know, that time reaches at least as far back as the ancient Greeks, whereupon we discover an intriguing relationship between the realms of natural science, religion and ancient mythology.

The Psyche and The Soul

The word "psyche" originates in Greek and later *Roman*[*] mythology, and refers to a most beautiful princess who was the envy of the goddess Aphrodite *(Venus)*. To cut a very long and complex story short: After being rejected by Eros *(Cupid)* for looking at his face (Eros and *Cupid* being deities of love), the princess Psyche is later reunited with him, and subsequently made immortal by Zeus *(Jupiter)* as the personification of the soul. Those who understand the subtleties of mythology will recognize profound truths in the dynamics of this tale that relate to modern psychological and religious concepts – truths that are no respecters of human wisdom or ignorance, nor of any artificial classification systems – a fact which will become clearer as we proceed.

Despite fundamentalist beliefs to the contrary, prevailing Western thought and Christian precepts in particular owe much to the enlightened efforts of ancient Greek philosophers including Socrates, Plato and Aristotle, who predated Christianity by several centuries. For as each in turn sought out the 'meaning of life' through both metaphysical hypotheses and empirical research – (studying such topics as absolute reality, cosmic principles, and the human soul) – no artificial academic barriers had as yet been erected between what we now understand to be two differing areas of operation; namely, science and religion. In those days, investigations into both observed and unobserved phenomena produced many profound hypotheses that theoretically linked the spiritual and the physical realms as mutually-dependant and complimentary features of existence. Those early philosophical definitions of 'soul, mind, spirit,' and 'ultimate cause,' remained the foundational material for many centuries of scholarly work including forming the ontological basis for most of Christian theology through the rise of Christendom, to the Protestant Reformation and beyond. In fact, it was not until the turbulent Reformation years when first science and later Protestantism challenged the prevailing Catholic worldview that the race towards classification, delineation, and separation of the sciences really began. Until then, the subjects of history, theology, sociology, medicine, mathematics and astrology were uniformly embraced under Church-sponsored scholasticism in a unified 'science of reality' genre (so-to-speak). But in the climate of revolution, rebellion, and reformation that permeated Europe from the Renaissance through the French Revolution and beyond, a new generation of enlightened thinkers – having freed themselves

---

[*] Deities in italics in this paragraph are the Roman counterparts to their Greek forerunners

of suppressive orthodoxies – demanded some sort of non-religious academic framework within which to reference themselves.

Metaphorically speaking, this is when Psyche (science) first looked at the face of Cupid (religion) with curious fascination – and was angrily rejected! In the ensuing hostilities firstly between humanists and *theists*,[*] and later between Catholics and Protestants, the various camps inclined towards ever-more distinct group-identities in a fearful and unsettling political climate. In a nutshell, this is how we inherited both Christian denominationalism and an independent academic world in the West.

In the short term of course, the establishment of academic divisions amongst the arts and the sciences has well served the needs of collective education – after all, the legacy of those taxonomies now forms the curricula of our modern colleges and universities. But there are drawbacks too. Rigid conceptual boundaries by definition must always exclude *something*, and in the case of post-Reformation science, one could say that that 'something' was its conceptual soul – a soul that was promptly adopted (or should we say kidnapped?) by increasingly partisan religious institutions.

A Divided Mind

To be exact, psychology did not so much gain a psyche and lose its soul but rather, in an uneasy and unspoken accord with the older 'science' of theology agreed to busy itself with the empirical features of the psyche, whilst the theologians ostensibly occupied themselves with the mystical aspects of the soul. As if by tacit agreement, the 'heart' of man was thus divided into two implicit concepts; (i) the scientific 'psyche' and, (ii) the spiritual 'soul'. This resulted in the eventual and disconcerting development of a 'soul-less' secular scientific institution in direct competition with an often wildly-irrational religious spirituality – each further compounded by increasingly hostile fundamentalist and sectarian leanings on both sides of the divide. Eventually, both scientists and religionists withdrew into 'safe' territory as it were: The scientists into their facts, figures and data, and the ecclesiasts into their mysteries, doctrines and dogmas – each with their own specialized infrastructures, and specialized lexica. In ever more acrimonious confrontations each tried to deny the integrity of the other, even going so far as to label science 'heretical' – even 'demonic'; and religion as a 'mass neurosis' respectively. In short, just like Psyche and Cupid there was no love lost between them. And just as any individual who attempts to deny or suppress either his logical-rational or spiritual-unconscious self will suffer

---

[*] Theist; one who believes in a personal God

symptoms of dysfunction, so, in the aftermath of this historic divide we may anticipate both the scientific and religious communities manifesting similar symptoms of collective dysfunction – only on a socially-magnified scale.

As we have indeed seen, the numerous dysfunctions associated with irrational religious beliefs, or associated with an *absolute* reliance upon material or scientific reality (which is arguably just a secularized form of fundamentalism), closely resemble the psychological and *psychosomatic* * symptoms of the schizoid personality. Such an observation naturally leads us to consider whether the politically-forced separation of the collective mind and soul of post-Reformation man has in any way led to the current state of society; wherein the imbalances arising out of *atheistic nihilism* † and religious fanaticism respectively, reflect the continued tragic estrangement of our collective minds and spirits?

If this is indeed the case; that our minds and spirits are unnaturally alienated at the collective level, then obviously the place to look for a remedy would be back to a time of good social health. In Greek mythology, that would be the time before 'love' rejected 'beauty' – or the spirit (Cupid) rejected the mind (Psyche), and harmonious unity existed between the two. Unfortunately however, there is no prevailing socio-political parallel with this allegory in recent history – at least not in traditional Christian circles. Religion has stoutly rejected her younger sibling science, and has yet to be reconciled with her.

In his insightful commentary on the relationship between the psyche and the healing properties of human love, American mythologist Joseph Campbell noted; "The only one that can heal me is the one who delivered the blow."[9] This can be read to imply that the assorted mental and social disorders that have sprung out of the forced division of the heart of man may indeed be cured by a reunion of the same. In other words, by finding a way to reunite the alienated aspects of science and religion whilst keeping their True core values – (with a capital 'T') – intact.

Unfortunately we cannot return to the golden era of Greek mythology, but we can try to understand the principles involved and apply them to the problem in perspective today. Translating the metaphor forwards into context, we may deduce that the real problem began when religion rejected science, most notably during post-Renaissance times which not coincidentally, is when the process of academic separation between science

---

* Psychosomatic; of or relating to the physical symptoms of a mental disorder
† Atheistic nihilism; (in context here) a skeptical philosophy denying the existence of God, gods, or anything non-substantive, that also rejects all moral or religious values

and religion in the Western world was formally set in motion. Naturally then, any potential solution requires that Cupid (religion) must accept Psyche (science) once again. For just as the spirit needs the mind in order to healthily inhabit the body, so does the mind need the spirit for the very same reasons. In this parallel religion represents the spirit, science represents the mind, and society represents the collective 'body' where both spirit and mind find their meaning and purpose. Either without the other results in excesses and imbalances: Soul-less nihilistic secularism on the one hand, and irrational superstition, naiveté and fanaticism on the other.

The same is true at both the individual and the community level. Gather enough soul-less individuals together and you will have a soul-less community.. and vice versa. For just as with any given individual, so it is with society in general. It is only in their healthy combination that either science or religion stands to truly profit the collective body of man – in harmony with (God's) natural law of course. For obviously, religious faith directed at the Universal Creator requires justification in natural law, just as human intelligence and creativity needs to be rooted in principles that correspond to reality. Even so-called 'abstract' thoughts or artistic creations derive their meaning in context of concrete reality, inasmuch as that which determines such things to be 'abstract' in the first place is their apparent lack of uniformity with established norms. But if something is declared 'abstract' then it cannot also be considered literal... and this is precisely where many existing religions falter. Wanting the credibility that comes with undeniable truths, but also needing the license of abstraction in order to justify tenuous religious claims, such belief systems will always feel judged and threatened by self-evident scientific truths; especially those that directly challenge longstanding and dearly-held beliefs. As we saw in Renaissance times, when presented with scientific evidence that challenged prevailing orthodoxy, the primal response from the church was to first deny the reality and then to demonize the messengers. Thus the agency that was supposed to reflect God's truth, justice and wisdom, instead rejected it and coldly cast it aside. Cupid scorned the truthful Psyche in other words – and in so doing, lost his position as the master of love.

Ultimately, just like Cupid and Psyche, True science and True religion are destined for cosmic unity. But reunion can only happen after the causes for the initial alienation are resolved and Cupid once again returns to a loving, rather than fear-based position. Therefore, in context of natural law in a physical world; for a successful resolution of the alienation of the mind and spirit of man, the religious world must sooner or later acknowledge the preeminent authority of science. For ultimately it is in physical reality, in the lives of everyday men and women, where the drama of religion (redemption, enlightenment, salvation, resurrection etc..) must be played out.

Regardless of what may or may not be happening in any 'spiritual' realm, we are unquestionably physical beings inhabiting a physical domain. In context of where we are in our development as physical-spiritual beings the scientific-physical arena is, by nature of its connectedness with sensory reality, our primary source of knowledge and truth... or at least it should be. For indeed, what sort of a God would place us in a physical universe and then refuse to communicate with us on a physical level? Certainly not the loving Heavenly Father of Christian myth. One would imagine such a Heavenly Father doing all in His (almighty) power to communicate with His 'lost' children.. right where they are – right now. Logical is it not? Remaining aloof and shrouded in nebulous 'spiritual' mysteries whilst only communicating to us through questionable religious mediums does not sound much like an 'almighty' nor enthusiastic, Heavenly Parent. Why would God continue to use such a divided, confusing, and improvable medium as religion to convey Universal Truth(s) – especially when considering its dismal record so far?

If we are to believe religionists' claims of 'special status' with the Creator, then the only logical explanation for God continuing to use religion as His primary source of communication is that He either can't or won't do otherwise. The first explanation makes the concept of an Almighty God invalid; whilst the second disqualifies the notion of Divine Love. Either God is Almighty and Loving or He isn't! And if He is not loving and almighty, then He is not the 'God' we have traditionally understood Him to be. In fact, any such deficient and unloving being would not qualify for either worship or obedience – save possibly out of fear, which as we all well know is the antithesis of true love. So, we may soundly conclude that if there is an Almighty and Loving God out there then He speaks just as truly through His creation, as He does through any claimed religious revelation – if indeed not more so. In fact, to take this to its most logical conclusion, and based upon the obvious fact that sensory reality is witness unto itself – then unless spiritual and religious claims can be validated against the backdrop of (God's) physical reality, they should not be viewed literally – nor taken literally. In other words, if religious claims fly in the face of known reality, then maybe.. just maybe, we are supposed to use our God-given intelligence and the evidence of physical creation around us to raise reasonable doubts?

In the absence of sufficient ecological knowledge in the past, it was understandable that certain dubious religious claims and creeds took root and flourished. But now we are wiser, or at the very least more knowledgeable of both the scientific and religious worlds. We must then with courage and True faith ask the question of ourselves: Could it be possible that religion, with all its mysteries and incomprehensible superstitions – is more the creation of ignorant societies than of a handicapped Creator? For surely any True religion has nothing to fear. True spirituality is complimented by scientific truth; not challenged by it.

Hence Cupid (religion), under the watchful eye of Jupiter (God) must put aside his misplaced pride and allow Psyche (science) to rise to her rightful place as the natural qualifier of human spirituality. Love, Truth, and Wisdom may then be reunited as the foundations for human interactions, and as the promise for future generations.

*   *   *

To summarize: Reasoning that it should be psychology, and not religious institutions that head up the collaborative, remedial, and integrative tasks associated with religion's social problems; we noted that although being the younger discipline of the two, psychology is rooted in the same philosophical sources as contemporary religions – especially Christianity and the major monotheistic traditions. Allegorically speaking, this makes religion and psychology older-and-younger brothers respectively – Cain and Abel if you like – and providentially speaking, the age of faith is now giving way to that of reason. But as long as fundamentalists and career religionists suppress or deny the inherent truths of science, they effectively reject God's messengers. Thus, 'Cain' attacks and rejects 'Abel' once again. Sadly yet ironically, it has nearly always been the preexisting religious institutions – more so than the secular ones – that persecuted the saints and prophets of the day.

In any event, from a strictly academic perspective psychology is by far the better trained, better-regulated, and more objectively-educated sibling, and is therefore the better candidate for the title 'Doctors of the Soul'. Moreover, carrying little historical baggage into the public arena, psychology still has the advantage of relative professional 'sinlessness'. With little to hide, and nothing to prove except quantifiable truth, the specialty of psychology is therefore uniquely placed to diagnose and treat the psychological aspects of religious dysfunction in an objective, professional, and ultimately productive manner – later to reclaim its destiny, with its soul still intact.

CHAPTER SIX

PSYCHOSPIRITUAL THEORIES

*A comparison of theories from traditional religious and psychological
perspectives, with a view to identifying complimentary parallels that have
the potential to link the worlds of religion and psychology*

The term *psychospirituality* is not yet in the English dictionary.[*]
Presumably, this is because the concepts of psyche and spirit are
generally considered to relate to the psychological 'mind,' and the
religious 'soul' respectively. As such, they are rarely used collaboratively in
the same context due to the long-established reticence of psychologists and
religionists to enter each other's domains in anything but a critical role.
Reversing this trend today, we coin the word 'psychospirituality' in a literal
and conceptual reunion of the psyche and the spirit, the psychological and
spiritual realms; yet remaining firmly based upon empirical principles.
Hence the word 'psychospirituality' instead of the word 'spirituology' – the
latter being a semantic arrangement that would indicate that we are
approaching the bridging union between scientific and religious theory from
a spiritual or metaphysical basis. Such an approach however would only
exacerbate the already confusing world of chimerical religious theory – a
chief generator of the very psychological problems we are attempting to
address. In fact, if scholars adhere to literary principles, the word

---

[*] Recently, the term 'psychospirituality' has grown in popularity amongst proponents of
religion-and-psychology specific theories, and amongst a handful of 'New Age' groups,
whose definitions and understandings of the term may differ from those presented here.

'spirituology' should never appear in any future dictionaries as anything other than a hypothetical oxymoron, simply because by the time we know enough about 'the spirit world' to base a quantifiable scientific theory upon it, any semantic taxonomy would obviously come from the scientific (and therefore not 'spiritual') lexicon. Hopefully that day will come sooner rather than later. The psychospiritual theory referenced here may therefore be best understood as an inclusive (but not all-inclusive) conceptual framework within which existing competing theories may find a place of union. A framework however, with built-in empirical 'filters' that only allow self-evident truths to pass, thus avoiding the exacerbations alluded to in previous chapters. Examples of those filters include empirical data, simple logic, and cosmic principles such as we see evidenced around us daily; a viewpoint reflected in the scriptural admonition to rely upon our sensory perceptions: "For the invisible things of Him from the creation of the world are clearly seen... so that they are without excuse." (Romans 1:20)

A Psychology of Religion
The presence of the True religious experience ('TRE') hidden like the proverbial "pearl of great price" amongst the muck and grime of so much human ambition, ignorance, and dysfunction within institutionalized religion, strongly suggests that even after science has evaluated all the possible psychological motivations for religious practice, there will still remain this so-far unfathomable dimension to religion (the True religious experience) that apparently operates under 'different' rules – at least as far as we can tell.

To briefly recap: The TRE is usually depicted as an enlightening flow of wisdom, peace, and universal cognition. Or described as "ecstatic, mystical, spiritual" or "transcendental". Reported in various faith traditions throughout history, the genuine religious encounter is experienced as an uplifting numinous event whereupon subjectivity and objectivity fuse as a unified whole. The individual mind, psyche, or spirit merges with that of the universe, and we "become perfect like (our) Heavenly Father is perfect" – at least in theory, if only for a moment or two (Matt 5:48). Such is the reported essence of the genuine religious experience – a phenomenon which, whilst differing across the board in specific interpretations is nevertheless universally consistent in many other ways. It remains this writer's conviction that careful scientific scrutiny of this inviolable 'True' aspect of the phenomena we call religion will provide the answers to such questions as the origins and reasons for religious behaviors, and illuminate the true role of religion both historically, and in relation to contemporary society.

This conviction is fortified by psychological research derived from Sigmund Freud's original detection of the realm of the unconscious in the late 1800s, and Carl Gustav Jung's subsequent discovery of universal archetypes and symbols – both of which opened the way for scientific bridging discoveries into the traditionally mysterious realms of religion and spirituality. Coining new scientific terms for age-old religious concepts, Freud and Jung brought the psychological mechanisms of the religious journey slowly into focus, discussing the concepts of God, spirituality, the soul, the mind and religion, in such terms as; "the numinous realm, the unconscious, the superego, ego and id, the individual subconscious, archetypes, the animus and anima, complexes and neuroses" …and so forth, thus introducing a new scientific lexicon for traditionally 'spiritual' subject matter. Having been reasonably settled in their respective fields for over a century, this invasion by psychologists into sacrosanct religious territory caused ripples of disturbance on both sides of the divide. The uneasy truce had been violated and predictably, Freud and his findings were censured and demonized. The eventual result was that both science and religion took up the call to either investigate further or defend existing beliefs, resulting in a rash of new definitions, interpretations, terminologies and classifications that have since been handed down to us, unfortunately, often causing more confusion than clarifications. For this reason, and in order to avoid exacerbating existing misunderstandings, the reader is now advised to review diagrams (♣ 1, 2, 3,) in the midsection, and table 'A' below, which jointly outline the central characteristics of the four theories that we will discuss in this chapter.

Table A: Psycho-Spiritual Theories - Thematic Comparatives

Freudian	Jungian	Religious	Psychospiritual
(un-named realm)	Noumenal Realm	God	Realm of Great Unknown
(Deep) Subconscious	Collective Unconscious; Archetypes	Spirit World	Collective Unconscious
Psyche: Id & Subconscious	Personal Unconscious	Soul or Spirit	Personal Unconscious
Psyche: Id, Ego, Consciousness	Consciousness	Soul or Spirit	Inspirational Self
Psyche: Ego, Libido, Superego	Ego Consciousness	Spirit or Mind	Thinking Self
Ego & Personality	Persona	Body 'The Flesh'	Active Self

The tabular form of the chart should not be read to suggest that there are *exact* delineations between the contents of these columns and rows in any direction – either within theories, or cross-theoretically. For indeed, as explained in Chapter Four, categories and classifications are at best limited forms of information gathering. In this psycho-spiritual sphere of operations, it is precisely because we cannot reach a consensus of appropriate concepts and terminologies that we need to consider the creation of a more accurate and accommodating classification system in the first place. So as we better comprehend the religious, Freudian, and Jungian theories through the following definitions and discussions, and gain a general understanding of prevailing beliefs in the respective fields, we should (it is hoped) be better placed to evaluate the potential for any 'new' bridging psychospiritual theory.

Not wishing to distract the reader unnecessarily, but equally wanting the reader to fully appreciate the implications of the materials presented here, let me plainly state my conviction that any initial reservations the reader may have about the validity or the importance of the psychospiritual theory will be unequivocally resolved in the following chapters. That being said, let me now endeavor to prove the point.

Religious Terminology

It should be clearly noted from the start that there are a great many ongoing debates within the various faith traditions as well as within the discipline of psychology about the true nature and meaning of such overlapping terms as 'mind,' 'spirit,' 'heart', 'soul,' and 'spirituality,' and of their place and meaning in the religious journey. For although these terms attempt to encompass metaphysical feelings, experiences, or concepts, and are therefore often technically imprecise and nebulous in nature, scientists and theologians alike acknowledge the existence of an experiential realm beyond – yet somehow connected to – the realm of consciousness.

Wishing to avoid a long and unnecessary exposé of complex and confusing religious terminology, the reader is invited to accept this writer's personal testament based upon several years of inter-religious and inter-denominational exchanges, that there is hardly a theologian or cleric, let alone a religious layperson, who has a comprehensive, literal grasp of the meanings of such terms (spirit, mind, soul etc) – and for very good reason. In a simple experiment conducted on a variety of denominational groups noted for their dogmatic views, including Roman Catholics, Seventh Day Adventists, Christian Fundamentalists, Mormons, Unificationists, and Jehovah's Witnesses, between eight and a dozen persons attending a topical seminar were unexpectedly invited to list three words or a short phrase to define each of the following: (i) God, (ii) heaven, (iii) hell, (iv) spirit or soul, (v) prayer, (vi) religion, and (vii) spirituality. Rather surprisingly, there was hardly an instance where two people in any particular denominational group listed the very same properties or definitions *even for any one item* on the list. On several occasions, none of the answers matched at all, thus accumulating so many abstract adjectives, nouns, and concepts, as to render the subject under discussion practically meaningless; if not as a philosophical topic then certainly, as a collective doctrine. The tendency on the part of the surveyed subjects to *sciolistic* * definitions was very high, and the subsequent discussions invariably revealed considerable confusion, unacknowledged questions, and/or bland unquestioned acceptance of *imperspicuous* † doctrines. This confirmed not only the relativity and subjectivity of beliefs concerning the abovementioned topics even amongst denominationally-orthodox thinkers but, in combination with psychology's traditional reluctance to engage such religious terminology – also demonstrates the urgent need for an intelligible taxonomy that can be universally recognized. The following chapters will attempt to present the raw materials for just such a taxonomy, based upon existing scientific knowledge and our new 'psychospiritual' hypothesis.

The Religious Theory
In this instance 'religious' refers loosely and generally to the monotheistic / Christian belief system that is admittedly not representative of all religions, nor even of all Christian denominations in their different interpretations of the psychological / spiritual / *noumenal* ‡ realm(s). However, because the main purpose of this collaboration of theories is to authenticate and more accurately define such phenomena as the True religious experience – (a phenomenon that is not denomination-specific except by interpretation), the general-Christian theory is chosen both because it claims the largest amount of followers worldwide and more importantly, because the author believes it is *generally* representative of many other religious theories, especially Judaism and Islam, and will therefore have points familiar to most readers. Once the findings of this book are independently confirmed, the resultant 'psychospiritual' hypothesis should (it is hoped) be equally applicable to all theories of the mind or spirit, whether scientific or religious.

---

* Sciolistic; a pretentious attitude of scholarship; superficial knowledgeability
† Imperspicuous; unclear; obtuse; hazy; not transparent
‡ Noumenal; that which can only be intuited by the intellect; not sensory

Meanwhile however, the classic difficulty when dealing with theology or other systematic forms of religious scholarship such as doctrines, creeds, or dogmas is that 'truths' are usually, albeit speciously presented in pseudo-scientific form. This leads the adherent to assume that 'concrete' religious declarations are actually more than educated guesses (at best). That is to say that the standard procedure for establishing and reporting a scientific truth is to follow the formula: (1) Observation; (2) hypothesis; (3) experiment; (4) report results; (5) others repeat the experiment and achieve the same results; (6) interpretation of results and, (7) formal documentation of facts.

Religion on the other hand often omits several of these steps, sometimes even pulling hypotheses out of conceptual 'thin air' or labeling them 'revelation' without any express observations, and then moving directly to formalized conclusions (stages 6 & 7) in the form of the aforesaid creeds and doctrines. Consequently, many long-established religious beliefs are eventually challenged by 'new' scientific knowledge and discoveries – which in a word is at least half of the religion-science problem. However, despite this tendency to leap to unfounded or poorly interpreted conclusions, certain general beliefs within religion do indeed correlate to scientific findings as we can see in the illustrations (♣ 1 and 2).

Very simply, the religious understanding of the mind and its workings revolve around the perception that we are variously; 'lost, separated, ignorant, sinful, disconnected-from-God,' and generally 'living in spiritual and moral darkness'. The salvific processes of resurrection, restoration, redemption, and/or renewal each depend upon accessing this estranged realm via the soul, mind, heart, or spirit; usually through the mediums of prayer, meditation, or spiritual counseling.

Parallel with this concept we see that psychologists also practice therapies that access the subconscious in order to facilitate psychological and emotional healing. In the sense of 'separateness-from-another-dimension' therefore, science and religion seem to agree on the existence of a somewhat 'disconnected' feature of human-ness: Science calls it the realm of the unconscious, whilst religion calls it the spirit realm. Of course, various religions refer to the spiritual realm by other terms such as 'Nirvana' or 'Heaven' or 'The Supernatural Realm,' or name distant planets in unseen galaxies where our 'Spiritual Ancestors' reside. Indeed, all religions and mythologies suggest the existence of a place or realm of greater goodness, wisdom, and truth that we are somehow intimately connected to (or separated from) and to which we should aspire.

Undoubtedly, many would contest the non-specificity of the above generalizations, but nonetheless, both the subconscious and spiritual realms as respectively defined by science and religion do have one central thing in common; neither is fully understood – right? This fact alone unites them in the *possibility* that they do indeed have much in common – if not in fact actually being one and the same thing? In any event, given our lack of knowledge on these subjects, it simply cannot be argued that they are *not* interconnected in some way. Similarly, the characteristics of the soul or spirit as defined in religious thought relate closely to psychology's definitions of the psyche, superego, id, or subconscious, as do the mechanisms of prayer, meditation, and mystical trances correlate to the measurable effects of hypnosis, hypnoanalysis, or other mental states induced in psychiatric experiments. Indeed, considerable research has been conducted comparing religious phenomena with known *neuropsychological*[*] factors in an effort to isolate the biological and the psychical features from the potentially 'spiritual'. As a result evidence continues to mount that helps to explain 'mysterious' religious phenomena in purely empirical terms.

For instance; during now-famous experiments conducted in the 1960s by psychologists Schachter and Singer, it was found that persons tended to interpret the sensations and sentiments experienced under controlled conditions as either 'religious' or 'non-religious' (for example) depending purely and specifically upon their environmental surrounds.[1] Obviously, psychological and emotional predispositions also played a part, as did the subjects' familiarity with expected norms – which in turn influenced their reactions. In simple terms, it was shown that people can quite easily be conditioned to interpret plain old normal events as spiritual / religious / supernatural... or whatever. In fact, it was far easier than had been expected. Such experiments obviously go a long way to explaining natural phenomena often considered 'mysterious' in religious circles, but equally, also raise new questions about universal parallels linking other types of religious experience that *cannot* presently be dismissed as purely physical or psychological phenomena. So although the findings of recent research often challenges religious interpretations of natural phenomena, they also add indirect weight to the theory of universality; that is, the theory that states that there is indeed a universal source of 'outside' stimulus common to us all, that suffers being interpreted emotionally, individually and subjectively – and sometimes, even religiously.

---

[*] Neuropsychological; to do with the relationship between the nervous system (esp. the brain) and cerebral or mental functions such as language, memory, and perception

Freudian Theory

As the father of psychoanalysis, Sigmund Freud (1856-1939) introduced the world to such concepts as the subconscious, the ego, the id, the libido, psychosexuality, the superego, and the interpretation of dreams; as he pioneered the study of the mind, its ailments and its healing. Amongst some of his most outstanding students were the psychologist Otto Rank who wrote *Myth of the Birth of the Hero (1909);* psychiatrist Alfred Adler *(inferiority complexes);* and Carl Gustav Jung (1875–1961) who, amongst other notable achievements first documented the existence of archetypes in the collective unconscious.

It is not necessary to enter into great depth into Freud and Jung's understandings of various psychosocial states in order to make our point today. But the brief (and admittedly inexact) summaries represented in Table A, along with the following concise definitions of Freudian theory should assist the reader in understanding and evaluating the general similarities and differences between their respective theories:

The Ego: The ego is that conscious part of the psyche or mind, that deals with realities, thoughts and behaviors, and is influenced by social forces. The ego is one of three components of the human personality, mind, or psyche, and is sometimes defined as one's concept of 'self' – usually comprising mind and body elements.

The Superego: Roughly corresponding to a social conscience, the superego controls and regulates instinctual impulses, urges and thoughts. The superego develops as the individual is exposed to value systems through the normal process of social growth.

The Id: The id is comprised of mainly unconscious, pleasure-oriented impulses that exert influences upon the individual; driving them towards immediate gratification.

The Libido: Often described as the manifestation of the creative energies of the Id – frequently in sexual expression.

The Unconscious: Also referred to as the subconscious; is that part of the mind that contains fears, feelings, wishes, memories, ideas, dreams and the like, that are not directly expressed consciously but nevertheless influence many conscious processes in subtle or covert ways, including being expressed as neuroses.

Psychosexual Theory: Hypothesis that suggests that all mental disturbances originate in sexually-related experiences or behaviors. Two of Freud's better-known theories in this area were the Oedipus complex and infantile sexuality.

Not everyone of course agrees with Freud's psychosexual theories. Some of the abovelisted terms and theories for instance have long since given way to advances in the field. Nevertheless the same fundamentals do persist. So, we review these Freudian themes mainly to understand the original tenets that gave birth to the discipline of psychoanalysis in the first place. By taking a brief look at the Psychospiritual Theory outlined in Table A and ♣ 1 for instance, we can see how Freud's *superego* and *id* concepts correspond fairly well with the 'inspirational and emotional self' whilst his notions of *ego* and *personality* likewise parallel the 'thinking self' and the 'active person' respectively. Although matching the various themes exactly is not possible, I hope the reader can acknowledge the general parallels. One of the beauties of diagrams of course, is that a picture is supposed to paint a thousand words, at which cue I will resist the temptation to over-explain everything and move on to the man who first coined the term 'archetypes'.

Jungian Archetypes

Carl Gustav Jung was directly responsible for a great many innovations in psychology, and although viewed as the natural successor to Freud for many years, Jung eventually branched out along different lines founding the analytical school of psychology and focusing upon groundbreaking work with universal archetypes. In particular, he focused on the analysis of dreams, where he showed how the accurate interpretation of primordial manifestations in dreams could lead to dramatic resolutions of psychological disturbances. He later developed such techniques as *word association*, and defined the *introvert* and *extrovert* personality types. A truly religious man, Jung also became famous for applying psychological understandings to the religious field, and for suggesting the possible universal synchronicity of all things. However, Jung's insistence upon empirical and academic integrity, instead of being viewed as an admirable trait by his religionist detractors led to a reactionary rejection of many of his precise scientific definitions of religious subject material. It was really only after his passing in 1961 that Jung began to receive the respect he deserved from the religious world. This was a great tragedy, for if the religious world had been more receptive to some of Jung's psychological explanations of religious phenomena, we would undoubtedly be living in a better educated and therefore less dogmatic world today. Having made this respectful comment however, our concern with Jungian theory today centers chiefly on his findings concerning archetypes and the collective unconscious, for as we shall soon see, there are remarkable connections between mystical experiences such as TRE's and Jung's discoveries concerning the collective unconscious.

Jung's professional journey into mythology, religion, and psychotic fantasies stemmed from his doubts about the comprehensiveness of his mentor's psychosexual theories in explaining mental and emotional disturbances, and led to the eventual discovery that there were apparently 'universal' and unconscious forces at work that were integral to the resolution of imbalances in humanity's search for personal fulfillment. Jung believed that prototypical, conceptual 'inhabitants' of the subliminal realms communicated to us through our dreams, our neuroses, our myths and our religions, and, being beyond the *conscious* influence of man remained theoretically 'uncorrupted.' Here perhaps we should underline the bridging potential of these Jungian themes between the traditionally-competing fields of psychology and religion.

Amongst Jung's most influential work was *Psychology of the Unconscious (1917)* wherein he first promoted the existence of these universal energies naming them "archetypes" – describing them as a form of unconscious primordial symbolism common to all humanity – a concept first discussed by Greek philosophers Plato and Aristotle who believed that reality consisted of such archetypes, or fundamental truth-forms, beyond the reach of normal sensory perceptions. Unfortunately for us, that is largely where these phenomena have remained, hidden in the silent shadows of the collective unconscious unnoticed, unavailable, and unfortunately unable to compete with the frantic distractions of everyday life in a very material world. I say 'unfortunately' because I do not subscribe to the belief that 'hidden truths' have been cosmically engineered to escape our understandings. But rather, that any such 'hidden truths' can only serve their cosmic purpose through human discovery and understanding. The fact that they remain 'hidden' is simply a testament to our collective unenlightenment; to the fact that human consciousness has not yet fully matured. Indeed, we will know when human consciousness is approaching maturity when there are no more hidden scientific truths or arcane religious mysteries to solve. So, taking into account the fact that we are still very much upon the collective journey to enlightenment; of particular interest to us today is the fact that Dr. Jung eventually concluded that the archetypal projections he found through his research were nothing less than manifestations of some ultimate truth-language. So, taking into account the fact that we are still very much upon the collective journey to enlightenment, of particular interest to us today is the fact that Dr. Jung eventually concluded that the archetypal projections he found through his research were nothing less than manifestations of some ultimate cosmic truth-language. In his own words, Jung defines archetypes as follows:

> The concept of the archetype... is derived from the repeated observation that, for instance, the myths and fairytales of world literature contain definite motifs which crop up everywhere. We meet these same motifs in the fantasies, dreams, deliria, and delusions of individuals living today. These typical images and associations are what I call archetypal ideas. ... They impress, influence, and fascinate us. They have their origin in the archetype, which in itself is an irrepresentable, unconscious, pre-existent form that seems to be part of the inherited structure of the psyche and can therefore manifest itself spontaneously anywhere, at any time.[2]

Jung goes on to explain; "The archetype in itself is empty and purely formal, nothing but a *facultas praeformandi,* a possibility of representation that is given a priori." Here he is referring indirectly to the inability of the subjective mindset to truly grasp and articulate objective realities. In more common language, Jung is explaining that although archetypes definitely exist in the unconscious realm, their 'true' original form is inaccessible and rather meaningless to us without being packed out with images and associations that the (subjective) conscious mind can relate to. He adds; "...it seems to me probable that the real nature of the archetype is not capable of being made conscious, that it is transcendent, on which account I will call it psychoid."

Basically, and with allowances for the ambiguity of the term, there are three levels of Jungian 'awareness' to consider here: Firstly (a) the personal consciousness. Secondly (b) the personal unconscious (or subconscious); and thirdly (c) Jung's realm of collective unconsciousness (see ♣ 1, 2, 3). Loosely speaking these three levels of human awareness correspond to our psychospiritual theory as: (a) our personal experiences and emotions in daily life; (b) our hidden dreams and suppressed fears; and (c) the common gateway to collective archetypes, human spirituality, and the Great Unknown. Each of us without exception has a unique perspective on life that generally aligns along these three levels (whether we are aware of them or not). Most of us in fact remain only partly aware even of the first level (a); hence the term 'consciousness' – although perhaps the term 'partial-consciousness' might be more appropriate? Not surprisingly, to access the deeper personal subconscious (b) usually requires medication or psychotherapy; whilst access beyond this realm (c) is rarely reported or documented scientifically.

Delving Deeper

One way to explain the mysterious realm of collective unconsciousness (c); (where Jung surmises archetypes emanate from) is to use the illustration of individual swimming pools in the back gardens of our various homes. Each swimming pool has been uniquely designed to reflect the likes and character of the owner; its shape, length and depth, the surrounding foliage and the decorations all represent the individual consciousness (a). This is the place where we 'swim' daily. We like to keep the water a certain temperature and, when we want to play a little we bring out our beloved rubber ducks and floating armchairs. This is my own personal pool where I feel safe and comfortable. It is what I know – what I am used to – what I am familiar with. It represents my culture and my personal history, and the 'stuff' of my everyday life. It could therefore be decorated with all manner of political or religious symbolism, family photos, or even sexy pinups for that matter. If I am a true-blooded American, then I may have a Stars-and-Stripes theme predominating. If I am a fun-loving youngster, then there might be a Caribbean bar with beer and dance music. If I am a little unsure of myself then the pool may be a bit secluded, and so on. The water of course represents my personal flow of consciousness, and the pool's environment symbolizes my cultural location, surroundings, and beliefs. It can be a fun exercise imagining what one's own psychological 'pool' of consciousness would look like – and how we would decorate it using our own specific social and personal paraphernalia.

The unconscious or subconscious realm (b); or more specifically the *personal* unconscious, is represented by the deeper water of the pool. Still part of our personal pool of course, but somewhat removed from the surface it is not such a comfortable place to be. Usually colder and darker, we don't hear or see so well there – let alone breathe or run around. Neither does it contain the familiar stimulations of the surface. Because try as we might it is very difficult bringing our personal 'stuff' underwater; especially material stuff of course, and/or the thoughts and images of daily reality. The more of that personal 'stuff' that we attempt to hang on to (our ego-consciousness and persona) the less chance we have of being able to descend below the surface. Rather like trying to dive underwater dragging our rubber ducks and floating beds with us. Or, in more realistic terms; trying to sleep whilst playing sport.. or dream whilst engrossed in a stimulating conversation for example. One activity is conscious – the other is unconscious, so they can't be done simultaneously. Accordingly, if we do wish to access the subconscious (or super-conscious) realms, we need to somehow 'let go' of our attachments to sensory and material things, and of our overriding need to 'be in control'. But this is harder than it sounds. That's why the subconscious remains such an unvisited realm.

Here we may recall parallels between the traditional mystical quest and the denial of the flesh; the 'letting-go' of the ego and materialistic preoccupations. As a result, the only time we visit this deep water of the subconscious under normal circumstances is in our sleep. But hypnotism, psychotherapy, and certain religious practices can also take us there. But having little or no sensory stimulation it is for most an unfamiliar, unappealing, and therefore often-uncomfortable place to stay for very long.

Then we have the realm of the collective unconsciousness (c); the place identified by Jung as holding those key motifs and patterns inherited at birth. 'Psychoid' themes as he called them that are common to all humanity. This then is the realm of archetypes that is somehow connected both to our unconscious mind (b) as well as to what I term the Realm of Great Unknown. In the analogy, this collective unconsciousness is like an even larger lake of water; pure and clean, that unbeknownst to us supplies all our personal swimming pools from a common source. Like a huge subterranean sea of consciousness if you like, where all our individual 'pools' (personas) are ultimately rooted. This accounts for the regular surfacing of particular myths and social patterns common to all cultures throughout history, as well as for the existence of subliminal archetypes.

But the access points to this universal flow of Truth are so deep and well-hidden in the depths of the psyche that hardly anyone knows about them, let alone has visited there. Those few who have made that profound journey have had such difficulty explaining the experience or translating the wisdom glanced there when they return to 'the surface' that we either deify them or crucify them – sometimes both. Not wanting to let go of our own ideas, beliefs or possessions, or, scared of being swept away from our own personally-designed pools-of-consciousness, we stubbornly resist the call to explore so deeply. Indeed we may even deny the existence of such a place. Rather than change the shapes of our own pools of consciousness to accommodate a greater truth, we would rather suppress, ignore, or deny that greater truth. But the call remains all the same. If we do choose to believe in its existence, it is often in a prosthetic sense, and we simply latch onto one religion or another 'in faith' as a newly-converted member. But most of the time all we have done is join another larger swimming club that has its own 'collective pool' where we all share the same shallow consciousness, and still don't have to dive too deeply. It's the classic problem of mistaking breadth for genuine depth. 'More' does not necessarily mean better after all.

The great difficulty that Jung identified, and the reason that he considered archetypes as being incapable of being made manifest consciously, was simply because any Great Truths being drawn from this uncorrupted source must be viewed through the murky perspectives of our personal, subjective pools of awareness. A personal consciousness that is all cluttered up with our own particularized junk, our individual perspectives, our subjective and biased opinions, our emotional baggage, and our personal beliefs. This applies to both the individual psyche as well as to the collective, or group dynamic. This is one reason why true objectivity is so vitally important, and why ignorance – especially selective or sectarian ignorance – simply cannot be allowed to prevail.

In his voluminous works on dreams, mythology, alchemy, religious symbolism, mystical phenomena, and the science of psychology, Jung continued to present proof after proof of this yet-to-be-consciously-deciphered archetypal realm that was 'speaking' to us from that place he termed "the collective unconscious". A place populated with mythological figures; heroes and heroines, mother-figures, crones, virgins, and tricksters, ..to name but a few. Amongst his most poignant discoveries was the uncovering of the presence of the *Animus* and *Anima* (♣ 1), the feminine and masculine subconscious archetypes of the male and female psyche respectively, whose functions he described as follows:

> The natural function of the animus (as well as the anima) is to remain in (their) place between individual consciousness and the collective unconscious (q.v.); exactly as the persona (q.v.) is a sort of stratum between the ego-consciousness and the objects of the external world. The animus and the anima should function as a bridge, or a door, leading to the images of the collective unconscious, as the persona should be a sort of bridge unto the world.[3]

Thus, Jung paints a picture of gender-sensitive conscious and unconscious 'doors' of the psyche, opening and closing under certain circumstances, revealing or suppressing 'truths' as the case may be – depending upon our state of consciousness. As previously mentioned, the strong inference is that this collective unconscious; precisely *because* it has escaped conscious human influences, contains universal truths that have not yet suffered corruption by human agency. However, the related implication is that under normal circumstances we are cognitively alienated from this archetypal source and, whenever messages from this collective unconscious are somehow channeled through human agents or agencies, there is invariably a corresponding subjective 'corruption' of the original content or theme. Although this subjective interpretation process *seems* unavoidable, the theoretical implication is that the human mind should be as 'pure' and free from any false, limited, or artificial interpretative bias in order to guarantee the most accurate interpretations from this uncorrupted source – a truly objective or 'open' mind in other words. But such a state of pure objectivity can only be achieved where there is a total absence of subjective thinking – where the preoccupations of the ego are replaced by a higher state of awareness. Interestingly enough, most spiritual exercises such as fasting, praying, meditation, and chanting are specifically designed for this purpose; to deny the ego and worldly desires and to open up the mind (or spirit) to a higher state of consciousness. Some might even call the process "connecting with God."

What is of greatest interest to us today though, are the recent scientific findings that confirm these altered states of consciousness amongst religious subjects whenever they enter into mystical states.[4] Measuring alpha, beta, theta and delta brainwaves with sophisticated equipment, researchers have tabulated distinct neurological changes in subjects such as Zen Buddhist monks and Appalachian serpent-handlers, as well as during certain instances of glossolalia (speaking in tongues) within contemporary Christian groups. During these experiments a general correlation was noted between the left and right hemispheres of the human brain, and the logical-analytical and creative-ineffable functions respectively.

Without going into too much redundant technical detail; suffice to say that certain mystical states conducive to triggering experiences similar to our definition of the True religious experience, were generally found to occur in the creative-ineffable right side of the brain. *[Note: Generally speaking, the brain is understood to be divided into creative (right), and analytical (left) aspects]*. And although subjectivity and objectivity as discussed in this work do not directly correlate to the split-brain hypothesis (for of course there are both subjective and objective aspects to both analytical and creative thinking); there is in fact an observable functional connection between materialistic self-preoccupations and analytical thinking. We cannot be deemed to be 'selfish' in other words if we are not *subjectively* preoccupied with ourselves. Creativity on the other hand usually involves a certain 'losing' of oneself in the creative process. Considering the aforementioned facts about the partisan religious mindset, it seems logical to conclude that the more 'open' creative mindset is generally more objective-altruistic, and is thus more conducive to mystical experiences simply because the subject's concerns are more universal than discrete-and-personal. Sure enough, experiments showed that it is in elevated states of *objective* consciousness that mystics receive their most profound experiences.

So what does all this mean exactly? Well, if we now align Jung's definitions of the archetypal realm with the religious understandings of the supernatural realm; and then compare Jung's understanding of subjective bias with partisan religious dispositions; we see some intriguing parallels between, (a) subjective (mis)interpretations of universal reality, and (b) partisan interpretations of religious truths. There are strong connections in other words between subjectivity, self-centeredness, sectarianism, and the subsequent misinterpretation of universal truths.

By further applying this Jungian understanding of subjective bias to personal, denominational, or ethnic interpretations of noumena, we begin to understand the psychological causes for the development of neurotic and psychotic religious attitudes, especially pathological sectarianism. The basic information we are all getting might be exactly the same but, filtered through our subjective perspectives and then coupled with copious doses of ignorance, pride, and religious zeal, we can all too easily manage to arrive at utterly different, yet 'absolute' conclusions.... and then of course we fight about them! As the maxim "a little knowledge can be dangerous" implies; limited or partial understandings of reality are often more dangerous than total ignorance, especially when fuelled by prideful self-confidence. When dealing with topics or beliefs that will have far-reaching effects upon future generations, surely only the wisest and most knowledgeable should dare to offer their opinions? If only it were so. Unfortunately we live in a world where ignorance, arrogance, and pride greatly outweigh knowledge, wisdom, and humility. One can only live in hope that some great revelation is imminent – one that will clearly illustrate to the ignorant and the arrogant their true levels of wisdom and understanding. In the meantime however, we are tantalized both by the evidence of the True religious experience, and the findings of psychologists such as Jung who collectively assert the existence of 'something else' whole, pure, and true... out there still.

But remaining 'out there' is precisely the problem. As long as transcendent truths remain 'out there' they remain subject to misinterpretations and the manipulations of the unscrupulous. "Out there" indeed is a suitable adjective to describe most religious hypotheses concerning "that-which-is-beyond-consciousness". Somehow, and despite Jung's declared belief in the probable "eternal transcendence" of archetypes, we have to find a way to bring their essence into the realm of cognition or, learn how to read their existing signs and symbols in the pages of history and in the natural world around us.

Although it could be argued that Jung's findings themselves are sufficient to such proof, the plain fact is that most people are not familiar with the details of archetypal spheres, and even if they were, still have no substantial proofs or evidence with which to support their theories. Sensory beings that we are, we want to see sensible proofs, and this (I am glad to say) is what a good part of this book is all about.

At the risk of sounding a little dramatic, let me simply announce the fact that those sensible proofs – at least in part, are outlined in the following chapters. The theory of universal truth suggested by the existence of Jung's subliminal archetypes can now be demonstrated in the conscious, sensory, and substantial realm, and once accepted, the laborious process of untying the metaphorical blindfolds of sectarian belief systems can begin in earnest. By demonstrating the existence of this archetypal realm through observable examples of its manifestation in daily life we have the beginnings of a tentative 'theory of truth' that will simultaneously achieve four main goals:

- Firstly, it will bridge the scientific and religious realms by adding something 'new' and dynamic to both perspectives
- Secondly, it will help clarify and fortify many existing scientific theories
- Thirdly, it will help neutralize human delusions, phobias, and superstitions
- Fourthly, it will expose and correct much religious misinformation

The specific aim of the following chapters is to establish a foundation for these goals by introducing a new and bridging perspective that will effectively rewrite – to a greater or lesser extent – the way we approach our various theories of truth. Comprised of both scientific and religious data, and introducing new findings in the fields of history, natural science, religion and psychology; we may therefore name that bridging perspective "the psychospiritual theory".

The Psychospiritual Theory
If nothing else, the acceptance of ascending-and-descending realms of cognition as defined in diagrams ♣ 1, 2 and 3 – if-and-when they are recognized across the scientific-religious board – will provide a primary locus of agreement and professional acceptance, and contribute to the eventual development of a unified, if not universal theory of truth. In this sense, the psychospiritual theory outlined in the following pages does not pretend to be a comprehensive theory of universal truth, but rather a systematic and partial pointer in that direction that may, hopefully, be considered some improvement upon the cacophony of existing beliefs.

This new psychospiritual theory meets the above-declared goals by firstly presenting a systematic, foundational formula of conscious *and* unconscious universal values and principles. Secondly, it promises to help simplify and unify established but complex scientific theories. Thirdly, it will help neutralize individual religious delusions through the compassionate and informed application of remedial psychospiritual theory. Fourthly, it will help to correct religious misinformation by offering an unbiased truth-source for the thorough and tenacious investigation of the sources and origins of religious sectarianism and its related doctrines (this latter topic to be wrestled with in more depth another day).[*]

Naturally, we cannot engage these mammoth tasks to any great extent in so short a presentation. However, we can launch the process with the unveiling of a dramatic series of synchronistic phenomena that confirms the foundational structures of the psychospiritual theory as illustrated in this chapter. Thereafter, we can re-present our findings as a more effective diagnostic in evaluating both the psychological condition of, and the environmental influences upon, the general religious population. Hopefully, such findings will also serve as a bridging model between science and religion, as well as a general source of information for all who would advance in personal consciousness.

---

[*] As an example of this area of study, see *Mariology: Resolving the Confusion,* a master's thesis by this author: http://color-of-truth.com

Diagram 1: Structures of Psycho-Spiritual Theories

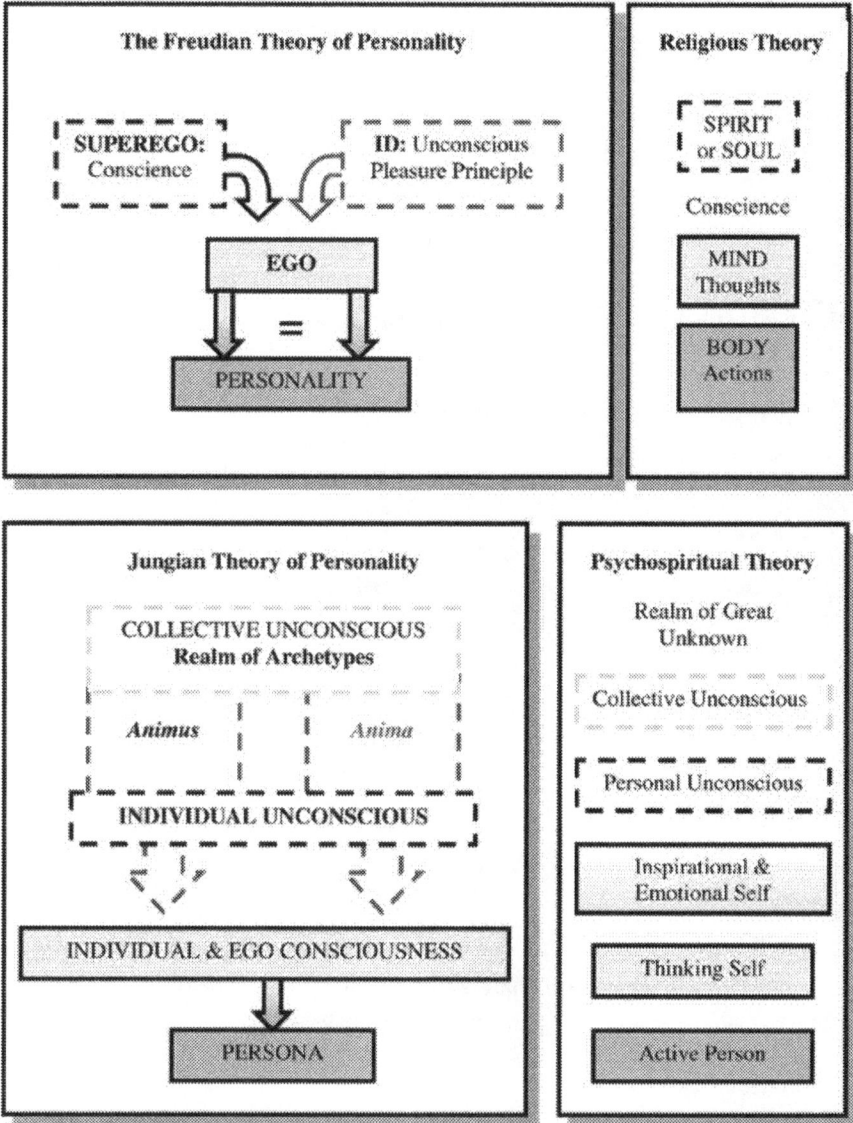

The Freudian Theory of Personality

SUPEREGO: Conscience

ID: Unconscious Pleasure Principle

EGO

=

PERSONALITY

Religious Theory

SPIRIT or SOUL

Conscience

MIND Thoughts

BODY Actions

Jungian Theory of Personality

COLLECTIVE UNCONSCIOUS
Realm of Archetypes

Animus

Anima

INDIVIDUAL UNCONSCIOUS

INDIVIDUAL & EGO CONSCIOUSNESS

PERSONA

Psychospiritual Theory

Realm of Great Unknown

Collective Unconscious

Personal Unconscious

Inspirational & Emotional Self

Thinking Self

Active Person

109

Diagram 2: Psychological and Religious Concepts

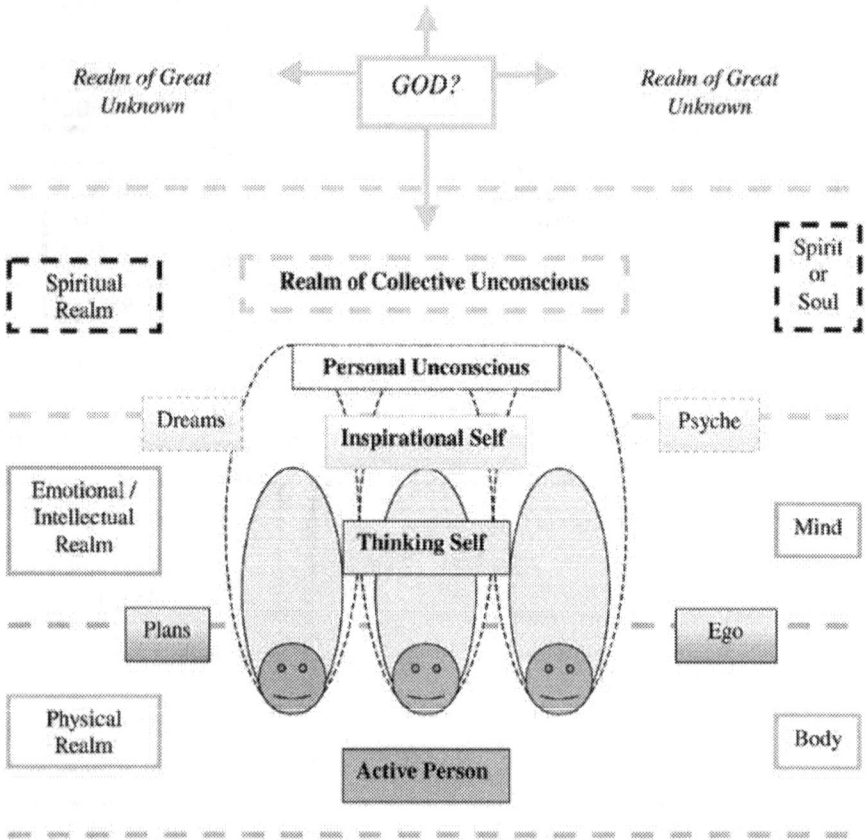

Religious beliefs and concepts, and scientific knowledge concerning the psycho-spiritual sphere can be contained in three general, thematic classifications that correspond sequentially to; spirit, mind, and body.

Diagram 3: Stages of Psychospiritual Interpretation

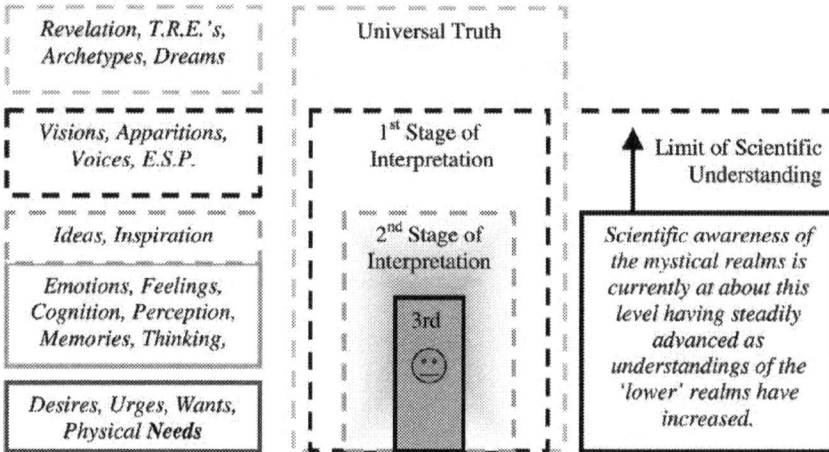

Revelation, T.R.E.'s, Archetypes, Dreams	Universal Truth	
Visions, Apparitions, Voices, E.S.P.	1st Stage of Interpretation	Limit of Scientific Understanding
Ideas, Inspiration	2nd Stage of Interpretation	*Scientific awareness of the mystical realms is currently at about this level having steadily advanced as understandings of the 'lower' realms have increased.*
Emotions, Feelings, Cognition, Perception, Memories, Thinking,	3rd	
Desires, Urges, Wants, Physical Needs		

Human knowledge has developed following the formula; body, mind, and spirit. Unfortunately, we tend to remain preoccupied with what we are familiar with, and as a result, most of our energies are invested at the 'lower' (red) levels of operation.

Diagram 4: Conceptual Values of White, Blue, and Red

White: *Spiritual, Origin, Soul, Inspiration, Creative. Containing All Colors, To do with inner spirit, or soul. Associated with the spiritual or noumenal realm. Our connecting point with God. The immortal aspect. The search for higher purpose, or The Divine. Pure religion*

Blue: *Emotional, Feminine, Contemplation, Sympathetic, Wisdom, Mental: To do with the mind, emotions, or intellect. Perception. Thinking. Affecting one emotionally. Desires and moods. Psychological. Rational. Planning. Conceptual.*

Red: *Physical, Masculine, Body, Action, Pragmatic: To do with the body. Physiological. Tangible perception. Matter. The five physical senses, sight, hearing, touch, taste and smell. Physically quantifiable.*

Diagram 5: Properties of the Color Spectrum

700 nm's

400 nm's

The visible color spectrum ranges from deep red at 700nm, to deep blue at 400nm.

Diagram 6: The Electromagnetic Spectrum

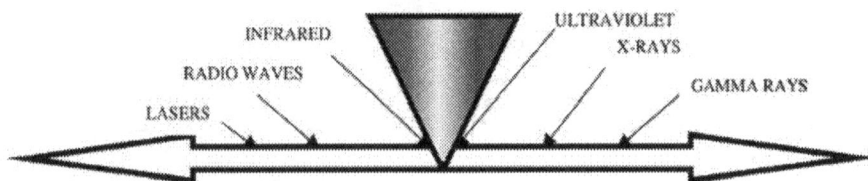

INFRARED

ULTRAVIOLET

X-RAYS

RADIO WAVES

GAMMA RAYS

LASERS

The visible spectrum comprises only about 1/60th of the known electromagnetic spectrum

Diagram 7: Conceptual Triads – White, Blue, Red

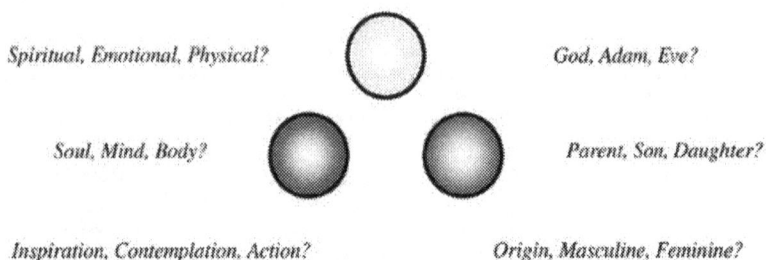

Spiritual, Emotional, Physical?

God, Adam, Eve?

Soul, Mind, Body?

Parent, Son, Daughter?

Inspiration, Contemplation, Action?

Origin, Masculine, Feminine?

8: The Standard Colors for the Four Primary Elements; Fire, Water, Air, and Earth

9: Symbolic Elements of the Greek Soul

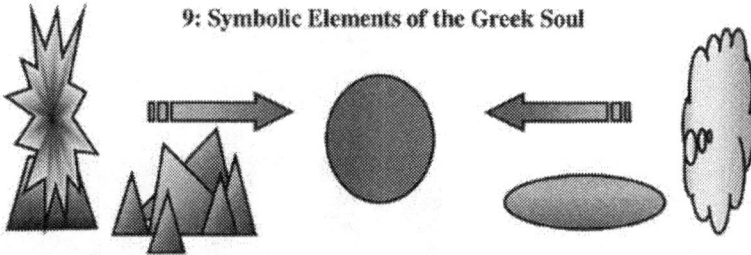

According to Ancient Greek philosophy, the immortal human soul was a mixture of fire (red) and water (blue). This matches with Bible references to the presence of God in fire, tongues of fire, water, and clouds, and has intriguing parallels with color-coded instructions to the Israelites regarding the construction of the Tabernacle and temple.

Diagram 10: Atomic Structure

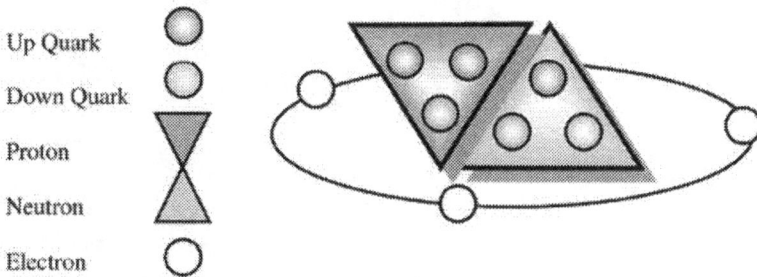

Up Quark

Down Quark

Proton

Neutron

Electron

The physical composition of the atom reflects triadic numbers and processes

113

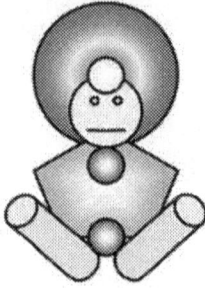

Diagram 11: Chakras   **12: The Cosmic Circle**   **13: The Individual Triad**

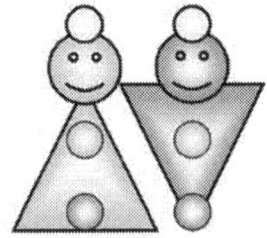

Diagram 14: The Hindu Trimurti

Brahma (Creator)   *Shiva (Fertility and Death)*   *Vishnu (Preserver of Life)*[1]

Diagram 15: Triadic Correlations in Eastern Traditions

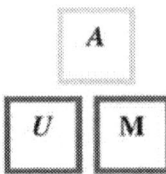

The sacred AUM symbol, the Tantric system, the Tao Te Ching, and the Hindu Trimurti are all loosely, albeit profoundly connected through unconscious archetypal recognitions

[1] Note: Frame colors added by the author for clarification

114

Note: Illustrated here are the political colors of the Arab League established in opposition to Israeli sovereignty. A handful of African nations such as Comoros, Somalia, Djibouti, Mauritania and Eritrea are currently in the Arab League (2004), but are not included here because they didn't officially exist before 1948.[1] The PLO is included because its origins were established before this time.

Diagram 16: Political Colors of the Arab League c. 1960

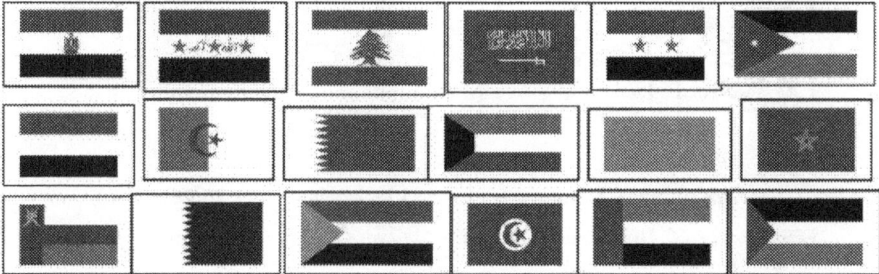

(L to R, top to bottom): Egypt (current H.Q. of Arab League), Iraq, Lebanon, Saudi Arabia, Syria, Transjordan (now Jordan), Yemen, Algeria, Bahrain, Kuwait, Libya, Morocco, Oman, Qatar, Sudan, Tunisia, the United Arab Emirates, and the P.L.O.

Diagram 17: The Arab – Israeli; Cain and Abel Dynamic

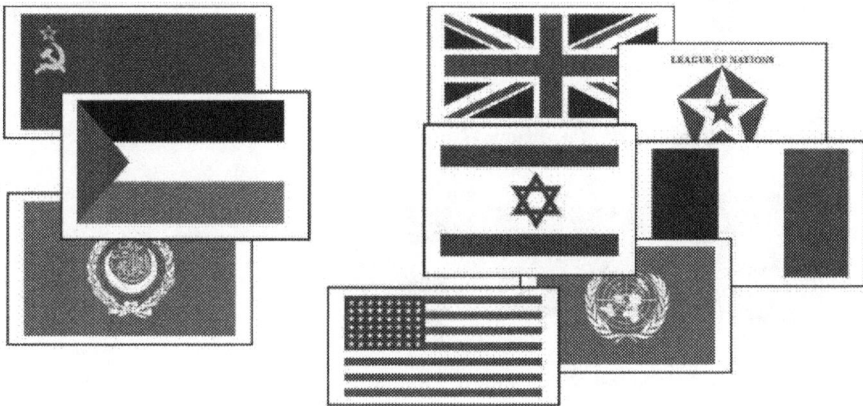

---

[1] The Jewish State of Israel was declared independent in 1948

Diagram 18: Pre-1800s Papacy and Holy Roman Emperors

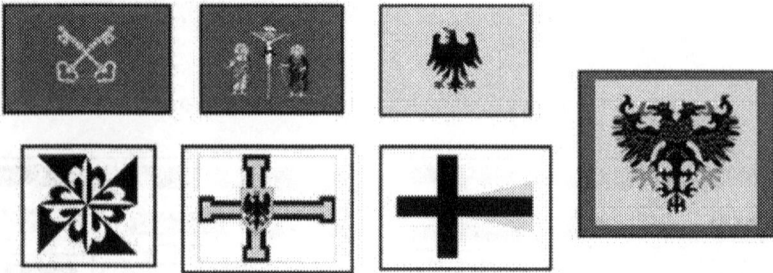

(Clockwise); French Papal Enclave c.1300, Papacy 1669, 14thC Holy Roman Emperor, 17thC Holy Roman Emperor, Teutonic Knights, Grandmaster of Teutonic Knights, Dominicans (Inquisitors)

Diagram19: Flags of France, Austria, Prussia, and Germany in 1918

Diagram 20: Traditional Colors of the Kingdom of France

Fleur-de-Lysee, and 'Trinity' flags, French Ensign 1660.   Royal Bourbons

Diagram 21: 'The Allies' and the 'Central Powers' during World War I

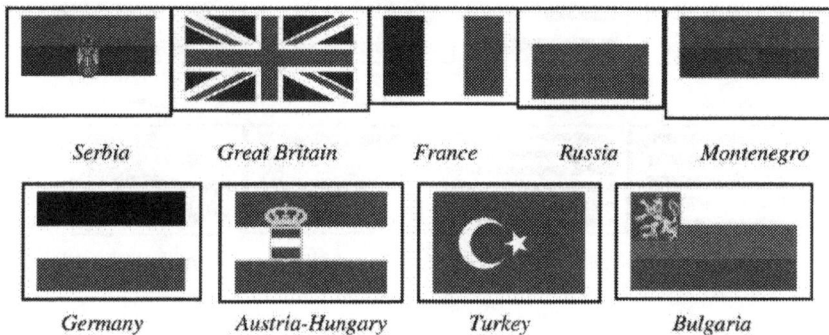

Serbia	*Great Britain*	*France*	*Russia*	*Montenegro*

Germany	*Austria-Hungary*	*Turkey*	*Bulgaria*

Diagram 22: The Asian Dynamic

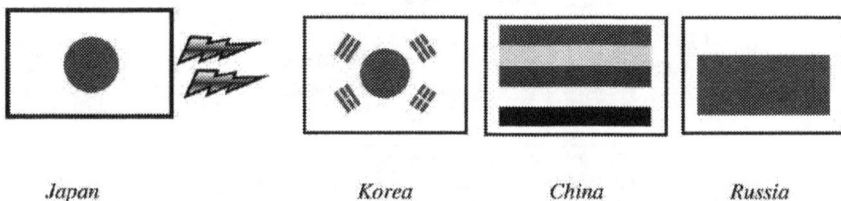

Japan	*Korea*	*China*	*Russia*

Diagram 23: The Twelve Red/White/Blue Nations of the Allied Forces

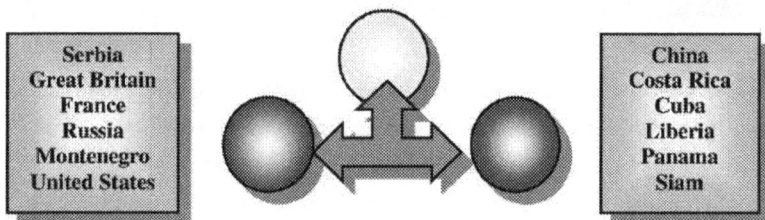

Serbia Great Britain France Russia Montenegro United States	China Costa Rica Cuba Liberia Panama Siam

117

Diagram 24: Eight More Allied Nations

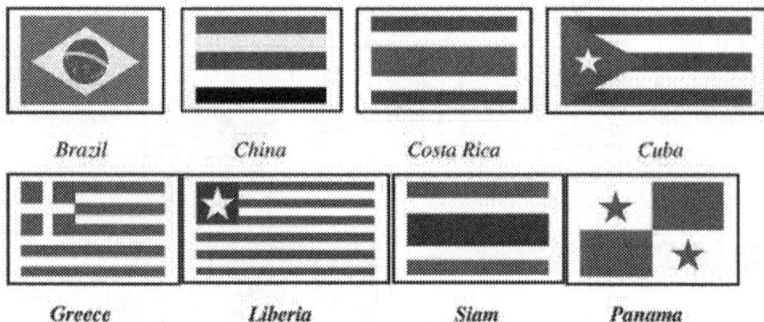

Brazil   China   Costa Rica   Cuba

Greece   Liberia   Siam   Panama

Diagram 25: The Remarkable Display of Post-WWII Historical Symbolism

(L. to R. top to bottom) England, United States, Australia, France, Norway, Russia, South Korea (WWI), China, Holland, Hawaii, Philippines, Guam, Wake Island, Midway Island, Hong Kong, British Malaya, Thailand, New Zealand, Luxembourg, Canada, South Korea (after WWII), and South Africa.

Diagram 26: Opposition Forces; WWI, WWII, Korean, & Cold War

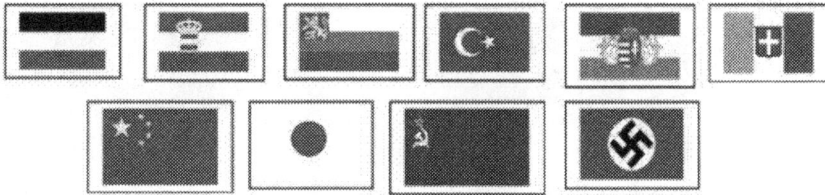

(L to R, top to bottom) Germany WWI, Austria-Hungary, Romania, Turkey, Bulgaria, Italy, Red China, Japan, USSR, Third Reich (Germany WWII).

Diagram 27: The Three Subdivisions of the Red Archetype

First male archetype, health, energy, vitality, male, power, greatness, pioneering, leadership, sexual energy, all things physical, strength, heroism, positive, the body, vigor, stimulating, passion, material prosperity	Lust, sins, dragon, fights-with- angel, devours-the-Savior, takes away peace, threat to God's people, mother of harlots Communism, war, opposition to white, absence of feminine, Fascism, Nazism, rage, force, anger	The hero, male, central figure, first-out-of-womb, birthright, red cloak, sacrifice, ritual, conqueror of evil, strong, valiant, true, savior, life, will, power, leadership, battles, martyrs, pioneers, victorious
(i) Original Male	*(ii) Perverse Male*	*(iii) The Hero Figure*

Diagram 28: Traditional Islamic Symbolism

| *Algeria* | *Tunisia* | *Pakistan* | *Comoros* |

119

Diagram 29: Solar and Lunar Symbolism in Religion

The 'pagan' influences upon both Christianity and Islam were based upon the sun and the moon respectively

Diagram 30: Jesus and Mary as Archetypes

Diagram 31: Monotheism's Triple-Triadic Archetype

Diagram 32: The Progressions of Truth

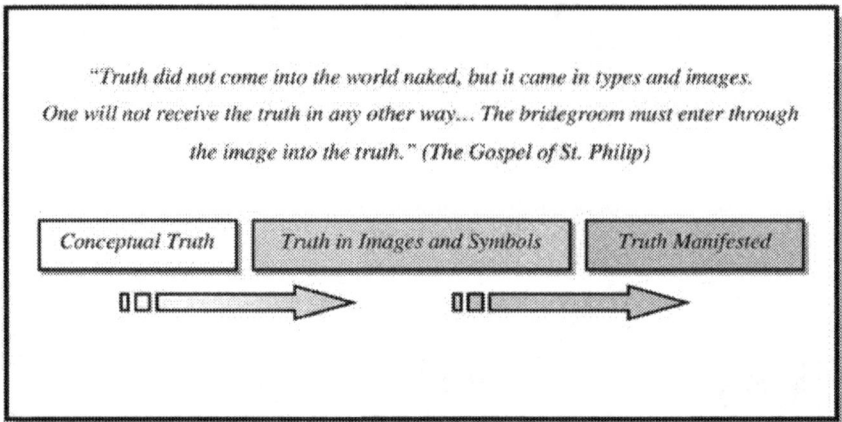

"*Truth did not come into the world naked, but it came in types and images. One will not receive the truth in any other way... The bridegroom must enter through the image into the truth.*" *(The Gospel of St. Philip)*

| Conceptual Truth | Truth in Images and Symbols | Truth Manifested |

SELECTED FEATURES OF THE TRIADIC ARCHETYPE: EXAMPLES 1-8

Remembering that each individual human hosts their own specific triadic sequence despite their primary designation as either male or female respectively (fig.13 ♣), so do many of the charted aspects, themes, attributes, or agencies listed here carry their own intrinsic triadic formulae despite being part of a greater or larger triadic theme.

Therefore whilst the propriety of many of the listed triads are clearly self-evident, we should also allow for the fact that, (a) this is not yet a fully developed science;(b) that all human taxonomies are ultimately somewhat limited and artificial; (c) that a certain amount of intersection and overlapping amongst listed themes is unavoidable; and (d) that some of the triads listed are not discussed in this particular book (see extra notes*).

We need also note that although the following tables display the information in a horizontal-linear mode, many of the triads listed might be better represented in vertical, triangular, or even circular mode, such as the spirit-mind-body triad (vertical descending), the white-blue-red triad (triangular), and the proton-neutron-electron (circular).

I also humbly acknowledge that alterations or adjustments may be necessary in the future in order to 'tighten-up', add, or even eliminate some of the more abstract triads, and I eagerly await suggestions from those who may be more experienced in any given field.

In short, please be patient with a very inadequate taxonomy, and simply observe the striking consistency of the triadic archetype phenomenon in so many shapes, forms, and disciplines.

Example 1: Science / Quantum Physics / Numeric

	Red	White	Blue
A	Deep Reds	Light	Deep Blues
B	Infrared	Color Spectrum	Ultraviolet
C	Proton	Electron	Neutron
D	Up Quarks	Gluons	Down Quarks
E	Electricity	Electromagnetic Spectrum	Magnetism
F	700 nanometers	One, 300nms, or Infinity	400 nanometers
G	Positive	Fusion / Union	Negative
H	Experimentation	Observation	Reflection

Example 2: Ontological / Thematic / General

	Red	White	Blue
A	Masculine Elements	Original Principle	Feminine Elements
B	Creation	Cosmic Truth	Knowledge
C	The Word	The Way	Wisdom
D	External	Eternal	Internal
E	Action	Concept	Plan
F	Energy	Inspiration	Reason
G	Body	Spirit	Mind
H	Justice	Life	Liberty
J	Blood	Oxygen	Water
K	Fire	Air	Water
L	When?	Why?	How?
M	Solution	Problem	Analysis
N	Achievement	Desire	Purpose
P	Achieve	Concieve	Believe
Q	Logos	Ethos	Pathos
R	Yang	Union	Yin
S*	Left	Center	Right

Example 3: Psychological / Psychospiritual

	Red	White	Blue
A*	Material	Spiritual	Social
B	Actual	Noumenal	Ideal
C	Reality	Inspirations / Dreams	Thoughts
D	Creativity	Unconsciousness	Consciousness
E	Extrinsic	Questers	Intrinsic
F	Personal Choice	Genetics	Environment
G*	Animus	Psyche / Persona	Anima
H	Masculinity	Integrated Psyche	Femininity

122

Example 4: Human / Relational / Social

	Red	White	Blue
A	Body	Soul	Mind
B	Physical	Spiritual	Emotional
C	Masculine	Creation	Feminine
D	Man	Love	Woman
E	Father / Husband	Parental / Conjugal Love	Mother / Wife
F	Brother / Son	Sibling / Filial Love	Sister / Daughter
G	Individual	Community	Family
H	Productive	Inspirational / Creative	Intellectual
J	Man	Union and Creation	Woman
K	Sperm	Conception	Egg

Example 5: Biblical / Judeo-Christian / Theological

	Red	White	Blue
A	Adam	God	Eve
B	Tree of Life	Paradise	Tree of Knowledge
C	Logos	God / Yahweh	Sophia
D	The Word	God	Wisdom
E	Messiah, Redeemer	Jehovah	Bride, Co-Redeemer
F	Burning Bush	Presence of God	Enveloping Cloud
G	Pillar of Fire	Mercy Seat	Pillar of Cloud
H	Temple	Ark of Covenant	Tabernacle
J*	Pillar; "Joachim"	The Temple	Pillar; "Boaz"
K	Outer Courtyard	Holy of Holies	Inner Sanctuary
L	Baptism of Fire	Baptism of Spirit	Baptism of Water
M	Charity	Faith	Hope
N	Flesh	Soul	Conscience
P*	The Son	The Father	Holy Spirit

Example 6: Other Religious / Mystical / Mythological

	Red	White	Blue
A	Body	Spirit	Mind
B	Healthy	Holy	Happy
C	M	A	U
D	Red Chakra	Crown Chakra	Blue Chakra
E*	Heart	Inner Eye	Throat
F*	Outer	Secret	Inner
G*	Sat	Ananda	Chit
H	Vishnu	Brahma	Shiva
J	Te	Tao	Ching
K	Jade Pure	Great Pure	Upper Pure
L	Yang	Nirvana	Yin
M*	Binah	Keter	Choma

N*	Ru'ach	Neshemah	Nefesh
P*	Lingam	Conception	Yoni
Q	Actual Truth	True Religious Experience	Conceptual Truth
R	Ritual	Meditation	Prayer
S	Charity	Love	Compassion
T*	Astlik	Vahagn	Anahit
U*	Hades	Zeus	Poseidon
V*	Horus	Osiris	Isis
W*	Inti	Viracocha	Illapa
X	Sun	The Heavens	Moon

Example 7: Historical / Political / Sociological

	Red	White	Blue
A	Industrial Revolution	Renaissance	Enlightenment
B	Products	Ideas	Plans
C	Mechanical	Artistic	Philosophical
D	Technical Skills	Morality	Academics
E	Industry	Government / Law	Education
F	Military	Executive	Legislative
G	Society	Religion	Science
H	Individualism	Universalism	Collectivism
J	Capitalism	Democracy	Socialism
K	Practice	Ideology	Theory
L*	Holy Roman Empire	Papacy	Kingdom of France

Example 8: Other Possible Representations

	Red	White	Blue
A	Sun	Stars	Moon
B	Earth	Sky	Oceans
C	Fire	Air	Water
D	Solid	Gas	Liquid
E	Core	Atmosphere	Surface
F	Hot	Cold	Cool
G*	Experiential	Attitudinal	Creative
H	Act	Feel	Think
J	Pragmatism	Morality	Ethics
K	Get	Want	Plan
L	Comprehend	Observe	Interpret
M	End	Beginning	Middle

* Examples 1-8: Explanatory Notes

2S: Left and right positions may be reversible

3A: Sociologist William James' social theory

3F: Religious personality types as viewed in the study of the Psychology of Religion

3G: Concepts from Jungian psychology

5J: Pillars of Solomon's temple were named 'Smiter' and 'Sustainer' respectively

5P: Although listed here in idealized format, the Christian Trinity has traditionally been conceptually devoid of the feminine (♣ 17)

6E & F: Aspects of the Hindu and Buddhist Chakra systems

6G: From Joseph Campbell's *The Power of Myth*, ancient Sanskrit language: "Sat" meaning 'being', "Chit" meaning 'consciousness', and "Ananda" meaning 'bliss or rapture'

6M: The crowning triad of the Kabala in Jewish mysticism (♣ 19)

6N: From Jewish mysticism's Zohar; the three aspects of the psyche or soul

6P: Hindu genitalia worship; 'Lingam' being the male organ; Yoni the female

6T, U, V, W: From the mythologies of Armenia, Greece, Egyptian, and Incan civilizations

7L: This topic is discussed fully in *The Color of Truth Volume II* by this author

8G: From Stephen Covey's *Seven Habits of Highly Effective People*

Table B: Sample of Possibly-Providential Numbers

40 hours	Jesus in the tomb
40 days	The Flood Judgment
40 days	Temptation of Christ
40 days	Battle of the Bulge – last German offensive in WW II
40 weeks	Of human pregnancy
40 years	Jacob's Birthright to Isaac's Blessing
40 years	David's reign, 7 yrs plus 33 yrs (also Saul and Solomon)
40 years	Moses' in Pharaoh's palace; 40yrs time in desert; 40 yrs time to Jordan
40 years	Charlemagne holds title "Protector of the Church"
40 years	Copernicus' age at major discoveries
40 years	Muhammad's age at time of visions, and wife's age at marriage
40 years	Duration of Great Schism – 1378 - 1417
40 years	Luther's Bible copied 100,000 times
40 years	Of Church sponsored witch-burnings in 16th & 17th Centuries
40 years	Existence of Berlin Wall
40	Generations between Abraham and Jesus (Matthew's gospel)
40	Antipopes during 1200 year period: Constantine to Reformation
40 camps	Between Red Sea and river Jordan during wilderness journey
400 miles	Abraham's journey to Canaan
400 men	Esau's army waiting to attack Jacob
400 years	Tabernacle serves as center-point of Hebrew faith
400 years	Moses to David
400 years	Reformation to Bolshevik Revolution 1517-1917
400 years	Ottoman occupation of Palestine 1517-1917
400 nm's	Nanometer measurement of deep blue color
40,000	Israelites do battle at Jericho
430 years	Israelites slavery in Egypt – before Moses
430 years	Between prophet Malachi and arrival of Jesus
430 years	Between Jewish revolt and baptism of King Clovis I
430 years	Between Emperor Constantine and Charlemagne
430 years	Between Reformation and Jews reclaiming homeland

Table C: Selected Examples of Appearances of the Number Twelve in Mythology, Astrology, Religion & Politics

Mythology / Astrology / Religion	Biblical / Political
12 Greek Olympian gods	12 Fountains at Elim (Exodus 15:27)
12 Egyptian deities (ennead & triad)	12 Stones on the Ephod breastplate
12 Roman gods and goddesses	12 Tribes of Israel (via Jacob)
12 Labours of Heracles (Greek)	12 Hebrew Judges & Prophets
12 Signs of the Western Zodiac	12 Months of Gehinnom (Judaism)
12 Realms of Norse mythology	12 Age of Jesus in the Temple
12 Gods of Norse mythology	12 Disciples of John the Baptist
12 Animals of the Chinese Zodiac	12 Apostles of Jesus
12 Cycles of Rta; Aryan mythology	12 Baskets of leftovers miracle
12 Divas (Hindu / Buddhist)	12 Girl raised from dead miracle
12 Yaksa Guardians (Japan)	12 Years of diseased woman miracle
12 Upper worlds; Polynesian myth	12 Angels; Book of Revelation
12 Avatars; Hindu Vishnu (messiah)	12 Gates of Heaven; Book of Rev.
12 Adityas; sun gods of Hinduism,	12 Stars in woman's crown; Rev.
12 Idols of Crom Cruach (Celtic)	12 Fruits of the Tree of Life; Rev.
12 Members of a modern jury	12 Days of Christmas (to Epiphany)
12 Months of the year	12 Disciples of St. Columba
12 Carbon; and triple-alpha Process	12 Carolingian French Kings (Vol II)
12 Colours; standard colour wheel	12 R-W-B coalition in WW I
12 Arabic tribes (of Ishmael)	12 R-W-B coalition in WW II
12 Yrs; Muhammad's visions to Hijra	12 R-W-B coalition in Korean War
12 Imams in Shi'ia Islam	12 Stars in European Flag

For a fuller exposition of the phenomenon of synchronistic data please see *The Color of Truth* series; *Volumes I, II and III* by this author.

Or visit the Color of Truth webpage: http://color-of-truth.com

PART THREE
A UNIVERSAL SYNCHRONICITY

(I)

Introducing newly-compiled data centering upon the phenomena of subliminal, chromo-numeric, semiotic archetypes; a recent and original discovery that fundamentally rewrites our ontological understandings of human history..

(II)

...and reviewing convincing evidence for the existence of these substantial archetypes at the individual, atomic, tribal, political, collective, and religious levels; with a view to applying the principles thereof to the resolution of religion-based social problems

CHAPTER SEVEN

CHROMATIC ARCHETYPES

An introduction to color archetypes in nature and society

As explained in Chapter Six, the main drawback to Jungian archetypal theory is its inaccessibility to the common man due to the relatively obscure subject material and the lack of substantial supporting evidence. Delving into dreams and the realms of the unconscious for one's data is all very well for the trained specialist, but for the rest of us who inhabit the conscious realms, such findings will always seem just a little arcane. Now, what *would* be useful for us base-dwellers would be the introduction of a simple, clear, logical, and highly visible common language that we could all understand without doctorates in parapsychology. A language that included 'all important things' in its embrace. A language so universal and obvious that its truths could not be misinterpreted – even by the cleverest of scholars.

Well, the very good news for all of us (except perhaps for sectarian enthusiasts) is the recent uncovering of just such a universal, self-evident language; a language that permeates most, if not all aspects of human endeavor. Evident all around us in the fundamental structures of existence, chromo-numeric semiotics (colors, numbers, signs, and symbols) saturate both the natural world and human society. Here in substantial form, is the evidence of Jung's subliminal archetypes. In a remarkable if not astounding discovery, it has been found that the physiological, psychological, and noumenal characteristics of man are reflected symbolically throughout creation with a stunning consistency. As we shall soon see, from the arts to the sciences, from spirituality to psychology, even incorporating religious and political history, this self-evident language simply cannot be denied.

Existing a-priori since the first moments of creation, this unified and interrelated correlation of colors, forms, and symbols is rooted in the very dynamics of primordial energy itself. Indeed, this primordial 'language' permeates life so thoroughly that – just like the proverbial goldfish that "can't see the water" – its very *omneity** has apparently prevented us from seeing it too. If I may be so bold.. here at last perhaps, is the evidence we have been waiting for. Man and his cosmic environment are apparently intimately – albeit so-far subliminally – connected by this universal, self-evident language; an analogous shared language between society, nature, and the cosmos, that promises stimulating insights into so-far unknown dimensions, including the upper reaches of the mind and spirit of man.

This archetypal-yet-substantial language will form the foundation of our psychospiritual theory, inasmuch as it relates uncompromisingly with both religious and scientific theory. Clear, unambiguous, and self-evident, the most dynamic features of our investigation will revolve around the 'sciences' of (a) chromonumerics, and (b) semiotics, in relationship to archetypal formulae. The former being the study of colors and numbers, and the latter, the study of signs and symbols. However, because we need to maintain conceptual clarity; because we are primarily interested in universal formulae; and because all visible signs and symbols are themselves constructed of chromatic and numeral structures, we may consolidate both areas of study under the same general title of "archetypal semiotics."

For the reader's better understanding this simply means that we are going to explore those symbols, signs, colors and numbers in history and the natural world that share similar or identical characteristics across social, cultural, or academic borders. In particular, we will be discussing those archetypal semiotic forms whose thematic 'values' share a universal appeal.

Archetypal Semiotics

The original study of archetypal semiotics is entitled *The Color of Truth Volume I: Patterns in Light* [†] and comprises the first of three volumes that jointly run to over seven hundred pages of text and diagrams. Those pages record symbolic patterns and their universal meanings throughout history, sociology, art, quantum physics, mythology, and ancient and modern religions. Naturally, in a relatively brief study such as this we cannot indulge in too much detail, hence only a select few examples will be proffered as proofs of the central findings of those volumes, to which end

---

[*] Omneity; wholeness, integrality, completeness
[†] See http://color-of-truth.com

131

the reader's attention is now directed to the brief summaries (as mentioned in the technical foreword) of familiar signs and symbols interspersed in the text throughout Part Three and denoted thus; '#'. Corresponding illustrations can be found amongst the color plates whenever the text is accompanied by the symbol '♣'.

Reducing the topical complexity further, we need only draw brief attention to the numeral aspect of chromo-numerics, as the application of this data to the specialty of psychology remains limited to the recognition of specific patterns that permeate history. Suffice for now to inform the reader that these historical patterns center upon major historical events such as the rise and fall of dynasties, nations, religions and empires; as well as other key social developments such as wars, revolutions, reformations and renewals, and are both statistically and thematically consistent with certain numeric formulas present in universal symbolism. Already recognized by Carl Jung as having archetypal values beyond normal knowledge, the numbers 3, 4, 7, and 10 (and their multiples) are confirmed here as having particular import in history inasmuch as they are attached in significant ways to historical figures or events, and, against any probability of conscious orchestration deny all the 'natural' odds of reoccurrence. If time and space allowed, I would be happy to list years of research statistics for the reader's perusal, but presenting such data in the unavoidably colossal table might all too soon become tedious reading. For now, I hope the few direct references made in the following chapters will serve to prove my claims of a distinct series of numeric patterns in history that reflect an archetypal design. Meanwhile, to view a short sampling of the numeric phenomenon please see Tables 'B' and 'C' (pages 126, 127) at the rear of the illustrations section.

We now open our discussion on chromatic archetypes with a brief foray into the realm of color before addressing the interconnected relationships of archetypes, symbols, colors, psychology and religion, in connection with the functions and structures of the human mind and spirit.

The Symbolic Spectrum
The first point to be clearly made is that light is visible energy, and color is that visible energy separated into different components, depending upon the length of the light wave (♣ 5). These visible light waves (color) are measured in nano-meters (nm) by special apparatus that identifies their numeric properties; "The longest wavelength we can see is deep red at 700nm. The shortest wavelength visible to humans is deep blue, or violet at 400nm." [1] (Please note the presence of the aforementioned numbers; 3,4,7, and 10).

132

For most of us color is perceived through our eyes, and we are able to identify a whole range of colors from violet to indigo, blue, green, yellow, orange and red. But what most people are unaware of is that this color range is only about $1/60^{th}$ of the known electromagnetic spectrum, and although we cannot 'see' the other aspects of the spectrum (such as radio-waves, microwaves, lasers and x-rays), we are most definitely affected by them physically (♣ 6). The implication is, that based on the evidence that radio waves, lasers and microwaves can be experienced *physically* and hence have effective substance in relation to the human body (think sunburn or TV dinners) then perhaps color, which is after all just another aspect of the electromagnetic spectrum – may also have previously unrecognized substantial effects on human beings.

In recent years many 'mystical' sciences have surfaced in the Western sphere that claim associations between sound, color, and parts of the body. The whole Tantric spiritual system for example, familiar to Hindus and Buddhists for centuries is centered upon this and other principles – whereby adherents believe that by surrounding themselves with the appropriate visual and audible stimuli they can positively affect their physiological, psychological, and spiritual well-being. The early skepticism of conventional medicine to such claims abated once it became known that light-frequencies could indeed be measured in 'waves per second' (Hz) – a discovery that effectively confirmed a 'physical' and therefore effectual aspect to color. For example, we hear sounds that operate between 16 Hz to 20,000 Hz,* but color operates on a much higher frequency, between approximately 400 billion Hz for deep red, to about 700 billion Hz for deep blue. This suggests that if we can respond emotionally to Mozart for example (or Megadeth if you prefer) – just because our ears are receptive to the frequencies of music, then why indeed shouldn't light-wave frequencies also be having a similar, although perhaps largely unnoticed effect upon us? Surely, the concept of experiencing color in myriad forms other than visually is not beyond possibility or comprehension? After all, who is going to argue that a 'silent' dog-whistle makes no sound just because we can't hear it? As we further recognize that human beings are not just physical beings, but also comprise 'mental' (rational and emotional), and spiritual aspects – isn't it reasonable to investigate the possibility that psychospiritual aspects of the human make-up are also subject to substantial, recognizable effects from chromatic, numeric, or semiotic influences – just as Jung discovered with the perennial occurrences of archetypes?

---

* Hz; abbreviation of 'hertz' – a unit of frequency, or cycle such as in light waves

133

Color Values and Meanings

Now things get very interesting, because although they have sometimes used different terminology for these categories, many eminent scholars have written on the topic of color as a form of energy that has substantial effect upon us; physically, emotionally, and spiritually. And although certain sources may differ in philosophical opinion about color-related matters their data and findings, even amongst the metaphysicians are strikingly consistent. Sir Isaac Newton, Paracelcus, Faber Birren, Johann Wolfgang von Goethe, Rudolf Steiner, Albert Einstein, Edgar Cayce, Faber Birren, Betty Wood, John Gage, and many more, have each hinted at the conclusions presented in this work.[*] The concepts are basically the same. Each has recognized that color contains within itself hitherto unknown properties, associations and meanings that await investigation.

Based upon such findings, not just a few modern psychologists have developed treatment programs utilizing color properties in some form or other.[2] To the best of my knowledge however, none of the aforementioned have yet formulated a universal theory centered upon archetypal semiotics, although many indeed have made groundbreaking discoveries in the field – for which we are greatly indebted. We will shortly view specifics of those findings, particularly concerning the colors white, blue and red. But if the reader is inclined towards succinctness and is willing to accept my conclusions or, has already read *The Color of Truth Volume I*, then he or she may simply view the summarizing table of color-values ('D') on page 139, and move directly to Part Four. For a more detailed understanding however the reader is respectfully advised to read the complete text.

The following summary of color values for white, blue, and red are compiled from the published conclusions of scholars and experts in the fields of psychology, world history, physics and metaphysics, including a variety of new age or modern sources ranging from color-therapists, to occult practitioners, to interior decorators, and incorporating my own broad-ranging research in this area.[3] The mythical and religious connections to these specific colors will be dealt with separately in more depth in Chapter Eleven. As with all classification systems, there will of course be some merging of concepts from color to color. For just as each has individual characteristics that give it its own specific identity, in reality, all colors merge in the electromagnetic spectrum to form true light.

Interestingly enough, it is impossible to accurately discern the 'trueness' of any particular color in isolation without the illuminating

---

[*] Please refer to Bibliography for a comprehensive listing

perspective of true light in the first place. Therefore, the first important principle that can be metaphorically deduced from the dynamics of the color spectrum is that one first needs to be in the universally-objective position (of light) before one can accurately determine true value.

The 'Color' White

Science tells us that when all colors are combined in light, we get the impression of white. We already know that the color spectrum ranges from deep red at 700nm, to deep blue (or violet) at 400nm. This means that white light incorporates and encompasses all the other colors combined, and can be represented either by the number range 300, or 1,000. That is, that the visible 'value' of white in the electromagnetic spectrum can be assessed as either the difference between, or the sum of all the colors between 400nm and 700nm. In relation to our ability to see colors, white therefore represents 'everything'. In relation to the source of color, white represents 'the origin', and in relation to the individuality of colors, white represents 'unity or wholeness'. As the source of energy for our planet, white light also holds the position of 'life-source'. Supporting these themes, in his book *Light, Color and Environment* (1969) [4] Faber Birren documents the results of scientific experiments that demonstrate the ability of light to affect breeding habits, and to influence the quality of the produce from captive animals (such as eggs, milk, fur etc.). This confirms the data that asserts that full spectrum 'white' light helps nourish, develop, and recreate all light-dependant beings.

In political history, one of the most notable uses of the term 'whites' was the description of the counter-revolutionary forces fighting against Communism in the Russian Civil War between 1918 –1921. In Asia too the Korean people reportedly earned the title "the people in white" from foreign invaders due to a perceived national spirituality, and because of the unusual fact that they have never aggressively invaded another country. In contemporary understandings of the color white, Edgar Cayce the spiritual healer says that white is the perfect aura. "If our souls were in perfect balance, then all our color vibrations would blend and we would have an aura of pure white". In her book *The Healing Power of Color,* color-healer Betty Wood also describes white as a most sacred color associated with "wholeness, purity, and innocence" and "spiritual authority." Whilst the Sherwin-Williams Co., who specialize in painting and decorating give this description of the influence of white on moods: "White purifies, energizes, unifies; in combination, enlivens all other colors."

Finally, in his fascinating book *The Secret Language of Symbols* (1993) psychologist Dr. David Fontana notes: "White represents purity, virginity and the transcendent… For the Tibetans, white is the color of Mount Meru, the mountain 'at the center of the world' embodying ascent to enlightenment."[5]

The Color Blue

The Encarta Encyclopedia lists deep blue and violet as the same color. This matches the thematic findings of this work, but a clarification needs to be made between the different shades of deep blue such as violet-blue and indigo-blue, and other often-confused shades such as purple and mauve – for reasons that will soon become clear. In this presentation therefore, 'blue' represents all shades between sky blue and deep royal blue, such as the blue of the United Nations flag, and the blue in the French flag respectively.

In recent history, we can see that none of the axis or communist nations central to 20th Century conflicts contained blue in their flags at the time of conflict (♣ 26 – to be covered in Chapter Ten). However, during the war years there was an unspoken tradition of prostitutes wearing blue as a badge of their profession – an interesting connection with female sexuality that could have some bearing on the naming of sexually-explicit blue movies? In scientific experiments conducted under colored glass by Dr. John Ott,[6] the results were almost exactly opposite to those carried out under red-tinted glass inasmuch as captive animals were pacified by blue: the pregnancy rate increased significantly; the ratio of females born increased 50%; whilst the newborn males decreased 50%; thus suggesting a direct correlation between the color blue and the female gender, and the color red for males. Blue light effected positive female results, whilst red light did the same for the males. David Fontana summarizes the color blue as:

> .. the hue of the intellect, peace and contemplation. It represents water and coolness, and symbolizes the sky, infinity, the emptiness from which existence arises… the color of the Virgin as Queen of Heaven… denotes faith, compassion and the waters of baptism. …the goddess of love.[7]

Three respected authors on the subject of color-healing and auras; Edgar Cayce, Ingaer Naess, and Betty Wood, collectively agree that "blue…moves us towards the more spiritual aspects of life and away from the physical level." Naess continues, describing blue as "a peaceful and relaxing color" having "a pacifying effect." It is also "spiritually stimulating, being the color of the soul, and of purity." Cayce reiterates these concepts stating that "blue has always been the color of the spirit, the symbol of contemplation, prayer and heaven". In the concluding color chart of his booklet *Auras* he attributes "spiritual, artistic, and selflessness" to the color blue. Betty Wood goes into considerable depth in describing the values associated with blue including its cultural association with "truth, revelation, wisdom, loyalty, fertility, constancy, and chastity" – concepts also reflected in traditional heraldry. Not surprisingly, Wood also connects blue with "the feminine principle, the Great Mother,... comfort, compassion, peace and healing." In an interesting note on a chapter about healing she adds that blue "is only superceded by its higher counterpart.. indigo, the ray of spirituality" (purple). This ascending relationship with the color purple will also be discussed in due course.

Our painter-decorators define the properties of the color blue on mood as, "relaxing, refreshing, cooling, producing tranquil feelings and peaceful moods". On the subject of moods, if we look at colloquial speech 'mood' is often a regular partner to the term 'blue'. For example; "..a fit of the blues, feeling blue, a blue funk, singing the blues, being in a blue mood..." ..all of which may be associated with the mind and the emotions.

The Color Red

In the visible spectrum, red has the longest wavelengths and is therefore the strongest color, the easiest one to see. For the purposes of this paper, under the designation 'red' we include scarlet and crimson, whose numeric values also fall in the 700 nm range and who ascribe to the same symbolic properties as deep red. In ancient writings and manuscripts, red was the first recognized color recorded. Even Aristotle only recorded three colors of the rainbow; red, yellow and green, suggesting that color awareness amongst humans began with recognizing red, and has developed along the spectrum as time progressed.

In recent political history, the most notable use of the term "Reds" is in reference to Communism or communist sympathizers. In the Russian civil war of 1918-21, the 'red' forces were in direct opposition to the 'white' forces. The Soviet Red Army, and the Chinese Red Army are also so named because of their political affiliations. Here we see a correlation between the color red and masculine-authoritarian regimes. Red also factored integrally in the colors of Fascism and Nazism, and perhaps somewhat surprisingly, was one of the two central colors of pre-Reformation Christianity (more on this later). As already mentioned, scientific experiments using red-tinted glass have reported some amazing results. In Birren's reports concerning Ott's experiments it is noted that captive animals became more aggressive under red light, their appetites and weight increased, and pregnancy rates decreased, although the ratio of male births increased. Ott also discovered that the human male is physically and emotionally stimulated by red radiation. In addition to these findings, modern color healers associate red with, "will, power, life, vitality and energy," but insist that red "is never used for any type of mental healing." [8] Also often symbolic of blood, battles and wars, heroism and courage, and pioneering leader-types, in medieval heraldry red was the color of the warrior, the martyr, and representative of courage and strength.[9] Thus, sexual energy and procreation, as well as all things physical are typically associated with the color red. Thus red is reflective of the strongest and basest emotions, such as rage, lust, and anger as well as the more noble masculine virtues. Fontana summarizes the properties of red as follows:

> Symbolizing the life-force as expressed through the animal world, red is the energy coursing through the body, the color that flushes the face and swims before the eyes in violent arousal. Red is the color of war and its god, Mars, and of the greatest of the Roman gods, Jupiter. It is the color of masculinity and activity.[10]

The recognition of the hostile aspects of masculinity brings a little more complexity to the possible symbolic interpretation of the color red, and the reader should be made aware that there are indeed mitigating factors that we will address in due course. For now though, the acknowledgment of the primary *masculine* and *active* aspects associated with the color red is sufficient to our task. On the darker side mixing red with black is considered "the worst possible combination... but red can be either positive or negative". Corroborating these themes, Cayce tells us that in ancient symbolism red represented the body (as opposed to the spirit), and in his color chart he gives us the three words, "force, vigor, energy".. to define red. Our decorators too list the effects of red on mood as; "empowering, stimulating, dramatizing, competing, and stimulating passion". Finally, there is the use of the word red in common language, such as 'seeing red' (anger), 'red-blooded' (strong and high-spirited), 'red-alert' (danger), and getting the 'red carpet treatment' (being treated with respect, or as a hero).

So, as we can see in Table D, and based upon our brief examination of color-values we see a consistent, historical, symbolic association with the color red, masculinity, and physical activity (both constructive and destructive); femininity and mental activities with the color blue; and high spirituality and purity with white. Now let's see how this pattern applies to other aspects of life.

Table D: Summary of Color Values

White	Spiritual, Origin, Soul, Inspiration, Creativity, Unity, Purity, Wholeness
Blue	Emotional, Feminine, Mind, Contemplation, Sympathetic, Wisdom
Red	Physical, Masculine, Body, Action, Pragmatic,
Purple	Sovereignty, Royalty, Royal Family, Sacred, Spiritual
Green	Creation, Balance, Reproduction, Center, Harmony, Union, Healing
Gold	Of Ultimate Value, Symbol of Kingship & Prosperity
Black	Absence of light, Death, Primordial Darkness, Chaos, Evil

Spirit, Mind, and Body

Referring back to our discussions in chapter six concerning psycho-spiritual theories, and for the express purpose of understanding color values in relation to human experience, it is now necessary to make reasonably clear distinctions between the categories of 'body' 'mind' and 'spirit' so that we may more accurately identify how specific colors may be affecting these distinct, yet interdependently-synchronistic aspects of human reality. In particular, we are watching for words or phrases that correspond with the study of universal color-values as listed on the previous pages. In the following abridged summary please bear in mind that certain terms like 'psyche' or 'persona' have characteristics common to all three theoretical constructs. (Please view Table 'E' on the following page now)

Leaping straight into the conceptual fray, we immediately notice a direct and substantial correlation between these three dimensions of the human being, and the value-definitions accorded to the colors red, blue, and white respectively. If we now pair the two sets of definitions, we arrive at a very interesting red, white, and blue triad, that neatly overlaps the 'spirit, mind, body' paradigm, and corresponds not only with the physical structure of the color spectrum, whose opposite ends are represented by red and blue respectively – but also with the color coding of our psychospiritual diagrams (see ♣ 1,2, & 4).

Obviously this color-coding was not accidental. For as we can now see, the masculine and feminine features that correspond to the physical-active and the emotional-wisdom spheres respectively should indeed be symbolized by red and blue, whilst the 'spiritual' or noumenal realm, as the source of 'true light' or truth, should of course be white. The sequential white-blue-red progression is also important, as we shall soon see.

139

Table E: Structural Properties of the Human Being

Physical
To do with the body. Physiological. Tangible perception. Matter. Sensory.
The five physical senses, sight, hearing, touch, taste and smell.
Action. Actual. Physically quantifiable.

Mental / Emotional
To do with the mind, emotions, or intellect. Perception. Thinking.
Affecting one emotionally. Thoughts, desires, and moods. Psychological.
Rational. Contemplative. Planning. Conceptual. Wisdom.
(Note: It is generally recognized that the human mind is subdivided into emotional and rational aspects).

Spiritual
To do with inner spirit, or soul. Transcendent. Associated with the spiritual
or noumenal realm. Our connecting point with God.
Mystical, unworldly. The immortal aspect. The search for higher purpose,
or The Divine. Pure religion (a very rare thing).

Thus we establish the existence of a provisional, conceptual triad that incorporates at least three dimensions of existence in harmonious, although admittedly rather general terms: (1) The spirit, mind, and body triad; (2) the origin, female, and male triad, and (3), the inspiration, contemplation, and action triad. When we add the fact that astrologists measuring the values of the cosmic spectrum have concluded that the overall general color of the universe is white, but that " The universe started out young and blue, and grew gradually redder as the population of evolved 'red' giant stars built up..." [1] we are left in no doubt as to the cosmic propriety of these three colors in a specific sequence. So, based upon these recognized consensual color values of white, blue, and red, we can now observe a formulaic progression that hints at a natural order that in ideal circumstances would originate in 'inspirational' white (contains all colors), through to wise, thinking-and-planning blue (the feminine, nurturing color), and finally to active, reproductive, physical red – the masculine energy-color. Temporarily putting aside any debates about exceptions to this general rule, let's simply take a look at these color-values in context with the few examples illustrated at ♣ 9, and see whether we may actually be "on to something?" ...as Sherlock Holmes would say.

The real question of course, is what does this tell us other than simply recording the fact that masculinity and femininity correspond to the physical and mental realms, and to the color spectrum in some subliminal dimension? What else have we got here other than a quaint, perhaps even intriguing theory that links colors, numbers, and general concepts?

The answer to this question is dramatic indeed, because this token display of archetypal properties in relation to man and his world is only the proverbial 'tip of the iceberg' so-to-speak, with the greater part of the interconnected meanings of universal semiotics yet to be exposed (see Tables 1-8 in the midsection for a preview). Indeed, the proofs to come suggest – if not indeed confirm – that our very development as a species is being paralleled subliminally-yet-substantially by this symbolic, archetypal language – a language that can but express its own inviolate truths; truths that patiently await discovery and interpretation by the mind and heart of man. But who (we might ask again) is fit for the task of interpretation?

When we consider the depressingly fractured and partisan state of religion with all its associated limitations and vices, we dare not risk potential misinterpretations or manipulations by exposing these raw discoveries to traditional religionists for their subjective interpretations. Deciphering these symbolic patterns is a crucial, possibly even vital development for man. In my opinion, for such a critical task only scientists of integrity will suffice – preferably psychologists who are well versed in religion and spirituality. They may indeed be clerics – but they must first be scientists. Their sacred allegiances must favor self-evident truths over any preexistent religious beliefs, and they must be possessed of a singular objectivity. Probably most ideal for the task would be psychologists of religion or other suitable experts or professionals whose consciences and intellects remain governed primarily by humanistic principles. In short; those with the minds of true scholars, and the hearts of true saints.

However, psychologists too have their limitations. As an intellectual and conceptual science that has hesitated to some extent to approach the nebulous noumenal realm with its associated 'religious' imagery, psychology has suffered somewhat from an overabundance of literalism and a parallel dearth of symbolism, and is yet a little poorly equipped for the reading. Psychologists therefore need to update their awareness, not only of traditional religious beliefs, but also come to understand the often complex nuances that make the religious debate so fraught with frustrations.

Now, with these new psychospiritual discoveries at hand, psychologists should also become experts in universal symbolism in order to carry out their practices with up-to-date integrity, for what the doctor doesn't understand, he certainly shouldn't presume to treat. But perhaps I am speaking too soon, for we have yet to fully expose the signs and symbols under question. With the readers indulgence then, we will now explore the biological, anthropological, historical, and psychological records for more dramatic proofs of the existence of this secret-yet-observable universal code, which – in the opinion of trusted peers and scholars at least – promises to contribute so much to our future enlightenment.

CHAPTER EIGHT

INDIVIDUAL, ATOMIC, & BIBLICAL ARCHETYPES

A condensed overview of parallel themes in global symbolism that unite these three categories based upon the previously discussed universal values of the natural white, blue, and red triad of the color spectrum

Although not yet fully understood, the fact that archaeologists, explorers, anthropologists and historians regularly unearth artifacts that contain culturally-diverse, yet globally-consistent symbols during their research and discoveries further confirms that we are indeed connected through time and space, beyond cultural and ethnic borders by certain universal concepts. For, along with colors and numbers, visible symbols are yet another aspect of universal language whose meanings transcend the limited world of words. In their consistent appearances and reappearances throughout history, in different cultural, religious, and historical settings we are offered a profoundly valuable insight into human psychological and anthropological development. Coupled with the meanings and values of colors as outlined in chapter seven, and supported by Jungian theory and empirical data, apparently arbitrary historical decisions such as choosing tribal colors, or selecting political symbols such as flags or insignia of office now takes on an altogether new meaning. As we are about to see, many such symbols reflect cosmic truths that reside deep in the collective psyche (or collective spirituality), yet despite their sensory and substantial forms have somehow uncannily escaped formal, conscious, universal understanding or recognition.

Pervasive enough to affect the very patterns of history, the forces behind these phenomenon undoubtedly have archetypal (or noumenal) origins, but these particular symbols differ from abstract Jungian archetypes in that they are consistent, visible and substantial, and as such represent astounding empirical insights for comprehending the development of the human psyche – and by implication, the very meaning of life itself. The challenge of course is to bring the profound meanings of these symbols out of their 'subconscious' places of origin, and into the collective consciousness of mankind where such knowledge can benefit us all. This is our task today. However, considerable caution must be exercised in the interpretation process. For if inappropriate values are ascribed, then many symbols that indeed contain profound insights risk loosing their full impact and credibility – an occurrence already sadly prevalent in many pseudo-religious settings. Therefore, in this brief study of universal symbol-systems connected specifically to the colors white, blue, and red, we will list only those examples whose meanings are confirmed by substantiations in other cultures or religions. Examples such as the sun and the moon or the rainbow for instance, or the fire, air, water, and earth symbols of the ancient Greek fathers referred to below. As a final point of clarification, please be aware that the following definitions are not offered as 'absolutes', but rather as amalgamations of core, consistent meanings, gathered from a wide range of expert and historical sources.

Symbolism and the Greek Fathers
Let us begin by taking a brief look at some striking connections between our central chromonumerics, and the combined sources of astrology, Judeo-Christian scriptures, and the metaphysical teachings of the Ancient Greeks.

To begin with, there is the numeric principle that centers on the numbers three and four, whereby we have twelve signs of the zodiac, divided into four groups of three. The twelve Olympian gods and goddesses that later transmigrated into Roman mythology are believed in turn to have originated in early Egyptian myth – where the numbers three and four also bore primary significance (see Table C, p 127). This three-four pattern in mythology and astrology also corresponds to the twelve biblical sons of Jacob and the twelve tribes of Israel, which were likewise represented on Aaron's golden priestly breastplate by twelve precious stones, also in four groups of three. Several 120-year sequences also present themselves in Biblical dynasties, including the Saul / David / Solomon series of forty-year consecutive rules, and Moses' previous three forty-year courses in the wilderness.[1] The twelve apostles of Jesus were also numerically connected to this theme, and there are some intriguing associations between the symbolic icons of the individual tribes of Israel, such as animals, buildings, plants and the like that also coincide with the signs of the Zodiac, but only in a couple of special cases. What is more, the signs of the Zodiac are grouped into four central themes each comprising three astrological signs that represent; Fire, Water, Air, and Earth respectively. Each of these four primary elements have their own identity within symbolism. But it is worth noting that in combination, these elements, represented by the colors red, blue, white and green, not only represent all of creation but encompass the full range of the color spectrum; red and blue at opposing ends, green in the center, and white incorporating them all. When we compare this to the viewpoint of the ancient Greeks who believed that life was made up of four factors; air (white), fire (red), earth (green), and water (blue), long, long before they had any understandings of the color spectrum or its apparent gender-related properties, we uncover an intriguing, and very balanced match between those ancient metaphysical theories and the (then unknown) laws of natural science (♣ 5, 6, 7, 8, 9, 10). The symbolism is uncannily accurate. The question we should be asking of course is how ancient philosophers could hypothesize so accurately about scientific matters that were then well beyond their conceptual reach. Could the answer lie in the perennial workings of psychospiritual archetypes one wonders?

The Individual Triadic Archetype

Already briefly covered in the previous chapter, the central theme of the human triadic formula that corresponds with white, blue, and red 'values' is the 'spirit-mind-body' progression. This illustrates the universal law that actions (red) must be preceded by thoughts or plans (blue) which in turn must be preceded by an idea or inspiration (white). The fundamentals of this chromonumeric law are self-evident: Concept, plan, and action.

However, the astute observer will immediately note that we live in a world governed by masculine passions, appetites, and expressions – not only in our social orders and institutions that are dominated by men, but also individually; in that we are primarily driven by the 'needs of the flesh' (red), and tend to allow this sphere to dominate our intellectual, emotional, and spiritual faculties (blue-and-white). This latter condition applies equally to women as well as men, for as Jung explained in his observations of the animus and anima, we are all comprised of a genetic unisexuality that pervades the mind as much as it does the body. In this sense, although the female has more of the nurturing and feminine (blue) traits than her male counterpart at the foundations of her psyche, she is still dominated by her female sexuality, passions, and desires, which are associated with the physical and sensual (red) values. In this manner, although men are to be identified by red, and women by blue, they both carry the intrinsic personal triadic formula of red, blue, white, within their masculine or feminine-based personas. Thus, as we see in ♣ 13, individual human beings are walking-talking expressions of their own (functional or dysfunctional) triadic formulas, whilst simultaneously being part of the general masculine or feminine elements of the triadic principle at the collective-social level.

Confirming this theme is the fact that the colors of the seven-part Tantric meditation system of yoga philosophy are not only formulated along the patterns of the color spectrum, but also correlate to the chromatic values of the personal archetypal triad. In the practice of yoga for example.. "Tantric experts learn from a guru how to raise their psychosexual energy (Kundalini) from the base of the spine through successive focal points (chakras)." [2] These chakras are seven mystical locations on the body, where it is believed that spiritual and physical energy interrelates. Hinduism and Buddhism for instance, credit chakras with a very high level of importance in the process of human development. From the perspective of this work, it is in their representative colors that we recognize a universal truth (♣ 11 – only three chakras shown). In his comprehensive work on symbolism *The Secret Language Of Symbols* (1993) David Fontana writes;

> Each chakra has a different color associated with it, from red, the color of raw energy in the base chakra, through progressively more spiritual colors, to white in the brow chakra. The crown (head) is sometimes represented as a blaze of brilliant color. (Haloes?) [3]

Many aspects of the functions of the various charkas thus confirm the thematic characteristics of color, including the ordered triadic concept of physical, psychological, and spiritual.

In other religious traditions colors have definitive values and meanings. As suggested by our findings so far, there is often an ascending order of spirituality associated with the red, blue, and white sequence, with full spectrum white rating highest. Technically speaking 'full spectrum' means all-the-colors-combined, so when the rainbow appears in a religious setting for instance, such as in auras, haloes, or charkas, it is seen as indicating a very high degree of spirituality. Key points to note are: (i) a rainbow is a religious symbol of hope; (ii) each color of the rainbow has its own symbolic value; (iii) each color of the rainbow has its own scientific value; (iv) collectively, the colors of the rainbow unite to form true light. The relationship of the colors of the spectrum to corresponding human attributes, which in turn match the locations of the different charkas, is further confirmation of the fact that universal symbols do indeed reflect both religious beliefs and scientific truths, despite our relative collective ignorance of the fact. Adding weight to this hypothesis are the mounting volumes of scientific data confirming altered states of consciousness amongst Tantric mystics. Without passing express judgment upon those altered states, when a tried-and-tested spiritual system parallels our findings exactly, one is obliged to concede to the proofs. Furthermore, in regard to a natural cosmic order that begins with spirit, then mind, and then body; when recognizing man's disharmonious relationship both with nature and within himself, we can surmise that a disproportionate preoccupation with 'the flesh' (red) effects a disruption or reversal of the cosmic order, resulting in a dysfunctional continuum affecting all things touched by man. This of course, is one explanation for our alienation from – and ongoing destruction of the natural order. We use and abuse each other and our environment essentially for selfish reasons, chiefly because our (red) base urges dominate our (blue-white) cognitions. Thus we operate out of selfishness, or ignorance, or both. Whatever those 'spiritual' directions are that echo mutely in our deep subconscious stand little chance of being heard above the din of worldly obsessions. Hence the emphasis upon 'control of worldly desires' in most religions – a spiritual principle emphasized, but rarely clearly explained – or even understood for that matter. Evidenced in such practices as fasting, celibacy, tithing, meditation and pilgrimages, this 'denial of the flesh' tenet, central to practically all of the world's major faith traditions, is a key component in the preparation for the True religious experience – but it is *not* the only way to access the higher consciousness. This is a most important point to note, and will serve as the basis for later discussion on the merits, and remedial potentialities of triadic psychospiritual systems.

 # The Triangle: Speaking of triadic systems, perhaps we should note here the importance of the triangle both as a figurative and an abstract symbol that is key to this work. Obviously, the triangle represents the number three, which in turn relates to the theology of the Christian Trinity, the Hindu Trimurti, and other religious triads that we will cover soon. Historical associations with the number three-principle are innumerable. Likewise, the design of the triangle corresponds in several ways to other conceptual trinities. For instance, David Fontana's book defines upward or downward-pointing triangles as being representative of either male and female.[4] This affirmation of sexual properties is very interesting considering the foundational place of triangles and sexuality in our gender-sensitive triadic formulas. And although it could be argued that the triangular design of the uterus, and the phallic symbolism of the pyramid represent female and male triangles respectively, for rather obvious reasons associated with whole human physiology (♣ 13), it is this writer's opinion that the symbolic positions are at least reversible.

The Atomic Triadic Archetype

The philosophical hypothesis that man is a microcosm of the universe is relatively well documented. Proponents of this idea draw attention to the fact that the Earth and the human body contain the same percentage of water for example – or that trees and rivers do the same job for the Earth's atmosphere as lungs and arteries do for human beings – or the fact that just like the Earth, we are warm, moist, and messy in the center and colder and crustier on the outside. It is an interesting, but mostly speculative theory – that is, until we consider the evidence of the triadic archetype that seems to confirm mankind's central position in the general 'scheme of things'. As the evidence for a multilayered, universal, triadic archetypal systems builds, the fact that humanity is very much a living microcosm will become apparent - not so much because humanity is physically 'special' in any particular way, but actually…because in fact we are not! As relative latecomers to the evolutionary stage, we are naturally comprised of many attributes of our vegetable, animal, and mineral predecessors. Human beings are a reflection of many cosmic attributes precisely because, like all other features of the universe, we are made of the same stuff – although admittedly in diverse forms, and in varying degrees of consciousness, or natural perfection. In other words, scientifically speaking, humans are simple, carbon-based life forms that operate along the same cosmic principles as planets and atoms – and everything else in between. If we accept this man-as-microcosm theory, then perhaps the same principles will apply in reverse? That is to say; that before we demonstrate how man is a microcosm of the universe, let us first show how he is a macrocosm of the elementary particles of matter. We now begin with a cursory brief on quantum physics, paying particular attention to the presence of any triadic patterns that may reflect archetypal themes.

The physical universe is comprised of atoms, which are the building blocks of energy, light, and life. Atoms join in precisely defined clusters to form molecules. Molecules (such as carbon) then come together to form 'stuff' which we can identify as separate entities, such as gases, chemicals, and solids. However, scientists now inform us that atoms actually contain three even smaller fundamental particles. These are: (i) up quarks; (ii) down quarks, and (iii), electrons. According to the latest scientific information, everything in the known universe consists of amalgamations of these three elements. Thus, the central make-up of an atom comprises a proton and a neutron, each of which contains three quarks. The proton has two 'up' quarks, and one 'down' quark, whilst the neutron has one 'up' quark, and two 'down' quarks. The proton and neutron, comprised thus of up and down quarks, then form the nucleus of the atom, around which electrons are active – which under certain conditions emit light and/or heat. It was the splitting of this nucleus that gave us the atomic and nuclear bombs (♣ 10).

We can see then that the fundamental elements of matter; quarks and electrons, operate in a series of 'quantum trinities': When protons and neutrons unite, they each bring three quarks, thus; three-plus-three come together to form the nucleus, making three again. Because the (blue) neutron disintegrates as an isolated particle, the (red) proton is considered the stronger element, and the life-center of the atom. In an interesting metaphorical parallel with human family dynamics; before the atom can stabilize and join other atoms to become a molecule, the proton (red) and neutron (blue) must not only bond together, but must then share their (white) light, heat, and energy-emitting electrons that are in orbit around them (white, red, and blue union). And whilst these particles are obviously too small to have physically determinable colors, they not only carry the abstract masculine, feminine, and union properties of cosmic law, but the study of the energies that bond quarks together in their elementary trinities is very interestingly called "quantum chromodynamics" a phrase, which like the word 'chromosome' indicates the presence of 'color values' in the study of the most elementary particles known to man. Although we could digress into related topics in support of these facts - discussing the periodic table, deoxyribonucleic acid (DNA), atomic weights, and so on – for now, the clear point to establish is the physical existence of these triadic structures containing archetypal attributes even at the most elementary physical levels known to man.

More Primal Symbols

 # The Sun: Probably the most primal symbol of all, and recognized as the preeminent male symbol, often representing God the Father. The association with fire and the color red (as opposed to cool blues) should not go unnoticed. As the source of all light and energy, it is natural that ancient traditions would gravitate religiously towards this symbol of life. The Sun is the symbolic male partner to the female Moon, not only in the practice of

149

alchemy, but also in Joseph's Biblical dreams (Gen 37: 9-10). In the symbolic language of Genesis, the Gospels, and the book of Revelation, the Sun is interpreted as symbolizing the archetypal father figure, in a family that consists of; Father Sun, Mother Moon, and offspring denoted as Stars.

 # The Moon: As mentioned above; in the mystical science of alchemy, and in a natural dualism associated with night and day, the Moon represents the feminine counterpart to a masculine Sun. Because of its association with the monthly menstrual cycle and ocean tides, the Moon has been labeled the 'queen' of the heavens in certain traditions. Paintings of goddesses such as "The Birth of Venus"[5] invariably contain moon symbolism, and as Fontana notes; "the moon goddess was almost universally perceived as the weaver of fate and the controller of destinies, in the same way that she controlled the tides, the weather, rainfall and the seasons."[6] The Moon was a symbolic factor in the worship of the Egyptian mother-goddess Isis, and often factors in images or reported apparitions of the Virgin Mary – another archetypal mother-goddess figure. The regular lunar associations with the color blue in literature should also not go unnoticed.

 # Water: Another primal feminine symbol. In all its many forms, from snow and ice, through rivers and oceans, to clouds and mist, water remains essentially a feminine symbol. In its opposition to fire as a primary element, and in its partnership with fire as one of the pair of spiritual components of the human soul in Greek philosophy, water has a clearly defined feminine identity. In its association with the moon, the tides, the menstrual cycle, and the various ancient goddesses of the sea, we witness further connections with the feminine principle.

 # Fire: Like its original source the Sun, fire is another masculine symbol that neatly fits the chromatic profile. One of the primary symbolic elements, it represents power, heat, and energy. When connected with the divine it is considered a positive force, such as in the life-sustaining power of the sun, or representing the presence of God in the legendary burning bush, or the tongues of fire at Pentecost. However, when associated with the destroyer, fire is the fuel of hell and damnation – another apt association with the physical and destructive properties of the masculine color red. The ancient Greek philosophers considered fire to be one-half of the elements of the soul of man, the other half being water (♣ 9). This in turn related to their concept of Logos or 'Word' as the masculine attribute (of God); and Sophia or 'Wisdom' as the feminine aspect. Very interestingly, this association of the dual elements of (red-hot) fire and (blue-cool) water with the Divine is also reflected in the Bible through:

150

- The pillar of fire, and the pillar of cloud leading the Israelites for forty years in the wilderness
- The burning bush and the mystical cloud over Mt Sinai (where Moses received the Ten Commandments), and..
- The baptism of water, and the baptism of the Holy Spirit (the latter as tongues of fire at Pentecost)

Yin-Yang: A relatively simple-looking symbol that is a visual metaphor for the universal principle of division and union, or harmonious dualism (*see back cover*). Also known as the Tai Chi, the Yin-Yang loosely defines the world of opposites that are mutually dependant upon each other for their identities and fulfillment. More simply, Yin and Yang stand for feminine and masculine, right and left, dark and light, and positive and negative principles respectively. The presence of black in traditional Yin-Yang symbols has mistakenly led to a philosophical acceptance of the belief that "good and evil" also coexist in a dynamic yin-yang-type relationship. But this understanding of 'evil' as a necessary, or balancing component of our world is now being challenged, and ultimately disproved. By the conclusion of this work, the reader will hopefully agree that 'evil' is not so much a harmonious partner in a cosmic, philosophical Yin-Yang relationship, but rather, that 'evil' is actually better defined as an attack on the Yin-Yang principle itself.

The Cross: Most Christians may be surprised to hear that the cross has been a religious symbol since ancient times, only later to become adopted by the growing Christian Church. In several ancient cultures, the cross represented the coming together of two dimensions, chiefly masculine and feminine. Occasionally, it also represented the intersection of heaven and Earth, with humanity at the central point. This corresponds to the Christological view, which places Jesus as this central point of union between God and man, further symbolized by the cross of the crucifixion. A thousand years before Christ however, the cross was an Assyrian symbol for the sky-god 'Anu', and the ancient Chinese saw the cross as a symbol for the Earth. Cross-symbols were also present in ancient Egyptian hieroglyphics. The native religions of Mexico and Central America had crosses as religious symbols long before the arrival of the Spanish Conquistadors in 1519, but the Catholic Spaniards couldn't accept the possibility that the cross was not a unique Christian symbol, so this gave rise to the legend that St. Thomas the apostle had reached this area in his travels – a very 'doubtful' possibility.

The Biblical Triadic Archetype

Having already alluded to the masculine and feminine symbolism present in the pages of the Bible in the pillars of fire and cloud in the desert, the cloud and burning bush at Sinai, and the tongues of fire at Pentecost; let us now move directly to probably the most intriguing and convincing evidence so far for the perennial existence of these universal archetypes. Because of all the psychospiritual evidence of a cosmic, universal plan, perhaps none is quite so compelling as the colors, numbers, symbols, and patterns to be found surrounding the three central, and interrelated symbols of faith in ancient Judaism: (1) the Ark of the Covenant; (2) the Tabernacle; and (3) the Temple of ancient Judaism.

Never before recognized in any publications,[*] the sheer weight of evidence to support this archetypal dimension of the psychospiritual theory is so overwhelming that one wonders indeed if noumenal hand(s) are not still coordinating the release of this information. Too voluminous to engage in depth here today, the reader is cordially encouraged to visit Tony Badillo's website on "Solomon's Temple" for some fascinating supporting findings related specifically to sexual, archetypal symbolism.[†] The observation of such symbolism in ancient texts will undoubtedly stir a new and heightened respect for the hidden qualities of scripture – perhaps even more so when we see previously indecipherable religious symbolism such as that surrounding the Temple of Solomon manifesting itself substantially in the forms and themes of subsequent history. This being a systematic work however, we will of course try to prove our points methodically rather than leap to any preemptive conclusions. To achieve this goal, we will now review a short but relevant fragment from the pages of *The Color of Truth Volume II: Parallels in Life*, edited for brevity, which illustrates the matching triadic chromo-dynamics in the history and structures of the Ark of the Covenant, the Tabernacle, and the Temple.

> ...the Ark of the Covenant, the Tabernacle, and later the Temple, were all structures of worship that were constructed following precise 'instructions from God' – the details of which are recorded in The Bible in the Book of Numbers. ... The Ark of the Covenant was a portable box-like article that could be carried by four men. ...The Tabernacle was a sort of temporary temple made out of tent-like materials erected in the wilderness, and the

---

[*] To the best of the author's knowledge
[†] http://home.earthlink.net/~tonybadillo/

more famous Temple (of Solomon) was the later-erected permanent center of the Hebrew faith. All three were central symbolic focal points of the Hebrew faith for a period spanning 1400 years, from the time of Moses, through David, until the final destruction of the Temple by the Romans in AD 70.

The Ark of the Covenant was covered with pure gold inside and out, with the figures of two golden cherubim on top of the lid. ...These golden cherubim formed a triangular space between them with their wings, and it was in this space that God would reportedly 'appear' to Moses, or to the High Priest. This triangular area was known as "The Mercy Seat". Inside the Ark itself rested "The Law" given by God to Moses. From Bible records, we know that the Ark was to be carried before the people of Israel in their wilderness journeys, led by the mystical column of either fire or cloud, but only to be carried by purified individuals. ...The Tent of The Tabernacle served the Israelites as the home for The Ark of The Covenant, and was the symbolic center of their faith for about four hundred years until the time of King David. This Tabernacle, (unlike the tabernacles in Catholic Churches today), was a large, semi-permanent enclosure, made to specific dimensions that housed the Ark. It was like a courtyard, partially covered by a tent. Whenever the Israelites set up camp, this Tent of the Tabernacle would be erected to house the Ark, and serve as the center of worship. The movement of the column of fire, or the pillar of cloud that rested above the Tabernacle, was the mystical-yet-substantial signal for the Israelites to break camp and move to another location. (Exodus 40:36). Interestingly enough, the Bible reports that there were forty such locations during Moses' time in the wilderness.

Solomon inherited the instructions for the building of the Temple from his father, King David. He set about building what must have been the most magnificent structure ever seen in Jerusalem, if not in the whole of the ancient world. Much of the interior was plated with Gold, Silver, and precious stones, according to the 'instructions of God' to David, and the exterior was constructed of huge, pure white blocks, mirroring the white fabric fence that previously surrounded the Tabernacle...

...and here we uncover some very interesting facts indeed. Because not only were each of these constructs made to very exact, and symbolically significant dimensions, but for some never-before-explained reason, Moses, David, and Solomon, who each served as leader of the Israelites for an interesting forty years also received specific directions about which *colors* to use in all the structural features. This ranged from the white color of the fence surrounding the Tabernacle, and the white exterior of the Temple – to the remarkable fact that only four colors were chosen for all the material coverings and priestly vestments. Those four colors were; white, blue, red, and purple. Without offering any explanation whatsoever, the Bible records the use of these specific colors time after time following 'direct instructions from God' in all manner of sacred rites, rituals, and functions. This included their use on the coverings of the Tabernacle, the gates of the Temple, and even the colors of the sacred veil in the Holy of Holies. Both the abstract color-symbolism, and the physical structures themselves reflect a stunning consistency. The very design of the Temple for instance is homologous with human biology, as are certain features of the Ark and the Tabernacle analogous to human growth and sexual maturity.[7] One can identify a human head, torso and facial features for example, and see a sexual progression between the more 'juvenile' Tabernacle and the more 'mature' Temple. The pillars of the Temple crowned by multi-seeded pomegranates for instance, and the entrances to the Temple and Holy of Holies are seeped in powerful sexual symbolism. Along with the red, white, blue and purple décor, this not only suggests an archetypal theme behind these important historical icons, but also suggests an archetypal author of the same. Whether that is understood in a religious or non-religious sense is of course a matter for further debate. The astute reader may have noted that the additional presence of purple is on account of it being a mixture of red, white, and blue, and therefore can be observed to symbolize the unified archetypal 'royal family' of white, blue and red.[*] Or, the symbolic reunion of God (white, holy, spiritual) with his restored children, both masculine and feminine; God, Adam and Eve; white, red and blue; spirit, body and mind.

The Circle: The humble, but indispensable circle is mentioned here chiefly because of its connection to the triadic principle and to certain key numbers in chromonumerics, in particular the numbers 3, 12, 18 and 36. When divided by three for example, a 360° circle produces three 120° segments. Figuratively speaking, if the start / completion point of the cosmic

---

[*] Purple is not a natural color. With the exception of mixing red, white, and blue, resulting in purple, mixing color pigments will have a different outcome to mixing colored lights.

circle is 360 degrees, then 180 degrees is the direction of opposition, which is indicative of Satan's traditional position in relationship to God. Interestingly, scripture records Satan's number as being 666, and 6 + 6 + 6 equals eighteen (180 degrees?). Similarly, two-thirds of a circle is 66.6%. The significance of this number lies in the unprincipled division of the cosmic circle, whereby the white (spiritual) aspect is omitted, leaving only male and female; body and mind; without the governing and balancing attributes of (Godly) spirituality (♣ 12). A personality or world centered upon physical and emotional impulses (red and blue) without regard to a governing morality is narcissism defined. Thus one third – the most important third of the human condition is theoretically absent, leaving only a dysfunctional 66% of the collective 'self' to blunder selfishly, ignorantly, and destructively through life. As already mentioned, it is no secret that the number 666 is traditionally viewed as the 'mark of the beast' – strongly suggesting an archetypal association with Satan, with evil, or with similarly compromised agencies and institutions. This is one reason given for the sixty-six days of ritual cleansing of an Israelite woman after giving birth – symbolizing the period of separation from Satan.[*]

Just as a provocative speculation; is there also any significance one wonders in noting that the much disputed Jerusalem Bible – translated in 1966 and in common use amongst many Christian sects today contains (only) 66 books – and remains the source of much theological animosity between Catholics and Protestants? And perhaps it is only just coincidence too that Vienna, the ancestral seat of the Germanic Holy Roman Emperors and the capital of Austria, the country that gave us Adolf Hitler, is the *only* city in the world that sits at a height of six hundred and sixty-six feet above sea level? (More on this later).[†]

*   *   *

As we now wrap up the first half of this brief study of the triadic archetype phenomena, perhaps it is a good time to display a few facts and figures concerning colors in the Bible, which is obviously central to our efforts to link the Judeo-Christian religious world with psychospiritual theorem. After all, for all we know there could be numerous other colors mentioned just as

---

[*] Leviticus 12:2
[†] See *The Color of Truth Volume II: Parallels in Life* by this author for the full discussion

frequently in the Bible, which would make much of what's being reported here relatively insignificant. But of course, that's not the case. Of the other key colors referenced in this work, purple is mentioned in the Bible twenty-eight times in fourteen books. Black and blackness appears in twelve books a total of twenty-three times. Green appears in nineteen different books but nearly always as an adjective, and brown only appears four times in the Book of Genesis alone. The color gray gets mentioned in four books; yellow only twice; and 'speckled' three times. Of the colors; orange, pink, indigo, violet, maroon, turquoise, lavender, teal, plum, auburn, blonde, peach, khaki, tan, beige, lemon, lime, bronze, mauve, or 'mottled' there isn't a sign (did we omit any?) But gold, silver and brass on the other hand, as ornamental entities, and not necessarily as colors, are frequently spoken of.

We will later review more specific examples of the colors white, blue and red in the context of world religions, but for now we should note that when viewing the above data from a purely statistical perspective; especially when compared with the seventy-four entries of white in twenty-three different books, and the one-hundred-and-twelve entries of red, scarlet or crimson in thirty-eight books, it's plainly obvious that the two-hundred-and-forty combined entries of red, white and blue indicate the special significance of these three colors not only in Judeo-Christian-Islamic scripture, but also in any future psychospiritual / chromatic theory. What is also very interesting from a subliminal-symbolic perspective, is that there is no mention whatsoever of the (feminine) color blue in the New Testament, despite the fact that blue is the third most mentioned color in the Bible as a whole. Is it just pure coincidence one wonders, that both the New Testament and early Christianity were distinctly patriarchal, masculine, and authoritarian?

When we match this information with what we have learnt so far - one begins to suspect the inklings of a profound and universal connection... and believe it or not, we haven't even really got going yet!

CHAPTER NINE

TRIBAL-COLLECTIVE ARCHETYPES

Continuing and expanding our search for evidence of the triadic archetype within the annals of some of history's most prevailing disputes

In this chapter, we will review the evidence for the existence of the archetypal triad at the collective or 'tribal' level, the latter term being qualified by the ethnographical content, as we shall soon see. For inasmuch as the individual is made up of spirit, mind, and body, so is the family, community or social group comprised of a collective spirit, mind, and body. Therefore society at large is subject to similar dynamics – both functional and dysfunctional as the case may be, according to whether the community functions in-or-out-of-line with the archetypal cosmic order. In other words, if the spiritual, emotional-intellectual, or physical aspects of any given community are out of balance, not only should we expect to see resultant imbalances in the social properties of said community; less-or-more violence, or higher-or-lower education standards for instance; but we might also anticipate such imbalances to be subliminally represented in social symbolism. More simply put, if there really is any 'meat' to our psychospiritual theory, then we should be able to see corroborating evidence amongst the symbols of everyday life.

However, we must make an important distinction here between arbitrary colors, numbers or symbols, that may occur anywhere and everywhere for any manner of reasons, and those chromonumeric semiotics that have profound historical, scientific or religious import. For example, the fact that a person happens to wear a white-and-blue tie to work does not automatically credit them with some sort of intrinsic 'holiness' or spirituality; no more than cigarettes in blue-and-white packages are less damaging for one's physical health than those in red-black ones – although there may indeed be a correlation at some level. No, during several years of personal research in this field, it has become increasingly clear that when considering the potential archetypal values of collective symbolism, there needs to be a preponderance of evidence in the form of clearly identifiable historical and moral (or immoral) character patterns, that support the chromatic value-interpretation. For example, the very fact that the Jewish people claimed to be the exclusive stewards of the Covenant with God adds considerable weight to the universal properties of the Biblical symbolism discussed in the previous chapter – especially because the Jews themselves were obviously *not* consciously aware of these modern chromatic connections over three thousand years ago. Conversely the fact that Hitler, as the arch enemy of twentieth century Judaism chose red and black symbols for the Nazi swastika and assorted Third Reich paraphernalia – as the docile Jews were shepherded to their deaths against the backdrop of the blue star of Israel.. these are the sort of symbols we can confidently state have archetypal meanings. Likewise, the fact that Satanists have recently registered a black-red-silver flag as their color symbol of choice despite being unaware of the archetypal values described here is of no great surprise (see rear cover). This chapter therefore, will endeavor to show how archetypal chromatic principles have been in operation at the community or tribal level at least since recorded history began, beginning with the age-old Cain-and-Abel dynamic. We begin at this prehistoric point because the mythic battle between Cain and Abel is so profoundly representative of nearly all dualistic or triadic-based human conflicts in history at both the personal and collective level, and because symbolically speaking, the Cain-Abel dynamic is particularly well illustrated not only in the embittered legacy of Ishmael and Isaac – the Arabs and the Jews; but also in the political ancestry of Europe and the United States since medieval times, and as such bears particular relevance to our discussion, and to our world today.

Remembering that the information presented here is both condensed and edited for brevity, but nevertheless remains directed towards a universal understanding of the human condition, the reader is advised to be alert to those symbolically significant numbers, colors or signs, that indicate substantial manifestations of the subconscious in historical events. As in previous chapters, we will make occasional diversions to incorporate brief explanations of specific symbols where appropriate.

We now open with a cursory exploration of the anthropological origins of the Semitic peoples (which incidentally includes both Arabs and Jews) in order to firmly establish a three dimensional connection between archetypal colors, and cultural, political and religious developments that extend throughout history to the present day.

158

The Sons of Abraham

Most *cosmogonic** myths acknowledge the ascent of man through one primary ancestor who somehow became separated from his divine origins. Different cultures variously describe this primordial 'Adam' figure as the *Cosmic Man*, the *Great Man*, and the *Man of Light*. In Biblical Hebrew for instance, the word 'Adam' means both 'humankind' and 'red earth.' Jung tells us that Hebrew legend describes Adam as being made of four colors of clay – a formula interestingly enough that does not contain the color blue.[1] Blue of course corresponds to Eve, the primordial woman. One reason we begin with this piece of mythological trivia is because we first need to establish a chromatic origin-of-man base before moving into a more specific discussion about particular tribes or cultures. The second reason we begin with the myth of Adam and Eve is to pose the fundamental question of whether or not religion actually existed a-priori in the Garden of Eden?

Assuming that the reader is beyond interpreting cosmogonic scriptures literally, and in order to avoid a prolonged discussion on the topic, let us go with the standard Christian belief in the Fall of Man which is generally representative of most cosmogonic myths. Very simply put, this 'Fall' theme, present in many ethnic and religious traditions worldwide states that man's current disharmonious (or sinful) condition is symptomatic of a state of separation from God (or Nirvana, or happiness) – a result of a primordial 'fall from grace' *after* which event, religion began. That is to say that religion, as an estranged attempt to communicate with or engage God, was simply not necessary in an environment where Adam and Eve "walked and talked" with God in the Garden before the Fall (Gen 3:8). Supporting this precept, the authors of Genesis inform us that Adam and Eve were banished from Eden immediately after the Fall – and their subsequent estranged attempts to recover that lost 'state of grace' or reunion with God, is what we might justifiably term the beginnings of religion. The ritual practices of offerings, prayers, tithing and sacrifices are of course unnecessary where there is Divine immanence – that's why there is no mention of such in the Garden. Why build a temple when one can walk and talk with God directly? It is only in estrangement from Ultimate Reality that religion finds its purpose and meaning, and any justification for existence.

Having already shown that the foundational icons of Judeo-Christianity are intrinsically linked with white, blue, and red symbolism, and having also shown that religion (when fulfilling its original purpose) is ultimately a remedial condition; we may conclude that any related

---

* Cosmogonic; pertaining to a theory of the origins and evolution of the universe

archetypal theme(s) must in essence, be restorative in nature. This is not to suggest that original and restorative archetypes are not essentially one and the same thing, but simply recognizes the fact that the presence of chromo-numeric patterns in early religious history suggests their use in this particular case (through the agency of religion) in a restorative, or remedial way. The subliminal color-symbolism thus shows the direction and forms that religion *should* be following, in order to restore mankind to his True origins. Or, if one prefers a more progressive view; the symbolism illustrates the foundational route that religion (or science) should pursue in order to guide mankind to his True collective destiny. Whether that destiny is salvific-restorative or progressive-devolutionary is a secondary debate to acknowledging the presence of these archetypal tracks.

As we shall soon see, whenever religious or social groups stray from these archetypal guidelines they display both the appropriate symbolism and symptoms of agencies gone awry. Moreover, precisely *because* the symbolism is subliminal, we must also conclude that mankind is *not consciously* responsible for its manifestation. More on this later...

So, using chromonumeric archetypes as a reference; religion's providential function is now better understood as that of a remedial agency that facilitates a specific social curative process – with very specific objectives. Clearly, the religious condition itself is not the objective, but simply a process (at best) that *leads to* the true objective, which is reunion with God, or a return – or an advance – to True Wholeness. This paradigm contrasts significantly with the misguided belief that religiosity somehow equals truth or wholeness; – or with the convictions of those who subscribe to the commonly-held assumption that religiousness is akin to the original state of grace in the Garden of Eden.

This teleological understanding of the origin and purpose of religion naturally leads us back to Cain and Abel, Adam's first two sons who, according to the Bible, were the first humans to make religious offerings and sacrifices. Without getting into a long and complex discussion about the possible mechanisms of the Fall, let's just follow the Bible story that informs us that Cain was a worker of the (red) earth, and Abel was a shepherd. As the first two humans born in the fallen world (as recorded in scripture), their respective *positions* have more archetypal import than their physical gender. Therefore, in the dynamics between (i) earth-worker and shepherd, and (ii) older–and–younger sibling, we can attribute the strong physical color red to Cain, and the nurturing and more 'dependent' color blue to Abel. The next thing the Bible tells us is that for some reason God favored Abel over Cain – although scripture is not clear on the reason for

160

this favoring of the younger son, despite the fact that it is a consistent theme throughout Bible history. One credible hypothesis however is that Cain, as the first born after the Fall, was considered 'claimed' by Satan and prone to the sins of pride and arrogance that his senior position brought. Separation from Satan required that he conquer these urges and submit to God's pleasure by respecting and honoring God's apparently unfair favor of his younger brother. Cain was being asked to perform an act of faith; of true filial piety; a personal, religious sacrifice if you like. If Cain and Abel had indeed united under God, then the reunion of the white, blue, and red properties that were initially established in the Garden would have been at least partially restored: Satan's (black) influence would have been rejected; and technically 'religion' would have ended almost as soon as it began. But by murdering Abel in anger and jealousy, Cain murdered the chosen representative of the intermediate color blue, thus also rejecting the light of God (white) and confirming the satanic color black in his inherited spiritual genetics so-to-speak – the color that denotes absence of light, love, and True spirituality. Hence, Cain ratified the colors red and black – the colors that modern chromatologists declare to be the "worst possible combination" in terms of healing, peace, and harmony. Cain's fratricide thus necessitated the continuance of religion as a 'medicinal' attempt to restore humanity to grace – or grace to humanity – or to put it chromatically; to replace the black with the white, and then reunite the red with the blue. This ties in very neatly of course not only with the red-white-blue color symbolism of the Tabernacle and the Temple, but also provokes very disturbing questions about the red-black color symbolism of those nations, religions and political agencies who have traditionally used aggressive, Cain-like methods to suppress their longsuffering neighbors (♣ 16-19, 26)

What must also be considered is the aforementioned reversal of the natural cosmic order whereby ideally the spirit directs the mind; which in turn directs the body. By the time of Cain and Abel though, the world had already 'fallen' into a contrary mode: The red, physical, aggressive energies dominated in the form of Cain – hence the urgings from God to surrender his base urgings of jealousy and resentment and 'do the right thing'. Cain was being asked to reverse the Fall by placing the (white) spirit above the (red) flesh, which would also serve to elevate his (blue) brother Abel over him. But Cain couldn't, or wouldn't listen. Symbolically speaking, when the next youngest son Seth took Abel's place as God's favored, we see humanity split into two chromatic camps: The red / black "accursed" descendants of Cain, and the blue / white descendants of Seth. (Gen 4:11). Not so surprisingly, Noah who built the Ark was a direct descendant of Seth through Enosh, and would 'restart' the human race after the Great Flood with his three sons – just like Adam and his three sons before him. Thus we see the color blue, complete with feminine symbolism (the flood-waters and the life-preserving Ark) directly associated with Noah – not to mention the later appearance of the rainbow when the providence was restarted.

From a religious perspective therefore, we can say that God 'restarted' humanity in an act of rebirth after the forty-day flood – a time period incidentally that is representative of the forty weeks of human pregnancy, and Christ's forty hours in the tomb amongst many other examples of symbolic rebirth (see Table B on p 126). Based upon this new foundation, Noah's eldest son Shem would become the direct ancestor of Abraham; from which point we can trace the origins of both the Arabs and the Israelites, and by association, the modern Muslim and Jewish faith traditions respectively.

In the following edited extracts from my own research the reader is invited to observe the traditional connections between the Cain and Abel archetypes, understanding of course that the color red is representative of the older brother; strong and masculine, with the added presence of black possibly signifying the corruption or abuse of that position. Whilst the color blue can be either representative of the younger brother position or, representative of a feminine-archetypal position such as the daughter, sister, wife, or mother (as in the original Eve).

The Arab peoples, and Arab Muslims in particular, trace their origins back to Abraham via Ishmael, Abraham's eldest son by Hagar, his wife Sarah's Egyptian handmaid. The Jews on the other hand trace their ancestry back to Isaac, Ishmael's younger half-brother, who was the first-born son of Sarah. This older brother-younger brother dynamic is an analogous repeat of the Cain-Abel story that continues to recur throughout history at all levels of society... [*]

In Genesis 4:20 - 21, Cain's descendants Jabal and Jubal are described as "such as dwell in tents,...and have cattle, and ... such as handle the harp and organ." This matches historian Emmanuel Deutsch's description of the Arabs as "masters of song", and of course, the Arabs have traditionally lived as tent-dwelling nomads. In addition, Cain is told that the ground will not yield up its fruit to him, which would match the desert-type geography of most Arab lands. Furthermore, there is the

---

[*] See Volume II of *The Color of Truth* for a full account of this historical phenomenon

lineage factor, ...where brothers in the Bible such as Ishmael and Isaac, and Jacob and Esau, are not only direct ancestors of the Arabs and Jews, but they also play out the roles of Cain and Abel again and again...

An angel comforted Hagar (in the desert), telling her in Genesis 16:12 that her son Ishmael would "..be a wild man; his hand will be against every man, and every man's hand against him; and he shall dwell in the presence of all his brethren." The angel then told Hagar to return and 'submit' to Sarah, which she did; but when Isaac was born to Sarah thirteen years later, Sarah cast Hagar and her son out once again, and this time it was permanent. At the point of despair in the wilderness, God speaks to Hagar and reassures her that they will be saved, and from there, Ishmael "becomes an archer, dwells in the wilderness, and takes an Egyptian wife". This repeated connection with the Egyptians, who are today both an Arab state, and predominantly Muslims, is particularly evident through Ishmael's line, for both his mother and his wife are Egyptians, and the daughter(s)* from that union both marry Esau, who was Jacob's twin brother, sired by Isaac. Jacob and Esau too were players in another archetypal Cain-and-Abel dynamic. Jacob would later be renamed "Israel", and father twelve sons, amongst whom was Joseph (with the coat of many colors). Joseph in turn was sold to Ishmaelites who took him to Egypt, and later, it would be the Egyptians again who served as the instruments of oppression for the Israelites during their slavery period. This historic oppressive connection with Egypt is still maintained in the Egyptian's leadership of the Arab League, and support of other groups that traditionally oppose Jewish interests. In addition, the religious significance of Egypt to the Muslim world is honored by the Muslims of Mecca who will only hang Egyptian-made black curtains around the Kaaba, Islam's holiest shrine.

However, returning to the story, it should be made quite clear that Ishmael and Hagar's sacrifice in favor of Isaac, was a

---

* The Bible lists different names possibly for the same daughter(s) of Ishmael; Mahalath and Bashemath

> very important aspect of the ancestral restoration of the crime of Cain against Abel. Ultimately, Hagar and Ishmael should have seen this 'unfair treatment' of Ishmael by Sarah and Abraham as an opportunity to achieve a great victory of faith and obedience, and submission to the Will of God,* rather than to be seen as a justification for historical brotherly resentment between the offspring of Ishmael and Isaac; the Arabs and the Jews.

This brief account of the religio-political origins of the Semitic peoples is also peppered with other, so-far unexplained references to the color red in conjunction with the older brother position as in Genesis 25:25 where Esau, one of Isaac's twin sons, is described as "red all over" at birth. Esau grows up to become a "cunning hunter" and lives a very *physical* lifestyle compared to his brother Jacob, his mother's favorite. Red is mentioned again as the color of the food ("red pottage") accepted by Esau in exchange for his birthright, an event that marked the formal ascension of Jacob (later called "Israel") to the elder-brother position.

Later in Genesis 38, Tamar gives birth to Judah's twin sons Pharez and Zarah in another key providential event. Zarah sticks his hand out of the womb first, and a *red* thread is tied to it; why red one might ask? Although Pharez emerges first, Zarah is considered the elder. These stories are all intimately, albeit subliminally connected to the original Cain-and-Abel dynamic in a restorative mode. Without annotating the fact, scriptures record many such examples of Cain-and-Abel reversals tied to chromonumeric symbolism, including several thematic, geographic, and political associations between the Arabs and the Jews.

If we now compare the modern political colors and relational dynamics of the Arab League – the elder of the Semitic brothers traceable to Abraham, we witness an uncannily accurate display of red-based symbolism appropriate to the older brother – more specifically, we see no blue at all (♣ 16). The Jews on the contrary – the people in the younger brother position whom God also refers to in scripture as "my (virgin) daughter Zion"[2] only carry the appropriate blue (and white) symbolism. When considering contemporary Middle East politics from a historical perspective, we see even more uncannily-appropriate vexillological symbolism present amongst the supporters of the two camps over the years. Supporters of the P.L.O. for example have included the Soviet Union and the Arab League, whilst on the

---

* The word "Islam" means 'to surrender to God's (Allah's) authority'

opposing side we have the United Kingdom, the League of Nations, France, the United Nations, and the United States (♣ 17). The colors alone tell their own story. Red, whites, and blues on the one side, and a distinct absence of blue on the other. Moral assumptions aside; what can certainly be inferred from this evidence is that major historical players are unconsciously adhering to distinct chromatic patterns along thematic, archetypal lines.

Archetypal Vexillology

There are other symbols common to vexillology (the study of flags) that repeat with intriguing consistency throughout history. In fact, it is here that we find some of the most striking examples of subliminal adherence to archetypal constructs. Given the evidence, it seems to me quite amazing that no coherent taxonomy of universal values has yet been accorded to our various political insignia. But the evidence is indeed there, recorded with dramatic consistency ever since Denmark first registered her national flag in the early thirteenth century. Many explanations are given for the respective color-choices of different states, and the reader is directed to the *Flags of the World* website for probably the most comprehensive selection where thousands of examples are shown. In some cases, the explanations directly concur with my own findings, but in most, the explanations given for political color and symbol choices revolve chiefly around associations with ancestral traditions or national characteristics. Hence, the direct archetypal connections are mostly overlooked. This of course is understandable, given that the nature of these archetypes has been distinctly subliminal, and that this association between subliminal archetypes and real political symbolism is, as far as I know, being published now for the first time.

Political flags have been around for a long, long time, with records of dynastic banners being flown in China centuries ago, and many other examples since of Lords, Kings and Emperors using banners, standards and other colors for identification. Some modern flags have clear connections to these centuries-old origins, whilst others appear to be the direct by-product of modern-day politics, and have relatively few historical reference points. The British 'Union Jack' for example, first officially hoisted in 1801 was born out of the colors of three nations of the United Kingdom; England, Ireland, and Scotland, and was therefore 'adopted' from these previously independent countries with their own national histories stretching back many centuries. In contrast, the modern Palestinian flag or the flag of the United Nations have only been around a few short years. As we will see however, both classes of flags – both ancient and modern – adhere to these archetypal parameters. Considering the fact that various techniques for applying heraldic colors to shields, banners, and coats of arms have been available in Europe at least since the early Middle Ages, our curiosity should at least be piqued by the chromatic consistencies between particular countries' symbolism and their respective political positions. To be fair however, archetypal vexillological patterns would have been very difficult to track before the tumultuous events of the twentieth century, for it is in the rise and fall of such institutions as Zionism, Communism, and Nazism that many of our chromatic speculations are confirmed. This gives us an opportunity to briefly digress for a summary of some of the symbols commonly used in political insignia.

 # Stars: Stars feature prominently in vexillology particularly amongst the political colors of those nations currently in the news; Israel, Iraq, and the United States for example. The star is a relatively versatile symbol tha often denotes abundance. In the Bible, stars are often symbolic of children or of the chosen people, such as in the reference made by Joseph in his dream in Genesis 37: 9. The Bible also refers to 'the day star' (II Peter 1:19) and 'the morning star' (Revelation 2:28), which some scholars have concluded are symbolic references to 'The Anointed One' – The Christ. However, in Isaiah 14:12-13, Lucifer is called "Son of the morning" which also relates to the morning star, the brightest of the heavens. But here, Lucifer is chastised for attempting to place his throne "..above the stars of God" (humanity).

In subliminal vexillology, the differing shapes, forms, colors, or configurations of stars also contribute to their symbolic significance. White for example, although sometimes ambiguous, can generally be assumed a positive sign. However, the five-pointed pentagram is regularly associated with magic and even Satanism; and when presented in very dark, red, or black colors on a state flag may indicate a propensity towards 'false' religion or indicate aggressive or suppressive oligarchies. This could include atheism, communism, fascism, oppressive fundamentalism, or even pseudo-religious despotism. When coupled with black, or red-and-black supporting themes, dark-colored five-pointed stars can therefore be an ominous sign. The six-pointed star such as that of Judaism on the other hand, may (optimistically) be interpreted as two interlocking triangles – possibly male and female, or yin and yang, which represent a cosmic propriety. In the case of the flag of Israel the 'spiritual white' and 'feminine blue' coloring only adds psychospiritual credibility to the Jews' longstanding claim to be the true and original 'daughters of Zion'.

Regardless of contemporary politics, and regardless of any particular individual thereof who may or may not be perceived to be

166

engaged in less-than-righteous activities; these color themes clearly support the aforementioned Cain-and-Abel dynamic – at least in a historical setting. Therefore, stars in different political forms and colors may be symbolic of various themes. On the one hand; Christ, Archangels, or the 'true children of God.' On the other; Satanism, Lucifer, and oppression. Alternatively, they may of course represent any individual or group whose character is reflected in the colors and configuration of the star symbol.

   # **Birds of Prey:** Like stars, birds of prey including the majestic eagle, can carry mixed symbolism in our various cultural histories. In certain cases all the admirable qualities of the eagle or falcon are used to denote merit; such as in the Bible in Deuteronomy 32:11 where the eagle's care for her young is held up as a virtue. However, the Bible also instructs against consuming any birds of prey as meat, including the more noble ospreys, eagles, kites, nighthawks and owls. These are lumped together with other "abominable" fowls in a category that includes vultures, ravens, cuckoos, cormorants, herons, lapwings, and bats! One possible reason for this sweeping demotion is the fact that it was 'birds of prey' that claimed Abraham's failed animal sacrifice (Genesis 15:11). This in turn suggests a symbolic connection between 'birds of prey' and the Satan archetype. With a little creative interpretation, it is relatively easy to thus explain the sending out of the (black) raven from Noah's Ark, preceding the (white) dove that eventually returns with an olive branch. In other belief traditions however, birds of prey may represent lofty ideals, even deities. In Egyptian mythology for instance the falcon represented the sky-god Horus; whilst the Hindu 'god' Garuda is half man and half eagle – whose enemy is the serpent. This relates closely to the Christian idea of God and Satan (as serpent) engaged in an everlasting cosmic battle. However, the political double-headed eagle of the (Germanic) Holy Roman Empire of Medieval Europe traces its origins to pre-Constantinian Rome, and could therefore be interpreted as a simple continuation from the first Roman Empire. It would appear on the surface then that eagle and bird-of-prey symbolism is ambiguous, that is, until we include the chromo-numeric dimension. In other words, the colors of our symbolic eagles and their surrounding paraphernalia play a good part in discerning their essential meaning in any given instance. An eagle with a white head and tail such as the American bald eagle for example which also carries the olive branch and blue-colored emblems, has a very different symbolic value to an all-black bird, such as the Viking raven or the double-headed black, and red-black eagles of Prussia, fascist Italy, and Nazi Germany, which traditionally represented aggressive military oppression.

Medieval Kingdoms

Following almost exactly the same thematic patterns as the Arabs and Jews, medieval Christianity also had striking and consistent examples of subliminal archetypes being expressed in national colors and Church agencies. Bearing in mind the popular belief that Christianity inherited its providential mission from the Jews in the first century C.E., it is truly fascinating to observe the political dynamics that played out between the Holy Roman Empire, the Kingdom of France, and the Papacy in Rome over a thousand-year period between 800 and 1800 C.E. Although these patterns are not exclusive to this point in history, the following illustrations have been chosen for their clarity and consistency.

First a brief history: The period we are talking about begins on Christmas Eve in the year 800, and the event is the crowning of King Charlemagne by the Pope as the first official "Holy Roman Emperor." This event marked the beginning of a geographic and political power-triad in Central Europe comprising what would later become known as France, Germany, and Italy; or more specifically; the Kingdom of France, the Holy Roman Empire, and the Papacy respectively. The previous eight hundred years of Christian history are riddled with complex political and cultural factors, but it is fair to say that Charlemagne was the first Christian King to unite substantially and effectively with the Pope, thus creating a secular-and-religious governing partnership, at least in principle, between Church and State that would exist in some form or another for the next thousand years. Events leading up to the crowning of Charlemagne are equally intriguing, but to enter into more detail would extend this chapter threefold, and in any event the evidence presented here should suffice to our needs.

In 843 C.E. Europe was divided between East and West Francia under Charlemagne's sons, with the East Franks constituting the Germanic Kingdoms which retained the title 'Holy Roman Empire', and the West Franks who would later become known as the French, becoming an often combative opponent of East Frankish territorial expansion plans. The third factor of course was the Papacy in Rome. Under ideal circumstances, the Papacy should have embodied the spiritual properties of moral guidance (white); the German Emperors as powerful secular rulers represented the elder brother properties (red); and the Kingdom of France stood in the younger, and feminine position (blue). Although history testifies to the abysmal corruption of medieval Christianity and the everlasting hostilities between the French and the Germans, many historical events nevertheless support the presence of tribal and triadic archetypes in the various political maneuverings over the centuries.

168

For example, there is the aforementioned division of Europe by Charlemagne's heirs into three distinct kingdoms (east, west, and central) which precipitated a thousand years of striking chromonumerics amongst the triad of France, Germany, and the Italian Papal States – each of which carried the symbolism appropriate to providential, archetypal agencies. Not only do we see the same patterns in Adam's and Noah's families repeated amongst Charlemagne's heirs, but we also witness a thousand-year Cain-and-Abel dynamic as well. France for instance, has traditionally referred to herself as the "daughter of the Church" and her traditional blue symbolism was born of the spiritual visions of King Clovis I, the first Barbarian King to be baptized (on Christmas Day in the year 496 interestingly enough).

In the 1400s France also produced the enigmatic Joan of Arc who, as a seventeen-year-old virgin from the 'valley of colors' led France to unprecedented victories over the (Germanic-ruled) English, waging phenomenal campaigns under a blue banner. In the eighteenth century France would also be the locus for the Enlightenment whose central focus on thinking, knowledge, and wisdom can also be affiliated with the color blue. Furthermore, after the eventual union of the French and Austrian royal families through Marie Antoinette and King Louis XVI, France would host the bloody and tumultuous French Revolution where the red, white, and blue tricolor was first hoisted in public. Why those exact colors one might ask?

Meanwhile, the Germanic tribes maintained their Cain-type symbolism to such an extent that one can see many direct comparisons between the German States and the Arab states of today: WWI German, and Egyptian semiotics for example are practically identical – as was their mutual hostility towards the Jews (♣ 16, 19). Both have paraded red-and-black symbolism with eagles or falcons in prominence, and throughout the whole thousand-year period of the Holy Roman Emperors, one finds hardly a hint of blue symbolism. The fact that the Hapsburg family held the position of Emperor in almost unbroken succession for the latter three hundred and sixty years (6 x 6) based in Vienna, Austria, surrounded by black eagle symbolism and red and black colors, adds considerable weight to the argument that they were playing out a dominant Cain-type role at the international level. Most intriguing perhaps is the fact that Vienna is the only city in the world that sits at a height of six hundred and sixty six feet above sea level!

Italy meanwhile, as the home of the Papacy should ideally have been represented by the colors white and green; white for spirituality and inspiration, and green for the central position between the red and blue agents at opposite ends of the spectrum – and so it was. Even today Italy continues to sport green and white in its national flag. Furthermore, the Renaissance movement that later gave birth to the Enlightenment began in fourteenth century Italy, giving us an interesting sociological triad of; (white) Renaissance, Italy; (blue) Enlightenment, France; and (red) Industrial Revolution, England, which at that time was ruled by the German House of Hanover.[*] This sequence allows for both a geographic as well as chronological interpretation of an archetypal model following the 'inspiration, contemplation, action' pattern. Thus we witness a chromatic-historical progression from south to north following the conceptual principles of the white, blue, and red triadic archetype.

The Christian Church of course, should have either used the color white exclusively in her symbolism or, if she were truly on providential course, would have adopted the Biblical combination of red, white, and blue. Interesting then is it not, that we find no feminine blue symbolism associated with the Papacy throughout this period.[†] In fact it was the color red – very appropriately symbolizing excesses of the masculine – that predominated amongst official Papal symbolism (♣ 18). Indeed, amongst those 'Christian' institutions such as the Inquisition and the Teutonic Knights who carried out so much bloody work on behalf of ambitious Popes, we see the color black being ominously added to the equation. Hence, the most convincing evidence for the presence of archetypal influences affecting European affairs lies in the traditional symbolism of these three respective regimes.

Even in this admittedly brief and somewhat generalized view of European history, it is remarkable to observe the uncannily accurate color-symbolism. The three successive Cain-type Germanic Reichs who were descended from Charlemagne's eldest son showed particular adherence to archetypal symbolism over a twelve hundred year period. Whilst persistently and aggressively resisting the direction of unity with the Kingdom (and Republic) of France for instance; the Holy Roman Empire, also known as the First Reich (800-1801 C.E.) and later the Second and Third Reichs (1871-1918 and 1933-1945 respectively) – each in turn had their headquarters in countries flying red and black insignia; namely Austria, Prussia, and Germany.

In contrast, throughout her history, France has interestingly labeled herself "the daughter of the Church" and her flags have invariably been

---

[*] The British Royal Family is directly descended from the German Houses of Hanover and Saxe-Coburg-Gotha. They changed their ancestral name to "the House of Windsor" in 1917.
[†] Blue symbolism associated with Mary is a separate matter to be discussed in due course

peppered with blue-and-white, and feminine symbolism. This corresponds of course with France's origins being descended from the younger offspring of Charlemagne, who, in the position of 'Abel' would be considered the more 'feminine' of the two state founders. Accordingly, although suffering the occasional despotic ruler France has enjoyed a remarkably 'blessed' history before reformation times, suggesting (if one believes in divine providence) that she was somehow being mystically 'groomed' to partner a successful Cain country at the appropriate time in history – perhaps even Austria-Germany after the French Revolution?

We should remember that none of these historical players could possibly have been aware of their respective 'providential' positions; patterns that could only come to light as the centuries unfolded and modern information-technology began to put it all together. Neither (according to extensive research)[*] did the individuals involved in selecting political symbolism have any *conscious* awareness of the deeper symbolic implications of their vexillogical color choices as covered in this work, operating solely (they believed) out of their own motivations, family traditions, or at best, out of a relatively poorly informed sense of political duty or religious faith. Certainly, there was no official recognition of the triadic archetype or of the Cain-and-Abel restorative formula, nor of the natural dynamics of the color-spectrum. On the contrary, the FOTW website records many diverse philosophical interpretations for the symbolism of selected flags. This leaves the pregnant question of how indeed could such symbolism repeat so accurately and consistently over clearly-defined time periods? Even today the three countries of France, Italy, and Germany continue to carry the appropriate archetypal colors in their modern flags; blue for France, green for Italy, and red for Germany. And at the risk of pointing out the obvious, once again we have the colors of the spectrum neatly displayed in their natural sequence (♣ 5).

---

[*] Research carried out on FOTW website: http://fotw.digibel.be/flags/ reveals no consistency in the records concerning historical color choices

CHAPTER TEN

GLOBAL / POLITICAL ARCHETYPES

Continuing with our theme of white-blue-red triadic archetypes let us now move to the modern / international level where we view the dramatic historical evidence of the twentieth century, through two World Wars and the Cold War, and on to current events. For any lingering skeptics amongst us, we will also evaluate the statistical likelihood of these chromatic phenomena occurring by chance, or coincidence.

At the outbreak of World War One in 1914, two major military alliances stood in opposition to each other. These were known as the 'Triple Alliance' on the one hand, consisting of Germany, Austria-Hungary, and Italy, and the 'Triple Entente' consisting of Great Britain, France and Russia. The Great War began when Austria-Hungary declared war on Serbia who in turn, called on her allies France, England, and Montenegro for protection. This also drew Imperial Russia, as the ally of France and England – and Germany on the other side, into the conflict. Thus within a matter of days, five members of the two hostile 'trinities' (the Entente and the Alliance) would each declare war on their opponents. Italy was the sole exception, choosing to sit out the first year of the war before eventually switching allegiances and aligning herself with the group of nations that would later become known as 'The Allies' or the 'Associated Powers'. Their opponents later to be known as the 'Central Powers' would eventually consist of Germany, Austria-Hungary, the Ottoman Empire (Turkey), and Bulgaria (♣ 21).

The discerning reader will immediately notice that amongst the major players in this global conflict we once again see a very clear unifying pattern amongst the colors of their national flags. Could it simply be 'pure coincidence' that the entire Allied coalition at the outbreak of war flew under red, white and blue national colors? Is it also only pure coincidence that we find no blue whatsoever in any of the Central Power's flags? Is there some simple explanation perhaps? Well, without even considering the prospect of archetypal influences or the evidence of previous chapters, let us deal with this particular historical occurrence in isolation and, considering the broad range of available colors in the spectrum, ask ourselves what indeed is the statistical likelihood of these five nations flying under the same colors at this particular point in history? Indeed, what sort of mathematical formula can we use to calculate this?

In fact, the likelihood of such an occurrence happening coincidentally is probably beyond reckoning. For in order to accurately compute the odds we would first of all need to find some reciprocal 'common-denominator' through which to quantify color, culture, politics and history. Provided we were successful in this endeavor we would then need to use the same value-system to appraise the characters of all the individuals who influenced the development of the flags at various points in history, (including their psychological states and all related environmental factors). Then, we would also have to somehow include time and space in the formula, and all manner of assorted variables both tangible and abstract... all in all a difficult task, I think you'll agree. When dealing with such a widely encompassing topic over such a broad period of time, there are just too many interrelated factors to be able to conduct a truly scientific, comprehensive assessment. Nevertheless, despite the absence of such a quantifiable common denominator we still have an important point to make and an issue to prove, so, in the spirit of pure scientific research, and in order to put the notion of 'pure coincidence' to rest, let's try to come up with the simplest formula possible and see what figure we arrive at.

Calculating the Odds

We already know that vexillological emblems have featured prominently in European culture since at least the thirteenth century. We also know that the techniques for applying heraldic colors to shields, banners, and coats of arms have been available in Europe at least since the time of stained glass painting which, although known in Egypt as early as the third century BCE, did not become established as an art form in Europe until the CE 800s.

Known then as 'painting with light' stained glass painting reached its zenith in France around the year 1200. The Encarta Encyclopedia informs us:

> The predominant colors used at this time were blue (especially for the background), red, yellow, and green. Violet, brown, and white with a green or blue cast were secondary, and pinkish shades served as flesh tones.

In addition, during the Gothic period, "A wider range of purples, dark green, and yellow hues were added to the French and English repertoire of colors". We are further informed that silver, tawny brown, olive green and mosaics of reds, blues, and grays were increasingly incorporated into medieval art forms and heraldry before the fourteenth century. So clearly, a wide range of colors were indeed available to artisans in the Middle Ages. Furthermore, in 1533 a manual "for the production of paints and inks" was published in Augsburg, Germany. This further affirms that the technical ability to reproduce a variety of colors upon assorted surfaces was clearly possible – at least from that time forwards. Obviously, the selection of recognized colors in medieval times was far fewer than the scores of different shades available to us today. Even so, it is clear that when craftsmen in the Middle Ages were directed to create banners, flags, shields, and stained glass, they usually had at least a dozen or so basic colors at their disposal.

Therefore, for the purpose of our investigation, and in order to ensure that our calculations remain very much on the conservative side, let's reduce these twelve basic colors to the seven already discussed. This gives us; black and white, red, green, blue, yellow and purple, which, considering the variety of colors available to our ancestors and in use in vexillology today – is a very modest selection indeed.[*]

Relating this selection of colors to the opening stages of the First World War, specifically to the five Allied nations of Russia, Great Britain, France, Serbia and Montenegro – and not even taking into account the statistical probability of any of these nations choosing a one, two, or four-colored flag – we can quickly calculate that with seven separate colors to choose from, any one of these nations could have chosen a tricolor from thirty-five possible choices. Therefore, thirty-four of the possible tricolor combinations are NOT red, white and blue! If we now multiply thirty-four (the flag options) times itself five times (the five nations), we get 1,544,804,416 different possible line-ups containing five tricolor flags that

---

[*] Technically, white is the presence of all colors, and black is the absence of color.

are NOT all red, white and blue across the board. In European mathematics that is odds of; one billion, five hundred and forty four million, eight hundred and four thousand, four hundred and sixteen... to one! Would anyone like to explain this phenomenon? Or would anyone like to place a bet on the likelihood of this happening again? There doesn't appear to be an obvious explanation for this, yet we can clearly see that for some reason these countries all chose red, white and blue, over any other selections, whilst their active opponents have no blue whatsoever in their flags.

So how is it that 'The Allies' all chose red, white and blue at this specific time in history? Please remember that vexillologists have no uniformed explanation why certain nations would choose certain colors. In fact, as already explained these uncanny coincidences cannot be accounted for thematically, with each nation listing different and often unconnected reasons for their particular choices; blue is for the ocean, red for the blood spilt on the battleground etc... Therefore, if we were able to factor in all the other personal and environmental variables previously mentioned such as time, culture, flag configuration etcetera; then the odds of this five-nation phenomenon occurring coincidentally would probably rise by several billions. I hope we are agreed that we do seem to have something of a mystery to solve...

The Odds Go Up

Countries from as far afield as China, Japan, and South America declared war on the Central Powers at various times during the four years of war from 1914 to 1918, but it was the full entry of the United States in April 1917 that would eventually decide the outcome, and this is where we will now focus our attention. It should be explained that in the course of the First World War, more than thirty different nations would become involved in one way or another, however, some of those nations such as Italy and Romania, would change allegiances during the course of the conflict, and others, (such as Belgium and Portugal) only had war declared *against* them without any significant response in return. Still others came in or out of the conflict at various stages, only cautiously "severing relations" with The Central Powers, and maneuvering for various political or nationalistic motives – as such they are not considered 'core' nations.

Shortly before the Americans arrived on the Western Front, revolutionary unrest in Russia had prompted the hasty withdrawal of the Russian military. The Tsar, Emperor Nicholas II was forced to abdicate, making way for the formation of the Union of Soviet Socialist Republics (USSR) by year's end, thus ensuring that the imperial red, white and blue would no longer fly at the vanguard of the Russian Army. As we all now know, the Soviet Union would nurture the growth of global communism under the dark-red communist flag, and become the bitter enemy of her previous democratically-inclined allies. Yet even as Russia transformed from a traditional 'Christian' Empire into a God-denying ideological State, the 'righteous and God-fearing' Americans planted their own red, white and blue *'Stars and Stripes'* on the European soil so recently vacated by the Russians.

Then, in response to the U.S. declaration of war on Germany in April 1917 – the same year incidentally that Carl Jung published his findings on the collective unconscious – the following eight nations also formally declared war on Germany: Brazil, China, Costa Rica, Panama, Cuba, Greece, Liberia and Siam. Once again we see a remarkable consistency in these nations' choice of colors. All of them contain white and blue, and six of the eight flags are red, white and blue, thereby bringing the 'coincidence' ratio up dramatically (♣ 24).

What is possibly even more remarkable is that despite a completely different set of cultural and political circumstances, the same color-related dynamic that was being played out between aggressive instigators and defenders in Europe was also evident in the conflicts of the Far East during this time. As another fascist-type political regime, Imperial Japan was unique in that she used the Allies' declaration of war against Germany to advance her own territorial interests in Asia, declaring war against Germany solely to justify seizing German-held territories in the Far East. Taking such actions, including occupying Chinese, Russian, and Korean land during this period without contributing materially to the war effort in Europe, effectively put Japan in an aggressive dictatorship class by itself, a situation that would continue through the Second World War. Once again, we see Japan's opponents sporting reds, whites, and blues (♣ 22).

Meanwhile back on the Western Front we now have fourteen different nations all having declared war on Germany either at the outset of war, or in conjunction with the Americans in 1917. All of these nations' flags contained blue and white colors, and *twelve* of them contained red, white and blue! Would anyone now like to compute the odds of this being mere coincidence? (♣ 23).

By now the reader should at least be intrigued, if not already convinced of the profound implications of these symbolic repetitions in history and in the natural world. But just in case any skepticism lingers, let us drive home the point with the following dramatic list of remarkable repetitions of the red-white-blue triadic archetype in recent political events.

Incidences After World War I (♣ 25).

- Three allied nations signed the Treaty of Versailles that officially ended the First World War; England, France and the U.S.A.
- Three nations were originally involved in founding the League of Nations (later to transmute into the United Nations); Norway, England and France.
- Three nations came under persistent attack from Japan; in the early-to-mid 1900s Russia, Korea and China.[*]
- Two nations opposed Hitler and Stalin's move on Poland in 1939; England and France.
- Three nations froze Japanese assets in the Pacific; England, Holland and the United States.
- On the same day that Pearl Harbor was attacked in 1941, Japan also launched attacks on The Philippines, Guam, Wake Island, Midway Island, Hong Kong, British Malaya and Thailand; each sporting red-white-blue flags.
- Resistance to Japanese aggression in the Pacific during the Second World War came chiefly from Australia, New Zealand, Britain and the United States.
- Sixteen nations collaborated in the Korean War against the Soviet Union, China and North Korea. Some supplied medicines and other logistics but the active forces comprised twelve nations; United States, England, Australia, Thailand, New Zealand, Netherlands, France, Luxembourg, Canada, Philippines, South Africa and Norway. Once again, all flying flags containing red, white and blue.

Does anybody out there still believe we are talking about arbitrary coincidence? Surely these historical facts seal the case for some sort of orchestrated, archetypal providence? For in contrast to those nations carrying red, white, and blue colors, their opponents also share one color-feature in common; no blue. Coupled with a predominance of reds, and red-blacks, described by color experts as "the worst possible combination" (in auras and color therapies), it seems rather uncanny that the flags of so many historical 'bad guys' from Fascists, through the Axis Forces, to militant Communists, to modern religious terrorists have also chosen (or

---

[*] Several flags underwent changes throughout this period – nevertheless maintaining archetypal integrity. For more detail see the Flags of the World website.

'coincidentally' ended up with) flags that contain no feminine, nurturing blues.* A brief review of the later conflicts of the twentieth century such as the Vietnam War, and even the current war against terror will expose many such typical archetypal patterns that go well beyond the realms of pure coincidence or simple cultural preferences. This presses home the fact that even international political events; the apparent outcomes of generations of ideological and socio-political inclinations and developments, are subject to subliminal, unconscious influences to a previously un thought-of degree.

It is particularly interesting to note that nations such as Russia, China, and Canada for example, when politically aligned with central allied nations such as the United States, France and England – also had red, white, and blue in their flags – later to lose the blue when internal politics necessitated their withdrawal from allied coalitions. And although the limitations of this book will not allow us to fully explain the numerical connections involved, there are equally striking chromo-numeric sequences surrounding these collaborations of nations that suggest further subliminal orchestrations. All in all, a very convincing argument for the existence of subliminal, yet systematic forces unconsciously affecting human choices even at the international-historical level. When we add the fact that several aggressive, male-dominated institutions and organizations such as modern neo-Nazis or radical Islamists continue to choose red and black as their predominant symbolism surely the point is made. Clearly, if we can unlock the true meanings of these visible patterns and themes in history in relation to universal norms, we will I believe, be one collective step closer to understanding the true meaning of human existence.

After observing the accumulated evidence so far, I believe it is fair to say that we either have an amazingly bizarre series of coincidences – bordering in fact on the incredible or, that 'something else' is influencing or directing this extraordinary phenomenon from the deep, collective, historical subconscious. This in turn forces the question: Could it really be possible that some plan, or cosmic formula – greater than any of the players or nations involved – is being played out despite our collective ignorance of its existence? Even from the limited evidence presented so far, it is clear that some force, or law, or active intelligence even, has subliminally influenced

---

* The pre-war Italian flag has blue piping bordering the Savoy family arms, which was removed after WWII. Furthermore, Italy's position was ambiguous throughout both World Wars and is therefore not considered a 'core' player in these formulas. R-W-B North Korea is a special exception as technically the country of Korea is still one – albeit divided into North and South since the armistice of 1953 after the Korean War. Nevertheless, the red 'dark-star' symbolism *could* be read as appropriate for an isolationist, aggressive, atheistic dictatorship.

the political color choices of nations – a previously unacknowledged and undocumented phenomenon. But how could this be? Or maybe more to the point; *what* could this be? And how exactly does this phenomenon relate to humanity today?

The central question then, is what indeed is this mind-boggling formula or 'plan' that is unfolding in history in spite of our understanding of ourselves as autonomous beings? After all, how could it be possible that we beings of 'free will' could simultaneously and unconsciously be fulfilling another, greater plan? A cosmic design that apparently affects nations and ideologies and individual destinies like so many pieces on a cosmic chessboard? Isn't this a fundamental challenge to our concept of personal choice and free will? Is there in fact any *further* evidence to suggest that there is really more than an amazing series of coincidences to observe here?

My firm and resounding answer to this is an emphatic YES! For the discovery of the triadic archetype shows that the reality that we perceive as a rather haphazard and disjointed collection of historical events has in fact left this sequential record in numbers, symbols and colors, that indisputably identifies a process and a theme for history – as well as suggesting a purpose and direction for individual human lives.

For a better understanding of that purpose and direction – and through association, any personal and historical violations of the same – as well as the resultant psychological and sociological repercussions in society, we now need to reexamine those perennial, and often unfathomable aspects of human culture and development that have straddled the known and unknown realms – namely mythology, and religion.

CHAPTER ELEVEN

COLOR, MYTH, & RELIGION

We now explore the symbolic values of the colors white, blue, and red
specific to mythology and world religions. Following this, we will
consolidate our findings concerning the substantial existence of universal
archetypes by readdressing our conclusions so far directly to the
comparative sphere of world religions.

Although it may appear we have belabored the point by presenting so many examples of the triadic archetype in varied settings over the last few chapters, we should remember that this is a recent, and previously unpublished discovery and therefore requires solid proofs for our hypotheses. Secondly, because the very credibility of the hypothesis hinges upon its universality, we must also establish the comprehensiveness of the triadic archetype phenomenon. Finally, because we are specifically dealing with the social dysfunctions and excesses of religion, we are obliged to present as wide-ranging a proof as possible in order to present a convincing scientific argument. Although extensive supporting data does exist in the *Color of Truth* series of books, in this abridged work we have admittedly only been able to present a limited selection of the symbolic proofs themselves. Hoping and presuming that this has been sufficient to the task so far, let us now approach the conclusions of this work by searching within religion and mythology for those symbolic indicators that will help discern the authenticity of contemporary religious traditions in relation to the proofs of universal archetypes.

Naturally, any such review (provided it is accurate) will be of immeasurable value in identifying and evaluating the environmental influences and causes affecting the psychological and emotional well-being of the adherents of such traditions, as well as providing historical indicators of the collective 'psychospiritual' health of society.

Religion and Myth

Although considered by some to be merely silly fairy-stories or legends, ancient myths are nonetheless intimately intertwined with religious thought. Indeed, the more one learns about mythology and religion, the more difficult it is to differentiate between them – and so it should be. Those that argue that ancient mythologies and modern religions differ in credibility, validity, or general orthodoxy are either ill-informed or selectively ignorant, since any cursory examination of cultural myths will invariably expose the central tenets, mysteries, and sacramental aspects of our modern faith traditions in some form or another. This is not an opinion, but a fact. A fact moreover, whose recognition and acceptance will contribute greatly to the ultimate diffusion of sectarian neuroses.[1]

Recalling our discussion on 'universal truth' in Chapter Four, this indisputable fusion of myth and religion confirms two very important points: Firstly it challenges the validity of exclusive or sectarian doctrines; and secondly, it strongly supports the Universal Truth hypothesis. Taken to the next level this naturally leads us to the conclusion that *all* truths are indeed united at source. As explained previously, the only reason we haven't yet arrived at this consensus is because of the ongoing, and debilitating condition of collective human ignorance that fosters the development of neurotic traditions (such as sectarian religions), and encourages infantile and fear-based dependency upon other authoritarian institutions. Nevertheless, as we learn more and more of the properties of science, anthropology, history, astrology, human relations, mathematics, art, religion, politics and so on…. we will it seems, be drawn to the inevitable conclusion that all our various 'categories' and classification systems, including ancient myths and modern religions, are at best simple and limited glimpses of One Great Universal Truth. A Universal Truth moreover whose principles, at least in part, are reflected in the colors, numbers, and symbols of the triadic archetype. Hence, the archetype-formulas presented in this work are ultimately just newly-visible manifestations of those *immutable*[*]cosmic laws and processes that we violate – individually or collectively – to our peril.

---

[*] Immutable; not subject or susceptible to change

181

Just as the relative balance and/or completeness of the triad of white, blue, and red 'values' in the previous illustrations consistently matched the character of the subject under scrutiny; the same rules generally apply to religious symbolism. In the following brief overview of religious color-values we will discover that in the acceptance or rejection of 'universal truths' as defined in this work, each of the various religions tend to reflect the appropriate symbolism. In other words, despite long, convoluted, and often corrupt traditions, the universal triadic archetype has borne subliminal witness to itself in each tradition's symbolism; either through its presence or through its absence. In particular, the omission of the feminine features of the universal archetype is not only reflected through matching symbolism (red, or red-black replacing blue for example), but is also typically associated with the existence or development of authoritarian and/or sectarian attitudes. In turn, these attitudes are invariably reinforced by an oppressive intellectual dogmatism – once again, another expression of (red-masculine) forces attempting to suppress the feminine (blue) aspects of the collective psyche. In a telling observation, we note the fuller inclusion of triadic symbolism in those religions with a *truly* familial, humanistic, or natural bent, such as several tribal or 'New-Age' religions, as well as many of the ancient philosophies.

So, as we now review the religious and mythological realms from our new and informed perspective, the reader will kindly excuse any repetition of facts previously presented as we reemphasize important symbolic, thematic, and historical connections.

White in Religion

Reinforcing our previous findings that white represents spiritual health we discover that in ancient Celtic mythology, white bulls, white clad priests, and white mistletoe were the center of a special 'cure-all' rite. Likewise, the Buddhist tradition considers white to be the color of self-mastery – a state that indicates a developing spirituality. The ancient Egyptians also considered white to represent joy, and for Native Americans white is symbolic of peace and happiness. Even in traditional occultism and magic circles the color white typically represents healing, blessing, truth, peace, purity, and protection.

Not so surprisingly these beliefs parallel Hebrew and Christian traditions, where we read in the Bible that the Priestly Levite tribe were "arrayed in white" singing God's praises in the Temple of Solomon (II Chronicles 5:12). Likewise, the High Priest may only be clothed in white garments whenever he enters the Holy of Holies, most notably on the occasion of Yom Kippur – the annual feast of atonement and repentance for the Jews. Other mentions of white in the Bible include the obvious connection with light, such as in the creation story; "Let there be Light!" (Gen 1: 3), and in association with primary sustenance through the miraculous delivery of the white manna – the food God sent to his people in the desert (Ex 16:31). In Daniel 7:9 "The Ancient of Days" (God) is clothed in white, whilst in Ecclesiastes 9:8 white garments again signify goodness. In the New Testament, the Holy Spirit is pictured as a (white) dove descending upon Jesus, which has metaphoric associations with the dove of Noah's Ark who similarly launched out to restart the new world four-hundred years before Abraham. Christ is also described as appearing "white as the light" during his miraculous transfiguration, and Matthew also tells us that the Easter Angel is clothed in white. In John's gospel, two angels are placed at the same scene also clothed in white, whilst in Acts 1:10 two mystical "men in white" are present at Jesus' ascension into Heaven. In the book of Revelation white is mentioned eighteen different times so, for the sake of brevity we will just list the central meanings: There are the multitudes "clothed in white" signifying either the faithful on Earth "like righteous saints" or the "armies of heaven" who follow the Son of Man whose hair is white (symbolic of spiritual wisdom) suspended on white clouds; or he who is "Faithful and True" riding on his white horse. We read of a "white stone" symbolizing the Christ-figure, and twenty-four elders dressed in white sitting in judgment in heaven. There are another seven angels in white, and the "Wife of The Lamb" too is likewise dressed in white. And finally, the last entry in the Bible mentioning white is God's heavenly throne of judgment. All-in-all, a ratification in the Bible of our central premise that white typically symbolizes high spirituality, true religion, and the direction of union with God.

Although not officially recognizing religious icons or religious symbolism, in the Qur'an and other Islamic writings the word 'white' is regularly used in place of 'dawn' or 'daylight', as well as in the form of white animals, birds, or clothing that represent goodness in opposition to 'sinful' black. The prophet Muhammad himself is often described as being dressed in white, as are angels who assist him in battle; as was the stallion that carried him to heaven from the Temple Mount in Jerusalem. Very interestingly, record is also made of the time when God allocated a white standard (flag) to Adam, and a black one to Iblis (Satan), representing the earthly battle between good and evil – which in turn was handed down to Abel and Cain and their descendants respectively.[2] This is of particular interest to us not only because it confirms the Cain-and-Abel dynamic in pre-*and*-post Abrahamic history, but also because the armies of seventh century Islam were recorded as flying black or green flags in battle, and Muhammad's own personal standard was an all-black flag that sometimes exhibited a falcon in its center. This of course *could* be symbolic confirmation of the Muslim-Arab world's providential 'Cain' position in relation to Judeo-Christianity as discussed previously. But caution must be exercised here. We should remember that the 'Cain' position is the position of direct providential struggle, and thus may respond in either direction; either for good, or evil. Of course, we would still expect the symbolism to follow suit.[*] Caution before judgment however, should be the rule of thumb.

In contrast to the disciplined orthodoxies of the monotheistic Abrahamic traditions Hinduism, with its abundant proliferation of colorful deities is religious amorphism defined. Yet in spite of its apparent lack of theological constraint, in certain key areas Hindu symbolism still adheres to archetypal principles. White for example, is generally understood to represent goodness, purity, and spiritual wisdom, as it does in Buddhism, Sikhism, and Zoroastrianism.

In contemporary religious understandings of the color white, spiritual healer Edgar Cayce says that white is the perfect aura. "If our souls were in perfect balance, then all our color vibrations would blend and we would have an aura of pure white."[3] Using religious terminology, chromatist Betty Wood describes white as associated with "wholeness, purity, and innocence and is a most sacred color, (representing) ..spiritual authority." [4]

To summarize therefore, we may conclude that white in religion and mythology has traditionally represented God, spirituality, goodness, wholeness, and purity.

Blue in Religion
In mythology and ancient religions blue has always held a special place as the color of the heavens and of the sea, and through association, the Moon and the archetypal mother figure. For example, the Greek goddess Demeter was clothed in a blue cloak, a tradition carried on in Catholic images of the Virgin Mary; whilst in Celtic mythology it was the color of the bard or poet-minstrel, which also has feminine overtones. Supporting this feminine / maternal / emotional / contemplative theme; in the Cabalistic tradition (Jewish mysticism), blue is the color of mercy; whilst in Buddhist thought, blue is the color of wisdom (again). The Cherokee Indians have a saying;

---

[*] The topic of archetypal Islamic symbolism is dealt with in *The Color of Truth Volume II*

"He is entirely blue" which is the equivalent of the emotional 'feeling blue' concept in modern English.

In the Bible the feminine theme is also closely affiliated with the color blue, especially in rituals associated with Israel's preparation as a bride for the Messiah. From Exodus 25:4 through 39:31 blue is mentioned thirty-four times in association with fine finishing work associated with the priestly vestments and with the Tent of the Tabernacle. It should be noted here that the priests of ancient Judaism saw themselves primarily in the role of custodians to God's chosen people – His 'daughter Zion' (blue). In Numbers 4: 6–12 for instance, "cloths of blue" are mentioned several times in reference to wrapping sacred items, and covering the altar with the food for offering to God. There are also two possible references to an association of blue with "whoredom" in Numbers 15:38, and Ezekiel 23:6 where we find blue affiliated with both the memory of whoredom, and with the act of adultery – but whether there is a direct connection to the acts of adultery and prostitution as opposed to a general connection with 'feminine sexuality' is an arguable point. Regardless, this does not challenge but instead supports the overall feminine theme of the color blue in scripture. As we have already shown, blue also featured in the building of Solomon's Temple along with red, white, and purple (II Chronicles 2). The only other references to blue in the Bible are descriptive of clothing and sails, yet the color blue is not mentioned at all in the New Testament; an omission that bears testament amongst other things, to the distinct patriarchal theme of early Christianity.

In Islamic writings, the Sufi disciples of Sheikh Hassan Asrakpush dressed only in blue garments, considering this a reflection of the color of heaven. Blue turbans too were the mark of the philosopher. But apart from this particular sect's use of the color, blue is noticeably absent in the Qur'an, and is even regarded a sign of hypocrisy in Rumi's Mathnavi, although possibly for its association with the abovementioned sect.[5] Blue does feature quite regularly in Mosque décor, in carpets, walls and such like, but rarely if ever features in prominent Islamic iconography or flags. Again, we should note the general masculine-and-militant nature of Islam and the corresponding absence of feminine colors and themes in its current constitution.

In our observations in Chapter Seven, we concluded that blue moves us towards the more spiritual aspects of life and away from the (red) physical level. Also "spiritually stimulating" blue is "the color of the soul, and of purity." Cayce reiterates these concepts stating that "blue has always been the color of the spirit, the symbol of contemplation, prayer and heaven". If we refer back to our psychospiritual diagrams (see ♣ 1, 2, 3, 4), we will see that the area occupied by the mind, psyche, and soul moves progressively from blue towards spiritual white as we move away from selfish individuality towards a collective spirituality. This not only matches Cayce's understanding of the soul's blue value, but underscores the chromatic connection between (a) red and selfishness, (b) passion and desires, and (c) flesh-centered masculine properties; and highlights the more contemplative and spiritual values associated with the colors blue and white. Furthermore, it reinforces the theoretical connection between the natural (ideal) development of the human being – spirit, mind, and body – vs. the obvious imbalances in modern individuals and societies which are predominantly focused on catering to the passions of the flesh. Naturally, the stronger color wavelengths (red) reflect the strongest (physical) urges.

Betty Wood describes the values connected to blue as "truth, revelation, wisdom, loyalty, fertility, constancy, and chastity" – concepts also reflected in traditional heraldry that likewise attributes the values of truth and loyalty to the color blue. Not surprisingly, Wood also connects blue with "the raising of consciousness to a spiritual level" and "the feminine principle, the Great Mother,... comfort, peace, compassion, and healing". Further confirmation of the archetypal association linking the color blue and the feminine. In an interesting note concerning healing, Wood adds that blue "is only superceded by its higher counterpart.. indigo, the ray of spirituality" (purple).[6] This supports our understanding that purple ranks high in symbolic importance – approaching equal status with white, in that it can represent the harmonious conjunction of spirit, mind, and body. Interesting too that purple is not actually a natural color, but is a combination of (masculine) red and (feminine) blue, with (spiritual) white?

Red in Religion

In mythology red regularly surfaces as the traditional color of the hero, such as in the color of Hercules' cloak (Greek and Roman), or Cuchulain's cloak (Celtic) – both of whom suffer remarkably similar adventures to the archetypal Greek hero Prometheus and another counterpart; Odin of Norse legend. The pattern of being tied to a rock or tree, being attacked by ravens or eagles (evil, Satan), journeying to the underworld and shedding blood in a sacrificial act is also common to other religious figures such as the ancient Persian god Mithras who strongly influenced Roman Christianity. Of course, the same themes are intriguingly present in Christ's passion story, who incidentally also wears a scarlet cloak in the gospel of Matthew (27: 28). Red was also the color of Set, the typhoon god of the ancient Egyptians, underlining a connection with force, or power.

Supporting these themes oriental philosophy places the red Chakra at the base of the spine, where it is considered 'the root' and source of sexual energy. Whilst in Buddhism, sacred chanting has a three-way connection with the color red and the heart. In Native American tradition, Lone Man (Adam) set up a totem pole and painted it red at the beginning of time, whilst in Cherokee symbolism red is symbolic of success in war, in play, and in love, and was the color of both the war-club and the shield. Edgar Cayce tells us that in ancient symbolism, red represented the body (as opposed to the spirit), whilst in his closing color chart Cayce gives us the three words; force, vigor, and energy, to define red. In occultism too, red is again associated with lust, strength, courage, power, health, energy, and vitality. Overall, a pretty consistent litany of masculine-physical properties.

In the monotheistic Sikh tradition, just as in our earlier findings, red is symbolic of egotism and selfish sensuality, whereas in the Qur'an, Muhammad is regularly described in conjunction with red tents or clothing – appropriate for a man of high position in a patriarchy. In the Bible too the words red, crimson and scarlet appear over a hundred times, beginning with a reference to Adam meaning "red earth" in Hebrew. As with white, there are two main uses of these words; either descriptive or symbolic – or a combination of both. In Genesis 25:25 for instance Esau, one of Isaac's twin sons is described as "red all over" at birth, and red is mentioned once again as the color of the food given by Jacob in exchange for Esau's birthright. Because Jacob and Esau are amongst the founding ancestors of the Arabs and the Jews, their stories as we have seen bear special import. Later, when Tamar gives birth to Judah's twin sons Pharez and Zarah (descendants of Jacob); Zarah sticks his hand out of the womb first, and a red thread is tied to it. But why red one might ask? This also has significant symbolic meaning connected to lineage. In Isaiah 1:18 sins are described as "scarlet" and "red like crimson" and in Isaiah 63:1-2 red garments denote might, power, and greatness. "Mighty and valiant men" (soldiers) dress in scarlet in Nahum 2:3, whilst a red rope is used to save Joshua's spies in Joshua 2. In II Samuel 1: 24 and Proverbs 31, scarlet clothing is a sign of material prosperity reflected again in the book of Daniel where the dream interpreter is "rewarded with scarlet". The one notable mention of red in the gospels, and the only time Jesus is associated with red is the aforementioned occasion when Jesus is mocked as a king in the scarlet robe during his torture, but interestingly enough, in the other gospels Jesus' robe is purple.

In spite of its obscure mystical language the Book of Revelation remains an official part of the Christian Bible, and some religious scholars continue to believe that the symbolic language contained therein does indeed have contemporary value. It should be noted however, that the six symbolic mentions of red and scarlet in the Book of Revelation are open to a wide variety of subjective interpretations, and as such have been the source of considerable acrimonious debate as differing groups interpret the allegorical language according to their own sectarian leanings. However, with the proofs of this work to guide us, connections with historical or contemporary figures or institutions can hopefully be more accurately discerned – depending of course on whether or not one believes literally in Bible prophecy in the first place. With a little imagination for instance, any of the upcoming figurative descriptions from the Book of Revelation could well be applied to political or religious institutions, both past and current, that have appeared in this presentation so far. Among possible candidates for these allegorical entities are certain features of; (i) the Imperial Roman Empire, (ii) the Holy Roman Empire, (iii) Roman Catholicism, (iv) corrupt Christianity, (v) Communism, (vi) Fascism, (vii) Fundamentalism, (viii) Islam, (ix) authoritarianism, or (x) secular materialism.

For instance, there is the red horse with the great sword that will "take peace from the Earth" in Rev 6:4; or the red dragon in Rev 12:3 that fights with Michael the Archangel and wants to "devour the child" (savior); and the woman dressed in scarlet, sitting on a scarlet beast who is "the mother of all harlots" and a great threat to God's people. If one is a Christian democrat for instance, then the red horse could very well be Soviet Communism – splitting the world with its 'sword' (militant ideology). If one is a regular Christian, then the red dragon is obviously Satan, or agents thereof. If one is a reform Protestant, then the woman in scarlet is clearly the Roman Catholic Church, and so on. We must remember amongst all this striking symbolism that the greatest danger is in making ill-informed subjective interpretations. The real 'enemy' is ignorance and enmity, and harboring pious justifications for hateful attitudes. We must resist the temptation to use this knowledge to further divide humankind. In every case, we should first apply these archetypal findings in a frank critique of our own cultures and faith traditions before ever daring to apply such to others – in doing so we may very well be surprised as to who in fact are really the 'good guys' and who are the bad. Again, caution and humility should be the rule of thumb.

In any event, we now know that whenever we see additional symbols of oppression such as black birds-of-prey, an absence of blue, and/or a predominance of red in any given institution's symbolism, we may be reasonably sure that we are looking at agencies of oppression, suppression, or destruction – of archetypal formulas and values – in some form or other. More often than not, it is the feminine-maternal aspects of society that suffer; our compassion, mercy, understanding, and willingness to cooperate, rather than fight and destroy. Recalling Chapter Seven: "Mixing red with black is considered the worst possible combination,… but red (alone) can be either positive or negative" – which brings us to a most important point of clarification.

Thematic Subdivisions of the Color Red
The reader will no doubt have noticed a broad array of sometimes-contradictory symbolic definitions within the range of the color red. From *sin* to *savior*, *priest* to *prostitute* ('harlot') and *Church* to *Communism* for instance. Coming up with just one central theme for the color red is therefore inappropriate, and rightly so. Because, especially in a religious context red is different to the other colors we are studying – having the confusing properties of representing three different archetypal categories which we will provisionally term here: (i) the original male; (ii) the perverse male; and (iii) the hero figure. Notwithstanding these three different classifications however, the common unifying elements of masculinity and physicality remains across the board (♣ 27).

This three-stage classification of archetypal red values fits particularly well with the traditional monotheistic understanding that mankind fell from a state of primordial grace, and has since been engaged in the struggle against evil in order to regain that state of original purity; for which role of course we need religious heroes, messiahs, or saviors. Hence we have an original 'perfect' male (red-white) who is connected to God, (i) namely Adam before the Fall. Then we have the perverse male figure (red-black) who has come under the influence of evil (ii). This category includes Adam *after* the Fall, his older son Cain the murderer, and of course Satan, as the (male) fallen angel of light and orchestrator of evil. Implicated in this second category of course are all human males who have not yet reached a state of 'perfection' or reunion with God. Such agencies as Nazism typify the worst of this category in a social-historical setting, but any excessive or violent use of masculine energies is symptomatic of this condition. It is no mere coincidence that traditional movie 'baddies' such as Count Dracula, Darth Vader, and the figure of Satan are almost always portrayed in blacks and red-blacks. The third category (iii) is the hero figure (red). Here we have salvific-oriented male figures such as Moses or Jesus, but it should also be noted that whether they subscribe to the fall-from-grace theory or not, nearly all religious traditions have central figures that fit this hero-mold.

189

In the context of red-white symbolism, all male figures that have attained a high degree of spiritual awareness and lived their lives accordingly may thus be viewed as 'hero' types, inasmuch as they have striven to reflect the ideal male archetype, or have contributed substantially to advancing that model. Based upon chromonumeric parallels this category would include Zoroaster, Abraham, Buddha, John-the-Baptist, Muhammad, Bahaullah, Gandhi, and many, many more who have in some way or other hosted the providential spirit – even if only partially and for limited periods of time. God's work is God's work, whether done at the local-personal or international-historical level. It is the role, and not the person that defines the symbolism. This rule of course applies equally to many mythological figures (think Prometheus, Hercules, Santa Claus etc..) as well as some of the secular heroes in history, for we must not forget that religion per se is but one of the features of everyday life that we employ to better ourselves. Moreover, religion is by definition a temporary condition in the history of humankind. Indeed as discussed earlier, the properties of true moral integrity are often found in greater abundance and consistency amongst the ranks of academics, scientists, and common people than in the narrow world of career religionists. 'Holiness' after all is descriptive of the Divine reflection, and as we noted earlier the Creator was first and foremost a scientist before ever He was a religionist (if ever indeed He was one). Perhaps we have been getting this whole 'being holy' thing back-to-front all this time?

Back in the real world; as we saw in our studies of political insignia the perverse male archetype is usually represented with the color red in conjunction with the color black, or at least without the presence of the color blue. And although the colors of the hero are definitely red *and* white – as were the colors of the original male (the Adam archetype) – the presence of white in certain red-black situations (such as the Nazi flag) may simply be due to the *absence* of color. Similarly, when red is present in isolation, it may only be representative of the male, or other masculine traits such as patriarchy, physical strength, or aggression. For as we all well know, many male hero figures in history from popes to priests, and from kings to emperors, have all too often succumbed to their baser traits. Thus, when assessing the potential values of red symbolism in specific situations, it is especially important to seek out additional evidence to confirm one's chromatically based assumptions. When it comes to the religious realm in particular, it is wiser to presume the possible presence of 'good' red symbolism in each case, given the conviction that it is indeed through the subliminal avenues of True religion (with a capital 'T') that any benign noumenal force has the best chance of getting through to us.

In the same vein however, the presence of dark or historically-destructive symbolism amongst the semiotics of any particular religious tradition should never be overlooked, for evil's best disguise is to masquerade as truth. Caution and humility however, should still remain the rule of thumb.

CHAPTER TWELVE

RELIGIOUS TRIADIC ARCHETYPES

We now undertake a brief but dramatic overview of triadic symbolism present in and amongst world religions today.

Naturally, we cannot but briefly allude to the specific theologies or philosophies underlying the symbolism of the various religions – nor would we want to get embroiled in the tortuous complexities of religious dogmas and doctrines, and their associated manifestations in religious practice – this book being a specific attempt to resolve some of the confusions that gave rise to such phenomena in the first place. Therefore, whilst recognizing that the information we are about to review is delivered from an objective, archetypal perspective, and as such may not be seen as fully 'orthodox' by any particular tradition's adherents; we will nevertheless endeavor to illustrate how the world's religions are in fact already subliminally united along triadic archetypal themes, and show how it is mainly due to the excesses and deficiencies of ignorance as explored in Part One that a religious consensus is not already in place.

As we shall see, the proofs of the triadic archetype strongly suggest that rigid orthodoxies and other modern interpretations of the Divine originally sprouted from the same archetypal origins but over time, have suffered many unqualified interpretations brought about chiefly by ignorance, and through liberal or conservative excesses respectively.

Hinduism

Hinduism itself almost defies specific academic definition, for not only is there no listed 'founder' of Hinduism, but there are no formal doctrines, such as we find in monotheistic traditions. This reflects the overall understanding amongst Hindus that 'God' or 'The Ultimate Reality' is beyond full understanding, but nevertheless is expressed in diverse forms and situations, according to environmental circumstances and the faith-position of the individual believer. Hence Hinduism displays an apparent multitude of discrete deities. It would be more accurate however, to recognize these deities as manifestations of the One Absolute Reality – only in different roles. As a result, we find many rich and colorful allegories in Hindu philosophy. Texts such as the Upanishads and the Vedas for instance were written several centuries before Christ, and the authors often used colors in their attempts to define both corporeal and mystical concepts, as in this extract from Volume 2 of the Upanishads referring to the path to Ultimate Reality (Brahman):

> On that path they say that there is white, or blue, or yellow, or green, or red; that path was found by Brahman, and on it goes whoever knows Brahman, and who has done good, and obtained splendor.[*]

But the very expansiveness of Hinduism, and the fact that it doggedly refuses to be trimmed and bracketed into logical creeds and dogmas makes it both a worthy model of universalism in principle, as well as an extremely difficult religious model to quantify systematically. Nevertheless, from the perspective of this work, it is very intriguing to discover a core triad known collectively as the Trimurti (trinity), that comprises three central deities accompanied by their consorts, who carry an assortment of characteristics that match the archetypal (religious) values of the colors white, blue, and red. With a little conceptual flexibility, and allowing for the inevitable thematic confusions when dealing with a million junior deities, the central premises of the triadic archetype can clearly be seen in this symbolism of the Hindu Trimurti (♣ 14).

Firstly there is 'white' Brahma (God the Creator) – from "Brahman" the Ultimate Cosmic Principle, who is interestingly partnered by Saraswati, the goddess of knowledge and wisdom (blue?). Secondly we have Shiva, another primary deity colored blue and associated with both procreation and

---

[*] Brahman is the Hindu name for Ultimate Reality

destruction and matched with his consort Kali, the goddess of power, destruction, and transformation. Thirdly there is Vishnu preserver of the universe, usually colored dark blue and associated with primordial waters or, sometimes colored black and reclining on a great serpent. Vishnu can manifest himself in avatars (human embodiments) in various colors. His consort Lakshmi is the goddess of love, beauty, and delight.

Although the symbolism, like Hinduism in general is somewhat difficult to pin down, we do see parallels between the triadic principle and the respective attributes of archetypal white, blues, and reds as discussed in this work. When allowing for the lack of constraint upon individual Hindus in matters of faith and religious expression, it is actually quite remarkable that the triadic archetype has still managed to hold its subliminal ground. Most important of all perhaps is the recognition that the Trimurti, as a core belief amongst Hindus, offers a common base both with Christian theology and quantum science in our search for universal truths.

This triadic core also presents itself in the sacred "AUM" chant. The AUM is the Hindu syllable of 'Supreme Reality' considered sacred in both its audible and visible forms. When chanted, the three sounds represent the Hindu Trimurti, and both Buddhists and Sikhs also consider it sacred. AUM symbolizes totality and completeness. There is an interesting literal connection between the sound of "AUM" and God-related terms in the English language such as: "Amen, Omnipotent, Omnipresent," and "Alpha-and-Omega." In scientific language 'AU' is the periodic table's sign for gold and may also factor in the word 'Aura' – the spiritual radiation phenomenon often associated with the concept of haloes. In Islam too the word "Amin" (amen), and the Islamic letter for "Allah" look remarkably similar to the literal AUM symbol, and during ritualized chants in the Buddhist tradition, each of the three audible sounds represents three aspects of the mystical process of communication which not surprisingly are:

- The Three Chakras; the inner eye, the throat, and the heart
- The Three Practices; the secret, the inner, and the outer
- The Three Colors; white, blue, and red (♣ 15)

Buddhism

Buddhism grew out of ancient Hinduism, refining its beliefs and practices along the foundations set by its founder Guatama Buddha in the sixth century B.C.E. Although officially rejecting monotheistic doctrines 'The Way' (of the Buddha) has many features in common with monotheistic traditions and not unlike Hindus, Buddhists identify with a broad collection of manifestations of the Buddha's characteristics. Some, known as 'Taras' are manifestations of the feminine (divine) or expressions of the female Buddha of Enlightened Activity. Once again a remarkable consistency is displayed when the color-symbolism relates to the characteristics, rather than just the stated gender of these deities. What must be taken into account of course is the fact that these applied mystical color-characteristics originated long before science had even discovered the color-properties of light itself.

In his book *In Praise of Tara: Songs to the Savioress* Martin Wilson translates Buddhist scripture regarding the origins of the primordial Tara as follows: "In the past, many eons ago... in the universe called Manifold Light, there lived a princess by the name of Moon of Wisdom-knowledge."[1] This moon-wisdom-knowledge theme exactly correlates to the feminine goddess-principle who, once fully enlightened, adopts the role of 'Liberator' (of the feminine traits) in a masculine-dominated world. Once again, this corresponds to the idea of an intermediary blue wisdom-entity seeking to redress the red, masculine, physical imbalances of patriarchal and materialistic societies. And although there are twenty-one different manifestations of Tara, she is nevertheless often referred to as "The Mother of all Buddhas:"

> Tara is known as the "Mother of all Buddhas." This is because she is the wisdom of reality, and all Buddhas and bodhisattvas are born from this wisdom. This wisdom is also the fundamental cause of happiness, and our own spiritual growth comes from this wisdom. That is why Tara is called the Mother. And Mother Tara has much wisdom to manifest many aspects, sometimes peaceful, sometimes wrathful, in different colours -- all to help sentient beings.[2]

The colors of each of the respective Taras is once again uncannily close to the chromatic values discovered in this work, with white representing high spirituality, enlightenment, and peace; red being an indicator of heroism and physical power; and whenever black appears, it is invariably associated with wrath, vengeance, and aggression – most notably when partnered by red. For a full listing of Buddhist Tara's color values, a visit to the website of *Amitabha Buddhist Centre* is recommended.

White, Red, and Blue: First of all there is the Tara who fulfills all active functions, her body colored white and radiating varicolored lights, holding the green flask from whence come all magical attainments. This is a clear association with light itself, the colors of the spectrum, and the position of the color green at the center of creation. Then there is the Tara 'white as the autumn moon' who defeats diseases and evil spirits, holding the white flask that pacifies. This same white flask is also capable of defeating all terrors, whilst bestowing good fortune, cleansing sins and obscurations, pacifying the poison of the 'lu' serpents, and dispelling poison and disease. Remembering that red is associated with things physical, active, and dynamic, and in it's pure form is also associated with the messiah or hero figure, we discover the Tara swift and heroic, who destroys hindering demons and heals injuries, her body colored red and blazing like fire, holding the red flask that protects from obstacles, and subjugates, tames, and defeats all 'du' demons and obstructions. And lastly, there is the Blue Buddha associated with the properties of wisdom, and the mystical blue "flask of knowledge" which subdues evil spirits.

There are two features of the color black identified in this work that are also common to Buddhism. These are (a) the connection with Satan, darkness, and the underworld; and (b), as an ominous portent when mixed with the color red. Although sometimes benign we see these two themes reflected in some of the Tara figures: There is "Tara the Terrifier" victorious of the triple world with frowning brows, who tames hindering demons, her body colored red-black holding the aforementioned blue flask that confounds ghosts and awakened corpses. There is also Mother Tara whose body is colored black, and holds the black flask that averts magic mantras, whilst a third red-black Tara holding a red flask defeats chi demons and enemies. Yet another red-black Tara is known as 'Tara the Pulverizer' – conjuring up a broad range of rather masculine images of the goddess. Here we see a good example of the principle of role over gender where symbolically speaking, the most important factor for determining the symbolism are the activities, rather than the gender of the subject.

Taoism
Another ancient tradition Taoism was developed from the Tao Te Ching, a manuscript believed to be written by the Chinese philosopher Lao Tse (604-520 B.C.E.), although scholars generally agree that a school of philosophy probably worked in collaboration to produce the Tao Te Ching. Taoism has brought to the Western sphere a spiritual awareness that promotes reverence and understanding of the natural order. In his *Anthology of World Religions* Huston Smith writes:

> The object of philosophical Taoism is to align one's daily life with the Tao, to ride its boundless tide and delight in its flow... a force that is infinitely subtle and intricate, ...it lives by a vitality that has no need of abruptness, much less violence. The Tao flows in and flows out again, turning life into a dance that is neither feverish nor unbalanced.[3]

The technical meaning of the word *Tao* is generally interpreted as 'The Way'; with the word *Te* meaning 'integrity and power'; and *Ching* referring to the sacred text itself. This conceptual triad again correlates to a three-system spirituality comprising an inspirational aspect (Tao), a theoretical aspect (Ching), and an active aspect (te). Again, this directly translates into concept, plan, and action; spirit, mind, and body; white, blue, and red (♣15).

Judaism, Christianity and Islam

We group these three monotheistic traditions together because in a very telling and historically accurate display of archetypal symbolism, each religion in isolation appears deficient in at least one central thematic aspect of the triadic archetype. This may indeed reflect a singular role for each tradition, but it could also indicate a lapse in universal understanding. Having already explored related political and historical material, and in order to establish this final point before moving to our conclusions, let us focus purely upon the striking symbolism of these three faith traditions – and see what it tells us.

Pagan Symbolism

We begin by informing the reader of the historical fact that both Christianity and Islam (in particular) are infused with a considerable amount of what orthodoxy terms 'pagan' symbolism – particularly, the sun and the moon respectively. From our (now) more enlightened perspective however, we can reasonably assume that this 'pagan' symbolism is in fact rooted in the same universal (archetypal) principles as modern religious orthodoxies – at least that is – those religions that function in accord with cosmic consciousness.

Chromatically speaking, Christianity and Islam also contain more than a peppering of 'dark and disturbing' signs and colors, but the specific study of religion's symbolic dark side must, for the sake of expediency be placed aside for another day.[*] Suffice it to say that the aggressive and destructive aspects of Christianity and Islam – by far the two most militant

---

[*] See *The Color of Truth Volume II: Parallels in Life* by this author

religions in history – can quickly be matched to corresponding 'excessive male' and authoritarian red-black symbolism in their internal, historical structures. Having made this brief clarifying statement, let us now draw the reader's attention to the fact that the primary colors of Christendom until the Reformation were red and white, and those of Islam were originally green and white – although black also featured very prominently in Muhammad's own tribal colors. In Christianity's case the red was chiefly inherited from the traditional colors of the (authoritarian and 'pagan'[*]) Roman Empire, and is directly associated with Mithraic sun-worship – the preexistent, exclusively-male belief system at the time Christianity merged with Roman paganism in the fourth century. Islam on the other hand picked up the crescent-moon symbolism that we see in political colors today from 'pagan' associations with the moon god Hubal, who was considered the greatest of the 360-or so gods of pre-Islamic Mecca (♣ 28, 29). Scholars inform us that the common name for Hubal as the highest deity was 'Allah'. In his book *In Defense of the Faith* David Hunt states;

> Allah is not a generic Arabic word for God but a name of a particular god among many deities traditionally honored in ancient times by nomadic tribes in Arabia. Allah was the chief god among the approximately 360 idols in the Kaaba in Mecca...Allah is a contraction of AL-ilah, the name of the Moon God [Hubal] of the local Quraysh, Mohammed's tribe...Allah's symbol was a crescent moon, which Muhammad carried over into Islam. This symbol is seen on Mosques, minarets, shrines, and Arab flags. [4]

Here we see a direct connection between Islam and moon symbolism, which, in Islam's early development was actually quite appropriate. For although it later gathered a reputation as a religion of barbarians (due mainly to Christian propaganda), Islam began as a compassionate and unifying monotheism that did much to elevate and protect the social position of women, and advanced learning and education in occupied lands.

If we now recall our exploration of symbols associated with the archetypal masculine and feminine, we begin to see an interesting dualistic model emerging between the respective sun and moon symbols of

[*] 'Pagan' is a relative term originally meaning 'country-folk' ('and their silly religions'). Before Christianity adopted the term as a pejorative, the Romans applied the term 'pagans' to the early Christians.

Christianity and Islam. It does seem most appropriate (from an archetypal-providential perspective) for feminine moon symbolism to be present in a religious movement (Islam) that aimed to correct a strongly patriarchal Christianity in the seventh century; a politically-oriented religion whose origins and character were not only distinctly masculine and authoritarian, but were also fused with Constantinian sun-worship. The question begs asking once again: Could it be possible, that despite the ignorance of such themes amongst early Christians and Muslims, that the noumenal, or subliminal influence behind this symbolism was somehow reaching out through (archetypal) 'pagan' connections (Mithrais and Hubal) to somehow achieve the balanced union of two great, but archetypically-incomplete religious movements, and two great but socially-imbalanced cultures? For although the colors don't seem quite right on the Islamic side, the symbolism is definitely there, and the rapid advance of Islam in those first hundred years between 632 and 732 C.E. was remarkable to say the least.

We should perhaps reiterate that despite the religious wars of the time, Muslim scholars effectively brought the Judeo-Christian world out of the Dark Ages, and unlike contemporary extremist attitudes amongst Muslim fanatics, expressed remarkable tolerance for both Christianity and Judaism. Hence the feminine traits of wisdom and scientific knowledge were very evident in the growth of early Islam – whilst being alarmingly deficient in the Christianity of the day. However, our archetypal male-and-female-union theory appears to stumble upon recognizing that there was no feminine blue symbolism in early Christianity, nor in the ancient or modern traditional colors of Islamic or Arab culture.

This lack of blue is a reflection of both the beliefs of Islam, which views Allah purely as a singular, masculine entity, and the social policies of the Arab-Muslim states, which generally suppress the feminine element in their societies. We are therefore left with the inescapable conclusion that 'archetypal wisdom' (blue) must at that time have been busy elsewhere – or was She? Maybe there's another explanation...

Let's take another look at the symbolism here. More specifically, let's look at what's *NOT* here. Based upon what we have discovered in this work so far and remembering that in the Bible the sun and the moon in Joseph's dream are recognized as representing his father and mother respectively (Gen 37: 9-10); and considering the fact that Christianity was overtly patriarchal and authoritarian at the time that Islam arose as a 'liberating' theology; we might justifiably expect to see signs of the feminine archetype trying to influence Christian society either from within or without, right?

With this in mind, when we look at the historical symbolic set up; with the sun and the moon, and the colors red, white, and green, we can see that we have two parts – of three possible, symbolic, archetypal triads:

- The color spectrum trinity of red at one end, blue at the other end, and green in the center. *Blue is missing.*
- The triad of red, white, and blue. Once again, *blue is missing.*
- The symbolic family of sun, moon, and stars. *The stars are missing.*

Maybe what's missing from the formula… is a blue star? (see ♣ 31).

Exciting, paradoxical, yet strangely probable; with a modest grasp of archetypal constructs it now seems very reasonable to assume that noumenal forces were attempting to orchestrate a benevolent union between three competing religious traditions who each had so much to learn from the others. However, it appears that this (if any) providential attempt at unity was not a total success. At least, that's what the current and historical enmities between Jews, Muslims, and Christians would suggest. The discrepancies of each of these three faith movements appears to have become exacerbated since the seventh century, with pride, arrogance, paranoia, and the scourges of sectarianism and nationalism reinforcing the negatives in each tradition – (please excuse the generalizations).

Thus we are left with (i) a Judaism that is for the most part still locked into Old Testament thinking *without* her (red) messiah, and who, like the archetypal female, has struggled both ideologically and politically to survive in an aggressive society surrounded by masculine reds and red-blacks (the Roman Empire, Middle Ages Christianity, Nazism, Communism, the Arab League); (ii) a Christianity that continues to be plagued with patriarchal attitudes and theological dissention (red); and (iii) a modern Islam that appears to have lost the compassionate flavor of its origins (no blue), and has for the most part exchanged its thrust for scientific knowledge and social justice (green) with a narrow minded, and often radical fundamentalism (red and black). Sadly, the symbols and the colors all confirm these facts with modern Judaism still carrying no red, and Roman Catholicism and Islam still displaying no blue in their vexillologies.

In the case of Christianity the original all-male Trinity of the early Church Councils has slowly transmigrated into a nebulous *androgyny;*[*] but in the oldest established branch of Christianity, namely Roman Catholicism,

---

[*] Androgynous; being neither distinguishable as masculine or feminine

we have witnessed the gradual promotion of the Virgin Mary (blue and white) to a position of co-redemptrix with Jesus (red and white). And although the theology and the Mariology surrounding this development is convoluted and confusing, the fact remains that the original, subliminal, triadic archetype as defined in this work has once again presented itself to the collective consciousness in sensory, albeit mystical forms: Christ as hero-redeemer and King, the 'Second Adam' and son of God; the original male archetype almost always depicted in red and white. And Mary, Queen of Heaven; also known as the 'Second Eve' fulfilling all the mystical requirements of the archetypal mother figure, invariably dressed in blues and whites both in popular paintings and whenever 'She' makes a mystical appearance.[5] Son and daughter under God; brother and sister; redeemer and redemptrix – not to mention mystical spouses in union with the Holy Ghost: Red, white, and blue (see ♣ 30).

With these striking illustrations even in the nebulous religious world bearing uncanny testament to our findings so far, we are presented with an undeniable record of substantial and/or sensory manifestations of universal archetypes across the whole range of human experience: The three-stage principles of concept, plan, and action, reflected in the human dynamic as spirit, mind, and body; in the atom as electron, neutron, and proton; and in industry and politics in the progression of ideology, theory, and practice, bear testament to a parallel subliminal dimension (see Tables 1-8 in the midsection). From mythology to quantum science; from ancient metaphysics to national symbolism; and from oriental philosophies to modern religions – all are enveloped by and infused with the colorful signatures of light and energy. When we further recognize the fact that imbalances or omissions in the respective symbolisms almost invariably reflect corresponding imbalances in human ideologies, agencies, or institutions, we are confronted with the stunning reality that some type of profound cosmic blueprint or intelligence is directly influencing our symbol-forms. Whether theistic and transcendent, or subliminal and immanent in essence, something (or someone?) is apparently maintaining a symbolic archetypal record, (if not also a balance) in history. The key of course is how to read, understand, and apply this knowledge to the betterment of human society?

Whilst being hesitant to make unscientific presumptions; but in light of the abundance of archetypal phenomena displayed throughout the political symbolism of the twentieth century, one could speculate that in the face of institutionalized religion's failure to substantially manifest universal principles in society, the noumenal force(s) behind this color-phenomena are somehow orchestrating these symbolic expressions in sensory forms so as to bring the realities of Universal Truth directly into human consciousness. Such a hypothesis fits with the understanding that institutionalized religion, as the 'official' representative of the noumenal / spiritual / unconscious realms, is now so compromised and consumed by the (red-black) excesses of the masculine – including sectarian indoctrinations and other materialistic concerns – that it can no longer access the noumenal realm on the scale necessary to serve the needs of an increasingly complex, and well-informed global society. Obstructed by the mechanisms, confusions, and corruptions of organized religion, the Energies and Truths of the noumenal realm can but persist in trying to reach us through more overt and conscious means.

Indeed it could even be, that religion as we have known it has served its primary purpose as an instrument of faith, and the fact that we are discovering these preexistent truths at this point in the social and technological development of mankind is an indicator that collectively, we may simply be progressing along natural, universal, thematic lines, from the child-like era of faith and obedience into the more mature and responsible age of knowledge and wisdom – thereafter to take our rightful place as 'Lords of the Earth' in a world comparable to the Garden of Eden. A world incidentally where there was – and will be – no need for religion.

In any event, and whichever hypothesis is closest to the truth one thing is absolutely clear: Someone or something is talking to us.

PART FOUR

CONCLUSIONS AND APPLICATIONS

Summarizing the central themes of the presentation so far, and offering some practical suggestions for applying the principles of the triadic archetype in the practice of psycho-spiritual disciplines as well as acknowledging the general educational and bridging potential of these discoveries – as a reforming influence in society as a whole

CHAPTER THIRTEEN

A TRIADIC SOCIAL THEORY

Applying the triadic archetype to the social setting, illustrating the key processes that form personalities, cultures, and societies, and establishing universal guidelines that may be used in determining the true value of the social forces, attitudes, and behaviors that ultimately shape human history.

Another potentially enlightening aspect of the triadic archetype is in its direct correlation to the formation, growth, and social development of the individual human: Exploring how each of us became who and what we are today, in other words. Having many parallels with the previously discussed 'body-mind-spirit' paradigm of the individual triadic archetype (♣ 13); the three areas of (i) genetics, (ii) social environment, and (iii) personal choice (respectively) can, in this triadic theory be identified as the key elements corresponding to; (i) the physical, (ii) the emotional-intellectual, and (iii) the spiritual development of any given individual in society. Obviously this also incorporates an underlying red-blue-white progression, at least theoretically.

Although apparently oversimplifying the complexities of human development to its bare minimums; with the clarifying backdrop of the triadic archetype to guide us we have here I believe, the potential for a newer, more structured, and arguably clearer understanding of the basic processes of human existence and the evolution (or devolution) of human society. At the same time, we may also be edging one step closer to a more realistic appreciation of the origins and ultimate potential of humankind in the cosmos at large. But first, some clarifications:

- Generally speaking, by 'genetics' (i) we are referring to our physical lineage and biological makeup at birth.
- 'Social environment' (ii) relates to our surroundings growing up; our culture, ethnicity, education, religion, social influences etc.,
- By 'personal choice' (iii) we mean exactly that; the choices we make throughout our lifetimes that will impact (a) our personalities, (b) our attitudes, and (c) our physical-material circumstances; spirit, mind, and body – white, blue, and red respectively.

As shown in Table 'F' there is also a prevailing 'past-present-future' theme inasmuch as psychobiological 'genetics' (i) can be seen to relate to our family histories and therefore to our individual and collective past. Our current 'social environment' (ii) concerns chiefly that which occurs, or is occurring in our lifetimes and therefore – historically speaking at least – can be seen to relate to the present. Finally we have the category of 'personal choice' (iii) which, inasmuch as it shapes not only our own personal futures but also that of future generations, naturally relates to the collective future.

Red	Blue	White
Body	Mind	Spirit
Physical	Mental / Emotional	Spiritual
Genetics	Social Environment	Personal Choice
Material / Actions	Thoughts / Attitudes	Personality
Past	Present	Future

Table F: Basic Concepts of the Triadic Social Theory

How this all fits together in a systematic theory of social development is of course the topic of this brief discussion. For insofar as the three successive elements of (i) genetics, (ii) environment, and (iii) personal choice can be identified and understood as *the* primary factors in human development and growth; we uncover yet another triadic-based model from where to appraise the individual, sociological, and historical significance of an apparently-disjointed humanity in an otherwise harmoniously-integrated universe.

The term 'apparently-disjointed' is used here in formal recognition of the general failure of society so far, to manifest a global socio-political model of freedom, health and harmony, that not only encourages the health and development of each individual, but also synchronizes with nature and with the cosmos at large.

As always, there will be some overlapping and blending of these categories just as in life itself, but to summarize: We arrive at birth genetically (or biologically) pre-formed (red). This is our physical connection 'with the past' – our ancestral lineage. Then, growing up in our respective social surroundings we absorb our cultural environments; our education, religion, and other social influences through intelligent cognition – automatic or otherwise – using our (blue) mental-emotional faculties. This is how we live consciously 'in the present'. Then throughout our lifetimes we make decisions ('personal choices') that ultimately form our personalities and characters, arguably symbolically colored somewhere along the white-to-black, good-to-evil spectrum, depending upon many interrelated factors. Arguably, this 'personal choice' aspect could be defined as our personal-spiritual contribution to the collective future of humanity, and is where the greatest potential for either good or ill lies.

To use a popular analogy; the first two categories (our genetics and our environment) concern our basic circumstances; "the hand we have been dealt" as they say in poker. Whilst the third category of 'personal choice' is "how we play those cards" if you like. In other words, despite being dealt a somewhat less-than-perfect hand in our genetics or social environments, we can still alter the outcome of this 'game of life' depending on how we play those cards. Even a poor hand can be turned into a winning one with the right approach and application. But we need to remember that I am not the only one at the table. With each decision made we affect not only our own game, but to a greater or lesser extent the games of everyone else at the table – either for good or for ill. Our personal life-choices in other words will also have an effect on others. But most of all, those personal choices define who we are as individuals; how we fit in as members of society; and ultimately who and what we become in life.

In understanding and cataloging the effects of these three factors on the development of the individual person – and then aligning our findings with the triadic archetype – we can, hopefully, approach a more universal understanding of the human condition; for without exception, all human beings have been subject to these influences since the advent of consciousness. Instead of using existing social or moral philosophies (including religion) to attempt to regulate the general health of society, I believe that a social theory that aligns neatly with the natural world – such as one based upon the triadic archetype – has a much better chance of resonating universally across religious, political, and cultural boundaries. Whether this particular social theory has the muscle to achieve the goal of a global consensus remains to be seen, but surely there can be no doubt that we need to be urgently investigating any and all possible solutions to the awful religious, political, and cultural divisions that threaten the very future of humanity. As with our earlier discussions about the merits vs. the dysfunctions of the religious mindset; and the profound social problems caused by elitist or sectarian thinking; it is I believe, in the recognition of our common humanity – as symbolized here in the patterns of the triadic archetype – that we stand the best chance of tackling these problems both at the individual and the collective level. With respect to all sincere attempts to qualify or establish a common morality amongst the world's religions and political ideologies; the great and continuing difficulty – it seems to me – has been the absence of a natural, scientific, and therefore global basis for that morality. Using a social theory of morality based upon the natural balance of the triadic archetype at least promises the *potential* for a global consensus. But instead, the difficulties of integrating the various cultures and religions of our modern 'global village' lies chiefly in each society's stubborn adherence to their own particular view of human morality – either in their socio-political or religious beliefs – as well as a parallel unwillingness to recognize the validity of another society's moral code. The much-debated problem of integrating Muslims into Western society for example, is a case in point that painfully illustrates the shortcomings of socio-political value systems that are based primarily on cultural or religious traditions – vs. universal principles. By identifying and then isolating the culturally-specific (or subjective) aspects of any given society's existing moral code; as well as those oft-disputed moral contrivances used either by religious or political authorities to control the populace; and then replacing such with a logical, natural morality, based first and foremost on a scientific understanding of our common humanity, we will I believe be taking the first vital steps towards the ultimate harmonious integration of the social order.

As we now explore the mechanics of 'being human' from this new perspective we should anticipate being confronted with some of the more profound questions concerning human psychology and spirituality. For example: "Are we each born 'perfect' or not? Is behavior inherited or learnt? What about physical defects or mental disease? How much are we a product of our social environments and how much is genetically inherited? Are we born intrinsically flawed as the religionists claim – spoiled by original sin – or is this supposedly-inherited 'sinfulness' some sort of genetic error? How then do we explain personal vices, criminality, or our proclivity for war? Are we psychologically incomplete perhaps? Or, are we lacking in some key feature of humanness that we mistakenly identify as 'sin', 'ignorance', or 'mental illness' as the case may be? Is there really some God-creature out there somewhere.. pulling the cosmic strings or not? Am I ultimately responsible for my own character and destiny or, ..is that already predetermined by my psychobiological ancestry? Where exactly does personal choice play a part? And what about gender and all its various manifestations in human society, especially when those flavors do not appear to fit into a wholly 'natural' model of life? What determines good or bad people – and who indeed is qualified to judge? How do we determine 'healthy' as a physical, psychological, or spiritual value? Given all the possibilities, what exactly is a 'perfect' person anyway? Is there indeed any such thing? And can I personally, ever realistically aspire to such a condition?"

Although any number of these questions taken separately could give rise to volumes of complex discussions – as indeed they already have – we will simply follow the guidance of the triadic archetype, identifying parallels and matching themes wherever we can, and see if this offers any new ideas or approaches in our attempts to understand what exactly it means to 'be human' today.

'Red' Genetics

Let's begin by clarifying the link between the physical-red aspect of our human triadic archetype and the matter of human genetics. For inasmuch as we are, most of all, the direct products of physical sexual intercourse between our biological parents then we must, naturally, carry their respective genetic blueprints in our genes. If my father is a tall, blond and muscular Norwegian for instance, and my mother is a short chubby Jamaican.. then I should not be too surprised if I turn out to be a medium-sized milk-chocolate version of their union, either with blond or black hair, or even somewhere in between. What would be highly unusual – perhaps even incredible – is if I, as the direct biological product of that union turned out to be a full-blooded oriental. Interesting perhaps – miraculous even – but unfortunately not at all likely. The key point to note of course, is that each of us is to a certain extent genetically pre-programmed, and therefore can anticipate certain features and behaviors common to our lineage: Size and shape, talents and skills, attitudes and character traits can all be traced, at least in part, to our lineage. For despite the colorful claims of myth and superstition, science has yet to verify the arrival of any natural object – vegetable, mineral, or animal – that is not a direct result of its formative origins. Even in the evolutionary process, the newly-identified skill, appendage, or habit of the emerging species is directly related to environmental changes in the lives of its predecessors. As far as I know this rule applies to all known aspects of life – all the way from planetary systems to atoms and molecules. Even ordinary water for example, although being an essential and arguably 'unique' component of life on Earth is itself a combination of two other elements; hydrogen and oxygen (H^2O). And as we have already seen, the energies of light itself which give shape and form to all consequent life forms, convey their particular subatomic 'characters' into those life-forms. Of course, this idea is at the very heart of the existence of color-based archetypal themes in the first place, and is the primary source of our triadic color theories.

But the main point here is to recognize that whatever 'uniqueness' or apparent 'specialness' any of us carry at birth can be traced almost exclusively to parental sources. So although we may each have distinct and unique physical characteristics that develop with age, we also invariably carry the biological signatures of our immediate ancestors – at least in part. So the first clear point of emphasis is to acknowledge that we are, at birth, the direct psychobiological products of the sexual union of two human lineages – each in turn with their own unique, yet multi-familial origins. Therefore, in the association with human lineage; in the onus on the sexual act of reproduction; and in the 'base' position in relation to environment (ii) and personal choice (iii); the theme of genetics (i) clearly carries the symbolic properties of red.

Keeping it simple for the time being, we will not digress into the (red) physical aspects of either the social environment (ii), nor of the realm of personal choice (iii), as this will only unnecessarily complicate matters at this point.* All we need establish at this juncture is that individual humans emerge at first chiefly from a biological, genetically-based formula (red). Whatever psychological or spiritual aptitudes we have at this early stage in life (blue and white) are still some way from becoming evident, and are of course heavily subject to environmental influences growing up. But our physical potential as strong workers, or great athletes or gymnasts for example is already in place; just as any physical limitations, weaknesses or handicaps will be too. Practice and training may improve that potential of course, but if we don't have the raw genetic material in the first place then all the training in the world is of no use. Likewise, short of radical surgery there is little we can do to alter our basic body types, ethnicity or looks. Although the womb is subject to maternal stresses that may affect the fetus to some extent, it is still primarily a *physical* environment for the growing embryo. Research may yet be able to prove a direct connection between the

---

* For the full discussion see *The Color of Truth Volume III: Principles to Live By*

psyche of the pregnant mother and the newborn – we already know that alcoholism and drug addictions can be directly transferred for instance. But whether this can be classed as a 'physical' or 'psychological' transfer is a debatable point that illustrates the challenges of trying to differentiate precisely between the two fields.

So, if we find ourselves dissatisfied in any way with our inherited genes, the only people we can criticize are our own direct ancestors. In the same vein however, we should realize that our very existence in the first place is a living testament to the durability and evolutionary success of our own specific lineage. Whether or not we should be proud of this of course, depends upon whether humanity is actually a blessing, or a blight on nature.

'Blue' Environment

Although there is of course an obvious (red) material-physical aspect to living in any given social environment, it is chiefly the (blue) conscious features that we are concerned with here. For if we consider the definitions previously listed under the heading of 'social environment' such as education, culture, social influences etc., then surely we can agree that the prime agent involved in being an active participant in human society is our minds. Social interaction is all about communication after all, and communication is almost always initiated by mental activity. Naturally, the (red) body is involved in socializing too, but almost always in a secondary or subconscious role; eating, shaking hands, hugging, fighting, unconscious 'body language', playing sports, dancing, or having sex might be other examples. In these cases, or when other physical urges dominate our consciousness, the mind is usually only temporarily disengaged and sooner or later reemerges to become the key agent in the process of normal socializing. On the other hand; language and speech, thought, the forming of opinions, learning and education, and generally negotiating the mechanics of society all require some mental agility and awareness. In ideal conditions the mind should lead the body, and not vice-versa. Hence the ideal progression is from blue to red (mind over body) rather than the other way around.

In a general sense then, one could say that our bodies simply serve as the material vehicles for the developing human mind (and spirit), which in turn are primarily preoccupied with human interactions, and with understanding our immediate worlds. Although it is of course very difficult to make a clear separation between the activities of the mind and the activities of the body – for after all, the human brain is itself a physical object engaged in electrical and chemical processes – nevertheless, and in order to facilitate a better understanding of this particular triadic model, we now need to draw some distinctions between the place of the body and ancestral genetics (i), and the intelligent mind and our social environments (ii). Making this distinction will also serve as an introduction to the topic of personal choice and human spirituality (iii), and prepare us for that convoluted arena wherein we will attempt to define the objective 'rightness' or 'wrongness' of those personal choices.

Flawed Origins

For the most part the triadic archetype as reported in our various charts and tables is clearly self evident, with multiple parallel connections running through so many areas of life and society. White, to blue, to red; or red through blue to white. But when it comes to human consciousness things get markedly more complex. This is chiefly because human consciousness (generally-collectively speaking) is not yet in true alignment with any natural model of the triadic archetype. With all the complexities of history and human development to consider, surely its no great surprise to learn that it simply isn't as easy as just 'one, two, three'. Instead of the usual linear, or circular triadic model that we see in other examples, we must now consider our triadic social theory in multiple dimensions. This is chiefly because each aspect of 'being human' at the individual level (body, mind, spirit) is, theoretically at least, explicitly influenced in various ways, (i) by our genetics, (ii) through our social environments, and (iii) by our personal choices in life. Having discussed human spirituality at length in previous chapters, we need only draw a parallel here between the concept of traditional religious spirituality – which is ostensibly designed to enlighten us and guide our behavior – and the notion of a global morality based upon the principles of the triadic archetype. I would of course argue that the latter holds at least as much, if not significantly more potential for actualizing 'the sacred' in our lives.

Table 'G' on the following page illustrates the three main themes under discussion whilst still allowing for their natural interconnectedness and their unavoidable influences upon each other. As always, I invite the reader's understanding in regards to the unavoidable generalizations and inter-blending of themes, especially in a new study like this. For indeed as already explained it is quite impossible to draw exact definitive lines between such complex and interconnected aspects of the human condition.

If we use the example of genetics (i), in relation to the mind (B) for example (see box 'B-i'), we can identify certain (blue) psychological, emotional, and intellectual traits that are also passed through lineage. This demonstrates the important secondary and tertiary 'red' 'blue' or 'white' aspects of each of the main categories respectively. Obviously I can only present a fraction of such examples in the table, but the reader is respectfully invited to now take a moment or two to digest the general theme which, as in the poker analogy, is the fact that despite our genetic lineages or social circumstances our lives really do rest largely in our own hands. There is always hope in other words. For when it comes to the area of personal choice we can, if we wish, choose to move in a completely different direction from that of our family traditions or cultures.

This of course is what separates us most of all from the rest of creation – from the plants and animals – who by and large do not have this 'conscious-choice' option open to them; at least not at the reflective level of human self-consciousness. For the most part theirs is an instinctual level of vegetable or animal 'intelligence' that rarely reaches above the needs of basic survival. But even so, this natural 'intelligence' (of the plants and animals) does not undermine the laws of nature. How then should we define so-called human 'intelligence' which in contrast, has resulted in so much harm, both within nature and towards each other?

Table G: Elements of the Individual Triadic Social Theory

	A: Body (red)	B: Mind (blue)	C: Spirit (white)
(i) Genetics (red) Inherited Traits & Characteristics	Body Type: Gender Health Race Ethnicity Athleticism Longevity Strong-or-Weak	Psychological Type: I.Q. Level, Intelligence Quick or Slow Learner Artistic or Pragmatic Leader or Follower Passive or Active etc.	Personality: (possible) Proclivity for Goodness or Evil
(ii) Environment (blue) Physical Emotional & Spiritual Development	Gen. Health: Nourishment Disease, Play Type of Labor Practical Skills Geog. Location	Local Culture: Credulous / Scientific Broad / Narrow-minded Universal / Sectarian Education & Learning Schooling, Social Skills	Local Religion: Traditions Mythology Moral Climate Hope-Despair
(iii) Personal Choice (white) Our Own Input in the Maturing Process	Lifestyle: Choices Food Active-Inactive Fitness Sleep Sex Smoking Drinking etc.	Level of Responsibility: Enlightened / Ignorant Attitudes & Principles Questing / Accepting Driver or Passenger Forming Opinions	Maturity Integrity Wisdom Ethics Morals Virtue / Vice Good or Evil

Hopefully the benefits of using such a social system in the various areas of education, psychology, sociology and general life-skills are self-evident. Most especially for psychologists, educators or analysts, this triadic-based system offers a practical structure for the delivery of their services in a rational and relatively uncomplicated manner. In particular for those who have to deal with 'the religious problem' in some form or another – either personally or as professionals dealing with others – this system provides a starting point for identifying the specific areas of concern as well as being in a format that can be easily explained to any particular subject by:

(1) Being an objective, non-partisan system of evaluation (of the general health of society) that is not intrinsically aligned with any political or religious moral ideology

(2) Having a systematic, logical and scientific basis that actually aligns in principle with the laws of nature

(3) Being comprised of three distinct-but-universal categories for the assessment, diagnosis or treatment of any given individual

This then is our theoretical starting point in building a multiple-triadic theory of human development. But it is of course only theoretical at this point, representing the *ideal* model of progression and development of the individual human from a social base of (white) morality or spirituality, through (blue) intellectual and social development, which in turn should govern our (red) physical environment. Unfortunately however, reality is very, very different. For in the case of humanity – and quite contrary to cosmic norms – we appear to be following a general red-to-blue progression with very little evidence of any collective (white) morality; at least not of a kind that resonates with the natural world, let alone with other societies. The reader will recall from the listed examples (on pp 120-124) that most mature examples of the triadic archetype operate on a white-thru-blue-to-red model.

This apparent red-to-blue (and then hopefully on to white) evolutionary tack strongly implies that mankind has yet to achieve that position of responsible stewardship of Earth so clearly suggested by our relatively-advanced intelligence. I say 'relatively' because relative to the plants and the animals we are obviously much more intelligent as far as a state of technical, mathematical consciousness goes. But unconsciously, instinctually even, the birds and the bees, the plants and the animals all share a common natural environment without endangering that precious ecosystem. We on the other hand, through the agents of pollution, deforestation, and various other abuses are wiping out countless native species, and even endangering the very existence of the planet. It could therefore be argued that despite our elevated state of consciousness and our physical dominance of the food chain, that we are in some way profoundly lacking in a fundamental *natural* intelligence so patently present in all other life forms. In other words, relative to our presumed advanced level of intelligence – we don't seem to be doing so well do we? The big question is why not – and how has this come to be?

Intelligence or Ignorance?
One answer to that difficult question of how we can be so 'intelligent' yet simultaneously so destructively ignorant of our world, lies in the manner we have historically used (or abused) that so-called 'advanced intelligence'. More simply, and considering the 'blue' theme surrounding the processes of the mind, it seems we have yet to collectively master (or should I say properly 'employ') so many of the 'blue' aspects and faculties available to us. Remembering that 'the mind' in context here incorporates both rational and emotional aspects, which range from the central theme of clear, logical thinking that ultimately leads to (feminine) wisdom, to the other cardinal aspect of blue; namely the feminine traits of compassion, unity, and maternal-type love that ultimately leads to harmonious societies. A maternal love not only of humankind, but also of the planet. It is no secret that the history of mankind has been precisely that; *his*-story, the history of *man*-kind, vs. the history of humanity as a unified partnership of both genders. Shaped by men, orchestrated by men, and compounded by the excesses of the (red) masculine, surely no-one can argue that the feminine aspects of humanity have suffered a chronically-underappreciated and largely unfulfilled role in the history of human society so far.

Admittedly, there has been a marked 'opening-up' of the collective psyche to what I call 'the cosmic feminine' in recent years. Most obvious perhaps in the decline of authoritarianism as a social model and the call to women's suffrage since the turn of the twentieth century; the advances in public education and the general intellectual empowerment of the individual should also not go unnoticed (blue). Reflected in the collected political symbolism of the more democratic nations who generally sport a red-white-blue theme (♣ 25), the marked increase in the number of female political appointees in those societies further demonstrates that the energies of the cosmic feminine are now being expressed as never before in human society. Probably most noticeable at first during Renaissance and Enlightenment years, and now becoming increasingly apparent in fields as far apart as sport and politics, and in the arts and religion, there is no doubt that the cosmic

214

feminine as I call her – the female spirit of the collective unconscious if you like – is gradually blossoming and unfolding in all areas of human society.

But perhaps this is a little too optimistic a view. For the very fact that this collective 'opening-up' to the feminine is so noticeable in the recent present is itself a disturbing testament to the suppression of the feminine in times past. How this collective empowerment relates to our development and maturity as individuals and to this particular triadic theory is discussed in more detail in *Volume III* of *The Color of Truth: Principles to Live By* – which in brief plots a gradual, and vital awakening of the feminine aspects of human society, leading (hopefully) to a full awakening of the collective mind of humanity in the not-too-distant future. But in context of this work, which highlights so many abuses and excesses of the (red-black) masculine in history; suffice for now to acknowledge that the collective 'blue' aspects of human history and society, which in turn relate to our current 'social environment' theme have not, until relatively recent times, had very much room for fruitful expression or development. Indeed, it is clear that practically all of the problems detailed in previous chapters – especially those associated with religious dysfunction – are by-products of the absence, denial, or suppression of the (blue) feminine traits of the human psyche. For according to the norms of the triadic archetype, in the journey to maturity it is the feminine aspect of the human psyche that should ideally be taking the lead over the masculine. The female aspect 'giving birth' so-to-speak to the (red) active aspect; thought before deed; communication before action; love before war... But with a very few exceptions, human society has so far been dominated by masculine, authoritarian energies, so often to the detriment of the feminine, and of society at large.

Without belaboring the point too much, I hope it is well beyond argument that there are some serious 'red flags' appearing when we consider humanity's current role in an otherwise harmoniously-functioning world. Long pondered by philosophers and scientists, the question of humanity's true role (if any) in our solar system is still open to debate. How exactly do we fit in here they ask? Why is it that human society is riddled with so many 'un-natural' problems? Are we just intelligent animals... Or some sort of alien species that somehow colonized the planet? Are we in fact the pinnacle of evolutionary creation or some sort of cancerous blight upon it? Did we haul ourselves from the primordial mud ..or do we really hail from divine origins? Do we really have the potential to be super-conscious, or is our so-called 'advanced intelligence' a misfit development of the evolutionary process, and we are in fact, actually suffering from some form of collective ecological retardation? What if any, is the answer to this conundrum?

Religion too has had its opinions and beliefs on the topic of course, and if we are being truly honest with ourselves we must concede that a theory of a once-perfect man who 'fell from grace' has some credibility – at least as far as explaining our ongoing state of social confusion and alienation from the natural world. But because we must stick with facts and logic, we cannot indulge the luxury of escaping into theology or mythology merely for an expedient answer. Besides, I don't believe we can ever approach our True potential (with a capital 'T') whilst remaining emotional and intellectual hostages of the debilitating notion of original sin.

But there are other theories out there – both religious and non-religious alike – some more or less credible: That we arrived from another planet for instance, either in primal soul-form or as a colonizing species that has somehow forgotten our origins. Or like the dinosaurs, that we are merely a temporary quirk of nature; a species that doesn't quite fit and therefore probably won't adapt quickly enough to ensure long-term survival. A misfit organism in other words, that is doomed to run a dramatic but relatively short course before some other genus rises to the fore. Or, there is the 'human intelligence was an accident' argument – or the pseudo-mythological belief that animals and angels mated thousands of years ago to produce our current super-or-sub-species. Or of course, that God the Creator simply 'made' us and then inexplicably hid from us, and is now awaiting the results of this seemingly-capricious experiment.

But I believe there is a more logical answer. To be more exact; a sequential chain of possible and plausible answers that are not only supported by the patterns of history and modern society, but which, surprisingly, do not actually conflict with mainstream religious theory – at least not in general principle. To briefly summarize; it appears that the patterns of the triadic archetype as expressed in the symbols and patterns of history and human development suggest that humanity is on some sort of learning curve. That we have yet to reach our full potential either as societies or as a species. In fact, recent research has plotted a prediction that the average lifespan will continue lengthening to about 120 years, and it is my contention that unless we end up destroying each other in some cataclysmic war or through more abuse of the planet, that there must be an inevitable integration of all societies on Earth. This most assuredly will require a moving away from the (red) masculine excesses and indulgences of today – and ever more towards a communicative, intelligent, and compassionate (blue) approach towards nature and to each other.

In short; any beliefs, ideologies, or political systems that do not (a) include a prevailing feminine-unifying theme (as defined in this study), or

(b) are sectarian in principle (either overtly or covertly), must be carefully examined as to their essential credibility and philosophical integrity. For it is my considered opinion – backed by the proofs of the triadic archetype – that any social structures lacking these key components cause far more damage than we ever realized. This damage includes the direct inhibition of the emotional and spiritual growth of individuals, as well as interfering with the healthy development of society at large. Not forgetting of course, the scourges of war and poverty, and the awful destruction caused by our abuses of Mother Nature, and the resultant long-term effects on the natural world.

Human Rights and Wrongs
Amongst those ideologies leading the pack, and perhaps most pertinent today is a popular but erroneous understanding within certain societies that they have the inalienable right – at both the individual and national levels – to exercise their particular 'rights' to behave according to their own specific beliefs. Those beliefs may be ideological, political, religious, or even sexual; and comprise those activities whose expression in society causes far more harm than good. This I believe is where we must begin our search for the root of humanity's divergence from cosmic law. Because it is in the individual's proclivity to insist upon one's 'freedom of expression' regardless of its effect on others or of its outcome on society at large, where we find the symptoms of a collective selfish ignorance – an apparently inherited state of mind that is both our greatest impediment as well as being potentially our greatest gift. This side-effect if-you-like of human consciousness – that is; our ability to reflect and ponder about ourselves as (apparently) separate beings – remains the biggest clue yet as to the source of our great many 'human problems'. For although all the other elements in creation possess some form of generic instinctual 'intelligence' that directs their activities, human beings are as far as we know, the only animals capable of conscious reflection.

In other words, we are the only psychobiological agents on Earth capable of self-examination, and therefore the only ones capable of conscious selfishness. Accordingly, because of this elevated consciousness and intelligence, we are capable of far more destruction than any other life form. All other aspects of creation exist as integrated parts of the ecosystem, but we are able to alienate ourselves both physically and intellectually from nature. We are more intelligent – yes. But are we really more 'aware' or 'enlightened' in the most crucial sense? Although we actually 'know' more intellectually about life, we are, arguably, – and relative to our advanced intelligence level – extremely ignorant and irresponsible beings.

Perhaps best exemplified in the material indulgences of those who believe that simply being alive is a license to self-gratification through the wanton abuse of material things, of others, and of the environment; the role of the psyche and the spirit has for too long been ignored. Obsessed with the pursuit and practice of (red) activities in other words, we have at our considerable cost disregarded for too long the side-effects of the (red) excesses on the (blue) psyche and (white) soul.

This is exemplified in our attitudes towards sex today, surely the most powerful of our 'red' urges. Despite much confusion about the real role of sexuality at both the individual as well as collective levels, most have never given serious thought to the connection between an individual's personal choices and the resultant effects on the community at large. Sex being the most primal urge that has the capacity to bring out the best or the worst in us, whilst simultaneously being a physical, emotional, and even spiritual expression of oneself, perhaps it is here we will find some answers to our apparent state of disconnectedness with the natural world. This leads us to a closer examination of human sexuality in light of current social norms, whilst all the time remaining acutely aware that with the apparent exception of humanity, nature does not freely suffer contraventions of cosmic law.

Human Sexuality

Arguably, no other discussion is so hotly debated at all levels of human society as the matter of personal rights when it comes to expressing one's sexuality. Whether in politics, religion, or in the business world, everyone seems to have an opinion about what is, or is not, 'appropriate' sexual behavior. Trapped between the fundamentalist leanings of puritanical religionists and the 'anything goes' liberalism of trendy New Agers (please excuse the generalizations) not to mention a very vocal gay rights movement; overburdened legislators struggle to reach an understanding of a complex issue that incorporates so many important moral, ethical, and material concerns.

The main reason for this being such a hot topic, and a reason I believe many may have overlooked, is that our core individual sexuality more than any other aspect of our being intrinsically defines who we really are. Indeed if we take sexuality to its purest form, there is a clear argument for establishing human sexuality as the essence of true spirituality. Again, in its purest form human sexuality equates with what the religious world terms 'the sacred' – the physical expression of agape love. Hence that unique air of intrigue and mystery when we first become sexually aware, and awake to the joys of erotic yearnings. But being exposed to human sexuality at its basest forms in so many walks of life daily, and coupled with certain religions' traditional stigmatization of sex as something inherently sinful, we have naturally (albeit subliminally) come to accept that traditional unhealthy tension between the terms 'sex' and 'sacred'. But paradoxically, it is precisely *because* our sexuality and our spirituality are in fact inseparable that accounts for the mysteriousness and taboo-like atmosphere surrounding sex. For although few of us are strangers to intimate physical sexuality, far more of us are strangers to the associated deep spiritual aspect therein.

In its purest form the natural act of sexual intercourse involves a sharing of one's innermost self, and a bonding of one's very essence with the body, mind and soul of another. This explanation accounts for the high levels of emotional distress first associated with 'immoral', 'inappropriate', or 'excessive' sexual behavior, where it is the body, and often only the body that is involved in what must now be understood as no more than a selfish act of self-gratification using another's body as the point of physical relief. Mutual masturbation at best. And before anyone rushes to judge me for using these terms indiscriminately, let me clarify that I am referring to these behaviors firstly in context to any given person's own unique sexuality, and secondly in relation to current social norms. Not so much what is and is not 'politically correct' per se, but more to do with one's own deep reactions. How did *I* feel after doing such-and-such for instance – not what does society say about it? Because if we think about it for a moment, there are two general areas of distress that arise when we engage in any behavior that (a) goes against one's own personal psyche (or conscience), and/or (b) that internally alienates us from society at large (the collective psyche). Both experiences raise very uncomfortable feelings that are rarely examined objectively, but nevertheless cause deep emotional stirrings that require a primal response. Indeed, it is in this innermost experience of personal distress that we first of all sense that something is amiss with our world – or at least with the way we are experiencing it. Our intimate core, our very identity, our sexuality-and-spirituality combined cries out in angst, and we can but fumble blindly around seeking a salve for our wounded souls.

Often we make the further mistake of seeking an answer in the (red) physical-sexual domain, and thus compound the problem; when the answer can really only be found in one's own understanding of one's sexuality – indeed one's very life – as something incredibly profound; as something in harmony with the pulse of the universe, and therefore something inherently 'sacred', wonderful, and beautiful that has to be cherished as well as properly understood (blue).

But as always the big question remains; is it society that is out-of-alignment? Or is it I? Is it my personal vision of the world that is perverse – or is it that of outside others? Is it authority figures such as my parents, the law, the status quo that creates the tension.. or is it my very own conscience expressing its distress? Is this the feminine aspect of my psyche stirring restlessly in her man-made prison perhaps, pleading to be freed? Or, could it be a combination of all of these? Surely, this is at the heart of the discussion about what is 'right' and what is 'wrong'; what is 'virtuous' and what is 'vice'; what is 'sinful' and what is 'good'?

Finding Balance

If we can somehow use the triadic archetype to determine, in ideal circumstances, the course for the 'perfect' human life, then perhaps we can begin to outline with some measure of credibility the parameters of what constitutes both personal and universal 'good health' – physically, emotionally, and spiritually. From there in turn we might begin to redraw our hitherto superstitious notions of right-and-wrong, and good-and-evil, and ultimately (dare I say it) even the very meaning of human life itself.

To reiterate; the key point to note in this tentative social theory is that 'personal choice' can trump the other two categories in every case. It may be very difficult of course, but certainly not impossible. Given the right direction and motivations there is no reason why any of us should feel trapped into repeating cultural or ancestral 'sins'. This is why a balanced education is so very important, and why false education that rests upon any form of sectarianism or religious exploitations is so very destructive. Because like it or not, we do assume the mantles of our environments in so many ways – but largely through a combination of innocence, ignorance, and the fear of being 'different'. Growing up in an inner-city ghetto for instance will provide a very different social environment to being raised on a mountain farm. But if for argument's sake we were to separate two identical twins at birth and position them in these two environments accordingly, then we would expect to see two very different personalities emerge at adolescence, right? But despite the different social environments their inherited genetic traits would still be there, regardless of how they responded to their social environments. They would still look very similar even if they no longer acted the same. Their (red) actions of course being very much shaped by their life experiences in their respective (blue) environments, along with the choices and habits they formed, could produce two quite different personalities. But if each twin were solidly grounded in natural moral principles (such as those of the triadic archetype) *before* they

220

took up life in their respective environments, then I would argue that their intrinsic *characters* at adolescence would not differ all that much. Being brought up on a farm or a city street would have produced very different memories and experiences of course, but if they were each grounded in the same behavioral principles (white) then their social environments would become subject to their own personal morality – and not the other way round. It's all about getting the sequence right: First a natural morality (white) that is reinforced (in ideal circumstances) by our social environments. Then, an intellectual-emotional understanding of that natural morality (white-blue) – which we then pass on to the next generation through our moral actions and enterprises throughout life (white-blue-red). Concept, plan and action; spirit, mind and body; morality, education and enterprise; white, blue and red.

Environments undoubtedly affect us as we grow up, but the key to true enlightenment lies in our unwillingness to let our personalities be shaped by our genes and environments alone. Especially when we can accept that the latter are very far from being ideal just yet. Given the right amount of information, direction, and motivation, there is nothing to prevent both of the proverbial twins having equal success and fulfillment in life. The main difference is that the one brought up in the inner city of today will probably have to fight his environmental influences with more determination and insight if he is not to succumb to its more negative pressures. But as we can all surely testify, there is hardly a person on the planet that has not had to battle their own personal demons in one form or another as each of us comes to terms with the realities of life. If we have actively used our intelligent minds (blue) to understand our genetic inheritance (red) and environmental circumstances (red-blues) as best we can – as many of the truly greats of history have done... then, after a lifetime of constantly trying to improve upon our inherited genetics and environments (correcting our ancestral and collective, personal and social 'sins') we can then begin to lay the (white) foundations for a new set of genetics and an improved environment for the next generation. I suppose we could call it a sort of 'psychospiritual evolution process', at least inasmuch as it is in fact an advancement towards true enlightenment rather than a step backwards into those traditional habits, superstitious beliefs, or elitist attitudes that run contrary to the laws of the universe. The same old (red-black) habits and traditions of course, that form un-natural (or perverse) social environments which are to a large part responsible for many of the religious problems and social dysfunctions outlined in this work.

In short, inasmuch as we are the natural and wholesome products of a universe that is continually reproducing and regenerating life, then surely the answer to the question of individual 'right' and 'wrong' lies in our personal alignment with – or alienation from – its cosmic norms?

In other words, although we tend to be preoccupied (i); with our own personal issues and desires; (ii) are driven and corralled by the whims of unsettled societies; and (iii) are invariably mystified and/or confused by various religious beliefs, then maybe we should take time to consider a more 'natural' set of values such as those expressed in the triadic archetype?

Finding ourselves so distracted, oppressed, misdirected and confused by conflicting value systems and beliefs, and in those preoccupations finding so much cause for personal conflict and distress... perhaps we should consider the other option, the cosmic option, and take all the energies and resources we usually invest in social interactions, personal 'issues', and religious speculations, and instead apply ourselves fully in that quest?

For, apart from the sudden arrival of proof that we are indeed some species of misfit aliens from another universe; then surely the full and logical understanding of the laws of our cosmos promises the best and most accurate way for us to truly understand ourselves and the beautiful world we inhabit.

CHAPTER FOURTEEN

TRUTH THERAPY

Where we return to the matter of psychopathic religious dysfunctions in society; attempt to define and classify the nature of human evil; and look towards a viable solution based upon the triadic archetype.

In the introduction to this work, we declared a belief that "scientific truth, when applied to problems of any type or description, will ultimately prove fruitful and beneficial." Upon this foundation, we have explored the signs, symbols, and thematic patterns of natural, anthropological, sociopolitical and religious history, with a view to reevaluating the personal and collective problems associated with religion in modern society from a new and innovative viewpoint. Chief amongst the problems identified was the tendency of religionists to operate in partisan groupings that foster addictive, subjective behaviors; authoritarian dependencies; and neurotic attitudes; attitudes that not only resist scientific truths, but are often unwittingly (and very ironically) in direct opposition to the declared humanistic principles of their respective religious founders.

Having now established solid, if not irrefutable proofs of the existence of archetypal principles and formulas that are (a); synchronous with the very fabric of creation; (b) are reflected symbolically in sociopolitical history; and (c) embrace both the scientific and the religious realms, it is now time to summarize our observations and findings using the triadic archetype as the central theme in our approach to society's 'religious problem' as defined in Part One.

Drawing upon our psychospiritual theory of Part Two in conjunction with the evidence for the True religious experience, we now build the case for an innovative application of universal principles in the treatment of religion-related disorders, before concluding this dissertation with the hopeful expectation that both the religious and scientific fields will pursue an increasingly more universal-and-unified, vs. limited-and-partisan approach to their respective social and vocational enterprises.

A Reminder of the Problem

Nobody argues about the existence of gravity any more, nor about the fact that the Earth orbits the Sun, simply because these physical truths are now both self-evident and well documented. However, several centuries ago when these 'mysterious' issues were still up for debate between the proponents of science and religion, it was the sharpest swords, and not the sharpest minds that dictated public 'truth.' More often than not the clergy were better armed than the scientists, and rarely hesitated in using those arms to prove their religious viewpoint.

Notorious in this regard was the Inquisition which, for over six hundred years managed to 'convince' the general public that her agents were the sole guardians of truth. Despite this intense suppression however, self-evident truths continued to speak for themselves and the Church found her doctrines and mysteries increasingly under question as the findings of brave scientists like Copernicus and Galileo were eventually published. This marked the beginnings of the polarization of science and religion that we are so familiar with today. Religionists retreated to the relative safety of revelation and theology where they set about shoring up whatever mystical doctrines the scientists had left intact. The secular humanists on the other hand, understandably disgusted with the longstanding corruption and power-mongering of the clergy, turned to their new scientific god for answers.

Thankfully, the ecclesiastical grip upon the academic world had been loosed at last. Gingerly at first and then more boldly, science took her first baby-steps as the natural successor to religious speculation, and the theoretical arguments, the bloodshed, and the proliferation of errors, superstitions, and deceptions that had flowed from the pulpits for centuries eventually slowed to a trickle. Coupled with the Protestant Reformation, the free rise of scientific enquiry gave license to many religious adherents to choose between traditional authoritarian dogmatics, and a new and 'enlightened' personal spirituality – which in turn, served to promote increasingly more objective standards in both secular and religious education. Not least of all, this ongoing process of religious and scientific enlightenment confirmed the personal graces to be found in the sincere pursuit of truth. The accessibility of the Divine to individual questers was finally realized by the multitudes – and with God thus within reach – who really needed institutionalized religion any more? Thus the 1200-year iron grip of the Christian clergy was finally and irrevocably loosed – never to regain its domination of society on such a scale again. The combination of individual enlightenment, logic and reason, along with the advent of the printing press, all helped to break the debilitating dependence upon a self-appointed and generally-exploitative clergy. Five hundred years ago it was the discoveries of science that prompted this great public awakening. In the face of ecclesiastic inertia, it was the innovations of the Renaissance and the Enlightenment that lifted Europe out of the Dark Ages. Hence my personal belief that the careful application of scientific truths will eventually untangle factional religious mysteries, resolve longstanding theoretical disputes, and nullify emotional superstitions. Nevertheless, we still need to remain vigilant so as to protect future generations from those who would endeavor once again to manipulate and mislead them.

In contrast to the unifying and enlightening properties of scientific discovery, orthodox religion has spawned so much bloodshed in history precisely because its extremely well documented doctrinal 'truths' are more often than not mysterious and inexplicable, rather than self-evident – a fact that fosters myriad insoluble theoretical disputes, factional infighting, and a plethora of psychologically and emotionally disabling beliefs that could variously be described as incredible, irrational, improbable, unsound, unrealistic, superstitious and illogical. Indeed, without official sanction as either 'sacred mysteries' or creeds, they would simply be recognized as delusional constructs – a deduction now categorically ratified in many cases by the march of science and the discoveries of the triadic archetype.

Indeed, it is through the discovery of the triadic archetype that we may solidly conclude that although religious *symbolism* (as a thematic language) undoubtedly represents something profoundly important associated with the collective human psyche (or soul); it is in the vain and inept attempts to preemptively categorize such universal motifs that we have tended to cultivate delusional beliefs and dogmatic statements of faith.

If we concur with Narramore's *Encyclopedia of Psychological Problems (1966)* that defines delusion as; "A belief which is out of keeping with reality.."[1] then we must designate all mental conditions that interpret reality in distorted forms as 'delusional.' And whether or not one espouses one's delusions with elegance, grace, pious conviction and perfect elocution, delusions are still delusions and are therefore by definition false and misleading. Such ubiquitous falseness prevails only at an immeasurable cost to the well being of society and humanity at large. Obviously, something must be done about it. Bringing the proofs of the triadic archetype to bear upon religious convictions is clearly a good place to begin our search for a remedy to pathological sectarianism and all its related poisons, both obvious and obscure.

Unfortunately however, enmeshed as they are with longstanding emotive cultural traditions, and often standing as the 'spiritual' foundations for huge commercial enterprises and institutions, questionable doctrines and traditions are unlikely to surrender gracefully – even to self-evident truths. For their ecclesiastical defenders too, the maintenance and protection of problematic religious beliefs has become far more important that the empirical validation of their supposed truths. This is true at both the individual and corporate level where, in a disquieting symbiosis each serves the interests of the other: The individual seeks the emotional and psychological security of the group, whilst the institution seeks expansion of the group's ideological, and associated corporate influences. Moreover, based upon the principle that deluded *and* dependent adherents constitute the 'most loyal' membership, genuine revelations of universal truth (and therefore liberating and empowering truth) must of course be avoided at all costs by the institution at large.

Hence the traditional enmity between certain branches of empirical science and established religion – in particular, the dichotomy between modern psychology and authoritarian religion. And whilst recognizing the legitimate functions of *genuine* authority – that is, authority that virtuously empowers individual members vs. authority that subtly suppresses, intimidates, manipulates and exploits membership for self-serving motives – it needs to be reemphasized that the human instigators of many great religions; Jesus, Confucius, Buddha, even Muhammad[*] – the ultimate human 'authority' figures in their respective traditions – were each definitively humanistic in principle in their day.

Their authority, based upon their evident (and humanistic) spirituality, came from the trust and respect of their followers. It was an authority of love, based in love, and delivered in love, which is very different in principle to the suppressive policies of certain religious groups today who nonetheless claim these icons as their foundations.

---

[*] Despite the much-publicized militant aspect of the spread of Islam; a number of modern scholars view the early years of Muhammad's religious ministry as definitively humanitarian.

Even corrupt authority however, fills an important need in the human psyche. American educator Wilfred Mc Clay recently summarized the authoritarian issue in American religious society as follows:

> The great problem of American life [is] the riddle of authority: the difficulty of finding a way, within a liberal and individualistic social order, of living in harmonious and consecrated submission to something larger than oneself.... A yearning for self–transcendence and submission to authority [is] as deeply rooted as the lure of individual liberation.[2]

Archetypically speaking, the authority Mc Clay is referring to is that traditionally associated with the Omnipotent Divine. But in the absence of full knowledge of that Divine or in our internal sense of separateness from that Divine brought about by personal, cultural, or other environmental effects – we formulate, or accept prosthetic authority. In some cases this may come in the form of submissive personal relationships or even in membership of secretive fraternities, complete with humiliating initiations and strict hierarchies; but most common of all is membership of a religious group whose image of God best meets our deep psychological needs.

The "self transcendence" spoken of by Mc Clay is none other than the fulfillment of human spirituality, the 'white' truly moral aspect of the human triadic archetype sadly absent from so many of our lives. Instead of feeling 'spiritually fulfilled' we have tended to experience the sacred as a disquieting urge from deep within – but don't want – or don't know how to reach it. In the subsequent unsettling void a profound emotional-psychical need develops and, being an intrinsic part of who we really are, simply must be acknowledged. Some try to smother those whisperings with worldly preoccupations, but most seek solace in religious leanings. With the psyche thus in subconscious collaboration it becomes relatively easy to submit to the dictates of authoritarian religiosity. And somewhere deep down inside, we feel a profound sense of release at the moment of conversion or commitment, which we mistakenly interpret as a 'spiritual experience' an epiphany, or a moment of grace. In truth, it is almost always a psychological submission of the kind described by Mc Clay, subtly camouflaged by the accompanying euphoria of religious sentiments and emotions.

But now, as part of the 'chosen' group I feel liberated from anonymity and insecurity. No longer meaningless or obscure, my previously perplexing world has been reduced to one of simple obedience, and I need only switch-off the irritating echoes of my previously questioning (and therefore healthy) mind. My natural, questioning, and often annoying spirituality is thus slowly seduced, enveloped and suppressed. I feel safe yes, but no longer truly unique and autonomous. To all intents and purposes it certainly feels like I have gained something. 'The community' will look after my spirituality; the pastor will give the instructions; I can assume a new identity perhaps – now that I am 'reborn' amongst the chosen people. I no longer need worry now that I am officially 'saved'. It all feels so safe and secure …and perhaps almost too easy.

To use an analogy; in so many ways this is not unlike the relief one feels when someone else volunteers to drive on a difficult stretch of highway. We worry at first, but we suppress our anxieties so as not to seem ungrateful. The driver is so very confident after all, and he has lots of experience – he even has a chauffeur's hat on – and the seats are so very comfortable… and the music is so very soothing... Eventually we convince ourselves that our driver is so skilled that we can place our *absolute* trust in him.. and we nod off to sleep asking only to be woken "when we get there…" Safe or not, our destiny now rests in someone else's hands. The analogy is complete when we understand that in surrendering to this type of religiousness, our spirits effectively take a long nap through life. Being truly spiritual means being really awake… not asleep.

Despite the cautionary admonitions of saints and sages, and the bloody evidence of religious history, in our ignorant and foolhardy certainties we nonetheless continue to accept systematic, absolutist, and specious religious beliefs that all but prevent the novel discovery of Truth. Symptomatic of mass neurosis, and undoubtedly linked to our aforementioned need to "submit" to something greater than ourselves – such intransigent religious attitudes are simultaneously both the cause *and* the effect of the problem. Indeed, the most disturbing aspect of such popular religion is not so much the fact that it facilitates mass neuroses, but that it insidiously presupposes to deny the fact, choosing instead to present itself as *the* preeminent healthy feature of society – a blatant falsehood whose prolongation and support is patently dependent upon the ignorance and/or neurotic delusions of its perhaps well-intentioned, albeit gullible adherents.

Cleverly, through the systematic indoctrination and psychological manipulation of the young and the unlearned, in combination with a strategy of suppression, denial, and censorship of scientific truths, many profoundly irrational religious beliefs have become so rooted in the collective psyche that it is now difficult to know where reason and reality finish, and religious mythology begins – even in our ultra-modern cultures. In the support or defense of questionable beliefs, many otherwise mentally healthy individuals have become unwitting psycho-spiritual casualties of the operational policies of religious institutions whose corporate interests are manifestly tied to the systematic and unscrupulous propagation of implausible, and often delusional doctrines. When speaking in general of traditional institutionalized religion vs. specific exceptions to the rule, the true (or psycho-spiritual) education, development, and empowerment of individuals has long since been supplanted by corporate goals and objectives, and by the unscrupulous manipulations of self-absorbed ecclesiasts. As we have sadly observed, empirical research indicates a direct relationship between authoritarian orthodoxies and; (a) sectarian indoctrinations; (b) resistance to scientific truth; (c) corporate corruption; (d) individual disempowerment; (e) delusional thinking; (f) addictive and obsessive behaviors; (g) prejudice and bigotry; (h) clerical abuses of power (political, sexual, and social); and (i) emotional and psychological immaturity in host communities – and from there to society in general.

In short, aside from the social benefits offered by charitable agencies and affiliated groups, sectarian and/or authoritarian religions foster neurotic and even psychopathic attitudes both amongst their membership and any competing heathenized 'others' and, being intrinsically compromised by their dependence upon these very same operational tactics, are obviously in no position to effect a remedy. On the contrary, any serious attempt to address this issue first requires that the false foundations of such religious institutions be exposed. Simultaneously however, and perhaps even more important; we must diligently ensure that their respective Truths (truths with a capital 'T') are protected.

The Baby and the Bathwater
If 'the bathwater' is the aforementioned collection of neuroses, psychoses, delusions, corruptions, and abuses associated with sectarian and authoritarian religions, then 'the baby' is the True religious experience. In attempting to compose a solution to society's religious problem we most certainly do not want to throw the baby out with the bathwater. Of course the bathwater must go at all costs. Likewise the baby must be saved, for it is the Original child of our collective psyche – our True spirituality. Too long submerged beneath the confusions of myth and religion and the perfidious calculations of dogmatic religionists, this child of our collective subconscious must now be allowed to grow, and breathe, and live amongst us; sharing those Original secrets previously only known to God and gifted mystics.

In our discussion in Chapter Three we concluded that mystical connectedness with the Divine was the true purpose and direction of religion. For despite cultural variations in expression and interpretation the T.R.E. remains common to all longstanding traditions, having been shared in one form or another by all the religious 'greats' of history. Moses had his burning bush, Buddha his Enlightenment, and Muhammad his visions for example. God only knows (literally) what episodes were visited upon Jesus during the many years missing from his biography, but surely, the reported descent of the Holy Spirit and the later supernatural Transfiguration would certainly qualify as True religious experiences. St. Stephen and St. Paul also had powerful mystical encounters, which they interpreted according to their time and culture, and one can see echoes of the transcendent in the biographies of many inspired others in history; from Francis of Assisi, to Joan of Arc, to Thomas Merton, and in the reported visions of Adventist Ellen White, or Joseph Smith founder of the Mormons, ...to name but a few.

Obviously there are far too many to mention here, but it should be clearly noted that this mystical phenomenon is not at all restricted to career religionists. Edgar Cayce's visionary abilities for instance, were considered no less than miraculous by his peers, and eminent psychologist William James' mystical encounters at the turn of the twentieth century whisper from every page of his groundbreaking work *The Varieties of Religious Experience*.[3] Equally the culture, environment, and religious persuasion of those encountering the transcendent, as well as the mildness or strength of the encounter naturally influences the subject's interpretation of the occurrence. In my own experience I too have been blessed by the companionship of questers whose passion for Truth has guided them beyond the limitations of stale orthodoxies and into the living light of the True religious experience. Indeed, the True religious experience as defined in this work continues to be a major focus of research for Division 36 of the American Psychological Association; the Psychology of Religion. This places the phenomenon in a unique bridging position between the corporeal and the incorporeal. Hence, recognizing that the T.R.E. is the one consistent aspect that not only unites different religious traditions and produces the most virtuous results, but is also increasingly being accepted as a 'real' phenomenon by the scientific community, we now turn in this direction for insight and guidance as we seek a noumenal-yet-empirical anchor-point from where to separate the productive from the destructive in religion.

Unfortunately though, one of the first problems we encounter is how to subtract the individual's subjective interpretation of the T.R.E. from the objective reality without getting embroiled in the usual acrimonious religious debates? Indeed who, amongst all the competing authorities, prophets, visionaries and pseudo-messiahs of contemporary religious groups is truly qualified to interpret these mystical religious experiences with clarity and integrity? Can we really trust any human interpretation any more given the factional history of theology and the perennial presence of subjective biases – let alone our differences in languages, traditions and cultures? Remaining as it does on the threshold of comprehension, drawing this spiritual 'baby' (the T.R.E.) safely and securely out of murky bathwaters will doubtless be a slippery task if attempted without some auxiliary bridging perspective, for we can be assured that the institutionalized religious world will not surrender its primary justification for existence willingly. Neither do we wish to exacerbate existing problems. For such a sensitive task we obviously need a *consentient** and unambiguous formula for identifying universal, immutable truths: An *omnipresent*† taxonomy whose significance is both self-evident and unequivocal, and can be recognized and understood by secularists and religious alike. In short; sensible archetypes. Coupled with the proofs of the True religious experience, the discovery of the triadic archetype will (optimistically) deepen our understandings of the universality of existence, and by association eliminate many delusional beliefs.

With this hopeful objective in mind we now turn to science for confirmation of our findings so far, specifically to the man who brought the concept of the archetype into the public realm; Dr. Carl Gustav Jung.

Truth and Archetypes
Remembering that he was not aware of the substantial symbolic phenomena presented in this work, we can nevertheless draw upon Jung's observations of the subconscious and his theories regarding psychology and religion when he declared:

> It is only through the psyche that we can establish that God acts upon us, but we are unable to distinguish whether these actions emanate from God or from the unconscious..[4]

Using data to explain that the access point for the True religious experience is via the unconscious, Jung goes on to state with conviction; "..empirically it can be established, with a sufficient degree of probability, that there is in

---

* Consentient; agreeing, concurrent, assenting
† Omnipresent; present everywhere simultaneously

the unconscious an archetype of wholeness.." One might even be tempted to interpret this as an archetype of holiness?

Having since uncovered undeniable patterns of symbolism that correlate to Jung's findings which, whilst being tied to the substantial world, evidently originate somewhere *beyond* consciousness, we may reasonably conclude that these multidimensional yet consistent patterns are no less than sensory expressions of Jung's "archetype of wholeness" which he further defines as, "producing a symbolism which has always characterized and expressed the Deity.."

We are thus left to contemplate the distinct and very realistic possibility that, put into religious language, such all-permeating symbolism such as that of the triadic archetype is no less than a historical 'message from God' – or perhaps even a 'reflection of God' experienced directly by some in the True religious experience. In scientific language, we may refer to the same in Jung's words concerning his interpretation of the 'God-image' or 'imago Dei' [*] as:

> ...an archetype of wholeness which manifests itself
> spontaneously in dreams, ...from the psychological point of
> view, a symbol of the self *(q.v.)*, of psychic wholeness..

...which in turn he clarifies:

> One can, then, explain the God-image...as a reflection of the
> self, or, conversely, explain the self as an *imago Dei* in man.

Yes, quite an astonishing assertion for a supposedly 'scientific' theory. But does not all the evidence add up? If we don't allow ourselves to become embroiled in religious semantics and can still maintain scientific objectivity the evidence clearly speaks for itself. Whatever it is we are experiencing in the themes, patterns and colors of the triadic archetype, it certainly resonates soundly with Jung's interpretation of a 'reflection of the Divine'.

It should of course be clarified that the "self" Jung is referring to is the unconscious or true inner self of an individual (the blue-white 'soul') as opposed to the persona, or outer (masculine) aspect of the personality. Very interestingly, in its sub-reference to 'self' in Jungian psychology the Encarta Encyclopedia refers to the anima as; "The *feminine* inner personality, as

---

[*] Imago Dei; Latin term constructed by early Church Fathers for what may be equated with the True religious experience

present in the unconscious of the male. It is in contrast to the animus, which represents *masculine* characteristics." [5] This not only corresponds to our subatomic findings concerning the structure of matter, specifically the role of quarks in the (male) proton and (female) neutron respectively, but we also have another direct reference to the converse human progression as explained in the previous chapter; from masculinity through femininity to spirituality; external, internal, eternal; red to blue to white.

These definitions of Jung's "archetype-of-wholeness" can be directly transferred to our discoveries concerning the triadic archetype. What Jung identified in the realm of the unconscious, we have today identified in nature, science, religion, history, mythology, art and politics. When subliminal patterns like this perennially replicate themselves, what else can they be called but archetypes? At last, we appear to have a fully consistent teleology that can encompass both the physical-scientific and noumenal-religious realms without compromising its intrinsic integrity. Even if we have had reason to doubt religious interpretations of these phenomena in the past, we can now trust our senses. Set against such a wide-ranging blueprint of existential themes, questionable hypotheses and theories in both scientific and religious fields may now be addressed with a reasonable degree of confidence that any longstanding erroneous features will be exposed.

Seeking Heaven …or a Haven?
In the meantime however, seen through personal, cultural, religious and environmental biases, our partial and understandably subjective interpretations of reality continue to color our understandings. This occurs to such an extent that even earnest and intelligent individuals often find it difficult to grasp the possibility that others who are receiving the exact same 'universal truths' from the noumenal / spiritual / unconscious realm could, with equal integrity, *consciously* interpret them differently.

Simple cultural or regional differences are thus declared heresy, as are all other apparently conflicting religious viewpoints, whose adherents in turn are regularly denounced as 'pagans', 'heretics', 'infidels', 'new-agers' or 'cultists' as the case may be. Those who utter such bland condemnations are usually quite ignorant of the facts or, are themselves devotees of some form of institutionalized religious excess. As filmmaker Robert Altman once remarked; "What is a cult? It just means not enough people to make a minority."[6] When writing about the Jonestown tragedy* the same sentiment was echoed by journalist Tom Wolfe where he said, "A cult is a religion

---

* Jim Jones and some 900 of his followers committed mass suicide in Guyana in 1978

with no political power."[7] What almost all traditional religionists fail to acknowledge of course, is that all the major faith traditions began their march to orthodoxy as local 'pagan cults', denounced and condemned by the mainstreamers of their day. How is it then that this crucial fact so often gets omitted when we receive our first well-polished indoctrinations into the world of religious orthodoxy? More disturbing perhaps is the willingness of the average adherent to accept the 'absolute truth' of any particular belief system without at least attempting to investigate the historical record for themselves? Amazingly, hordes of converts still flock enthusiastically to the pews offering their hearts and minds – indeed their very souls – to pernicious institutions whose foundations are soaked in blood, and whose ideologies remain rooted in mass deception. Choosing to accept rather than enquire; and choosing the security of the group over the loneliness of the personal quest; many religionists have not only withdrawn from the sincere pursuit of universal truth in exchange for partisan security, but evidently also choose not to acknowledge the rather obvious fact that self-centered or sectarian religious viewpoints are fundamentally idolatrous – inasmuch as one is placing one's own limited, subjective opinions (or those of the group) above those of an undeniably 'universal' God.

Neither are the larger religious groups that operate along similar lines necessarily 'more objective' just because they are in a larger, collective, or longstanding traditional form. For it is the *quality* of the reasoning and not its age or volume that dictates its veracity… at least that's how it *should* be. By deluding ourselves into believing that membership of the established religious group is a step further away from the (sinful) egocentric or subjective bias, many of us fail to recognize that we have done little more than exchange a *personal* egocentric subjectivity for a *collective* egocentric subjectivity. Choosing the camaraderie of prefabricated religion over the relative loneliness of the individual quest, such religionists fuel social religious problems through this (perhaps unwitting) combination of spiritual apathy, intellectual laziness and moral cowardice. Although most disturbing when manifested in supposedly 'spiritual' institutions, this tendency to surrender moral and personal integrity for the security of the group is a critique that may justly be applied to most segments of society.

The key to understanding this debilitating state of affairs lies in the word 'integrity' for indeed, it is precisely a lack of collective integrity at the conscious level – in relation to the natural cosmic integrity of the collective unconsciousness – that causes such variances in our perspectives and interpretations in the first place. If only we pursued Ultimate Truth with the same tenacity that 'Truth' has apparently been pursuing us; or with the same enthusiasm with which we defend our sectarian perspectives. Perhaps then the debilitating void of human ignorance would not nearly be so ruinous to humanity and the suffering world we inhabit. Just as religious beliefs associated with natural phenomena (such as solar eclipses for example) could not be challenged until facts and data disproved the existing superstitions, the same rule applies to modern deliria couched in the intimidating language of religious dogma.

By implication, the evidence that illuminates universal truths also exposes many of the so-called 'absolutes' of the religious sphere as little more than capricious hypotheses: Hypotheses whose most useful social function it seems, has been to provide a refuge and a sanctuary (if not also a haven) for neurotics, dogmatists, religionists, psychotics, manipulators, megalomaniacs, the deluded, the superstitious and the uneducated – a necessary humanitarian service perhaps, in a fearful, disturbing and mysterious world.

As Sigmund Freud once noted:

> Devout believers are safeguarded in a high degree against the risk of certain neurotic illnesses; their acceptance of the universal neurosis spares them the task of constructing a personal one. [8]

I suppose then it could justly be argued that if we didn't have religion to accommodate all the colorful varieties of personal and collective dysfunctions so often ritualized and worshipped as 'spiritual and holy' in the ranks of religion, then the rest of society might indeed be overwhelmed with the burden. Could that be what's happening today perhaps? How else do we account for suicidal terrorism; for the moral collapse of the clergy; for the awful epidemic of child abuse; for ethnic cleansing and religious wars; for masochistic 'end-timers' who literally can't wait for Armageddon to come? Indeed, how do we account for the downright craziness of it all? Is this the inevitable overspill of the accumulated mass-neuroses that have been nurtured and developed for centuries in hallowed halls – now facilitated by high technology and the interconnectedness of the modern world?

This is not of course to suggest that religion is exclusively inundated with dysfunctional characteristics in comparison to secular institutions. For indeed Erich Fromm puts forward a very credible argument that suggests that in a truly dysfunctional or fearful world it is actually the neurotics vs. the 'well-adjusted' who are technically the most mentally healthy.[9]

But this presentation is not about 'adjusting' to an imbalanced world but about bringing our dysfunctional (human) world *INTO* balance with universal norms, and therefore draws specific and particular attention to the dangerous and self-deluding properties of those popular forms of religion that presume any sort of absolute authority, exclusivity, or inimitable claim to truth. For as we have already seen, such elitist claims only lead to more and not less ignorance; greater alienation from universal norms; and increased levels of hypocrisy, arrogance, prejudice, bigotry, intolerance, and related emotional, psychological (and spiritual) disorders. The obvious question remains; if universality is not the one common denominator uniting all of natural existence, then what is?

Insofar as we judge creation itself to be intrinsically 'good' then naturally we must also consider an ethic of universality to parallel that goodness. Likewise, inasmuch as the triadic archetype is a true reflection of the properties of light; is universally consistent all across the natural world; and is a symbolic reflection of the 'Imago Dei'; then surely we must conclude that it too is universally 'good'. Conversely, any ideology that is fundamentally narrow-minded, sectarian, exclusive, or self-absorbed is by this definition definitively 'not good'. Indicted by anti-social policies, doctrines or practices, any such Church, Mosque, Synagogue or Temple – regardless of how passionately it may declare its own holiness – and regardless of how ardently its adherents may believe in it – any such agents of division are not serving any Creator-God of this universe. Who they are in fact really serving is debatable, but it is primarily only themselves in some protracted form, and may even constitute direct opposition to the very same 'Lord' they so zealously call upon for succor.

What a tragic irony to suddenly and shockingly realize that one's lifelong devotion to one's faith may not only have been in vain.. but worse still, that one was perhaps inadvertently working 'for the other side'; a topic that now brings us to a clarification of the troublesome subject of evil.

Defining Evil
In Chapter Eleven we alluded to the mistaken notion that the yin-yang symbol common to oriental and new-age traditions represents the cosmic battle between good and evil. It does not. Although interpreted thus by many, when read in context of this work the yin-yang is actually an archetype of goodness-and-wholeness, inasmuch as each half represents a collaborative and co-operative 'other' fused in eternal symbiotic union with its counterpart. Although usually depicted in black and white, a more chromatically-accurate portrayal would employ the colors red and blue for

masculine and feminine respectively, set against a background of white – as seen in the South Korean flag for instance (♣ 22). In our theory the yin-yang symbol is only fully complete when conjoined with the 'Origin' principle represented by white; thus making it a triadic, vs. dualistic symbol.

Chromatically speaking, as far as traditional yin-yang coloring is concerned black represents 'non-light' or 'the absence of light' or even 'the absence of color', and therefore is symbolic of anti-light. (White) light represents wholeness, completeness and perfection, therefore black as 'non-light' is naturally symbolic of evil – although not exclusively so. But certainly black as a non-color does not belong in any chromatic symbolism representing 'wholeness' or cosmic balance. And as we mentioned earlier, it is not mere happenstance that the traditional male villains from Dracula to Darth Vader to Satan – each are represented by a combination of red (masculine) and black (evil). So, if we are to take this subliminal color-symbolism thing at all seriously, we need to view the presence of black or red-black in religious iconography at least with some measure of caution. In the case of traditional yin-yang symbolism however, it was probably far more practical and expedient to simply use 'dark' and 'light' coloring, which in turn has given rise over time to an erroneous black-and-white theme. For the yin-yang, when comprised of red-and-blue segments on a white base is probably the best popular expression of the triadic archetype. The design also matches the configuration of quarks in the proton and neutron where each is mutually dependant upon the other, and where each contains some signature of the other in its essential form (♣ 10). Evil is not a part of that symbiotic harmony. It is an attack upon it, and not always a consciously-orchestrated attack either. Evil after all is neither the exclusive product of demonic legions, nor an intrinsic part of creation. Evil can be the product of ignorance as much as the product of conscious human choices, but undoubtedly man is always the agent. Evil is that which proliferates by attacking archetypal principles. Or to put it another way; any attack upon archetypal principles constitutes evil. Certain types of institutionalized or constructed ignorance can thus be termed 'evil' inasmuch as they attack universal harmonies and subsist upon the fallout – religious sectarianism being one clear example of just such a social cancer.

The medical analogy for evil would indeed be 'a social cancer'. Described variously in medical dictionaries as "a malignant growth that multiplies indiscriminately, feeding on surrounding tissue which it destroys as it grows." Reminiscent of the story of mankind perhaps – a classic definition of aggressive selfishness and reckless consumerism? With a little imagination we could apply this analogy to many social forms, but instead of debating its origins – whether in the diabolic depths of hell or in the compromised hearts of men – we would be better employed identifying evil's cloven footprint in our own daily lives and societies.

A common misconception amongst religionists is that God punishes us by allowing 'evil' things such as disease and death to happen to us. But death, disease, and general daily difficulties are not in themselves 'evil'. They may indeed be the direct result of evil influences, but in-and-of themselves many such human experiences traditionally attributed to evil forces are simply the more distasteful, yet equally necessary facets of natural existence. Enlightened souls rarely see death or disease for example, as anything more than life-challenges to be met, befriended, and conquered. Death compliments life – especially a fruitful and productive life. Death is simply the beginning of the next stage of existence – whether that is in spiritual form or simply in our physical return to elementary particles of nutritious matter for other life forms. In truth, death as we envision it doesn't actually exist. Life continues with or without our personal conscious awareness. We just change forms again, that's all.

Ideally, the yin-yang exchanges of light and dark; hot and cold; summer and winter; and life and death, occur cyclically and constantly so that no one principle continually dominates the other or determines the other. Inasmuch as this is not the case in human society we invariably see social imbalances that equate to serious collective dysfunctions: Excessive patriarchies, violence, war, materialism, and sexual suppression for example. When present in religious institutions (as is sadly so often the case), then radically patriarchal institutions such as Middle Ages Christianity, modern Roman Catholicism, the Taliban of Afghanistan or radical Islam for instance not only display the same internal dysfunctions and excesses of the masculine in their histories, but as we already noted also lack the feminine blue in their symbolisms. By relating these values to sectarian religious thinking, we can immediately see that any such ideologies are in breach of the principle of interdependent opposites – at least in part, if not in all of their operational policies.

Three Stages of Evil
If we are then agreed that the principle of interdependent opposites is indeed 'good'; including proton and neutron; male and female; sun and moon; fire and water; light and dark; summer and winter; etc.. each set against the (white) background of the third enveloping 'divine' principle – then any deliberate and calculated attack upon these principles may surely be defined

as evil? Indeed even 'accidental' attacks, by nature of their consequences may also be described as evil.

In this sense, pollution of the environment is evil, as is cigarette smoking, insofar as we are attacking the ecology and our own genetic balance with poisons and carcinogens. Our state of relative ignorance of our crimes is inconsequential to the result; therefore in such cases we are at least guilty of evil *action*, even if it is only at the unmindful level of physical evil. We take evil to an altogether different level of course when we add conscious understanding and premeditation to the mix. Now we are at the secondary stage of *cognitive* evil. This is when evil becomes truly dangerous, for now we are employing the mind as well as the body for evil means. By the time evil pervades the individual to the point of possessing his psyche or soul, we have reached the stage of evil personified. Thus evil intentions (i) lead to evil plans (ii) and then to evil actions (iii). Spirit, mind, and body are completely preoccupied by evil intentions, motivations and actions, and we become the direct agents of evil in society.

One point of clarification needs to be made concerning the dynamic between individual evil and institutionalized evil: Using twentieth century Nazism as an example; that institution of the German Third Reich that systematically set about 'cleansing' the world of millions of unwanted *untermensch,*[*] we are faced with the disturbing reality that institutionalized Nazism could only flourish with the assistance and support of the German population at large. Undoubtedly many of those normal, church-going individuals were unaware of the atrocities that were being committed in their names, and were no doubt horribly shocked to discover what was really going on in those so-called 'labor camps'. Nevertheless as members of the infrastructure that elected and supported Hitler and company, they were at very least the unwitting assistants to a massive social evil. The question that must be asked of course, is whether or not such persons should be defined as intrinsically evil because of their (perhaps unwitting) association with an undoubtedly evil institution? Once again, we turn to the triadic archetype for an answer, for evil – like goodness, also leaves its symbolic signature behind either by its presence or its absence. In the case of Nazi Germany the ominous black eagle and the odious red-and-black swastika is surely evidence enough.

As in all subjects discussed in this work so far, we have approached clarification by first applying the triadic model to the subject: spirit, mind, and body; concept, plan, and action. In the case of political evils such as

---

[*] Untermensch; ('under-men') German word for the lower classes or sub-species

Nazism or slavery for instance, we can identify three distinct levels of evil that progress from the physical-active level, to the thinking-planning level, and on to the level of absolute, intrinsic evil. Obviously, the greatest level of culpability lies with those who are intrinsically evil – the creators, orchestrators, and implementers of evil ideologies. In like manner however, anyone and everyone who is involved with the proliferation of evil in our world is also technically 'guilty' at some level. What most of us fail to grasp is the very disturbing reality that through simple ignorance, neglect, or apathy, we too may become unwitting agents of evil. Indifference in the presence of evil constitutes complicity. Whether active or passive collaborators, or whether ignorant or aware, the results are unfortunately the same. Our excuses and justifications will not bring millions back to life, no more than our ignorance of the toxins in tobacco smoke will stop cancer from spreading. This is why true education is so immensely important, and why false ideologies and indoctrinations are so very dangerous. 'Good' people (as opposed to evil ones) are those who seek to exempt themselves from any and all environments where they may be used as agents of evil. They seek to bring their own lives and the lives of their communities into harmony with universal principles. But this can only be achieved through a thorough and objective education based upon universal ethics and morals. We need our minds as much as our spirits to achieve 'good person' status. Far too many well-intentioned saints and religious scholars have inadvertently supported evil ideologies simply because they suppressed their intellectual searching in favor of misdirected 'blind faith' in a religious system. As we have shown, a well-intentioned pious fool is just as vulnerable to evil manipulations as an apathetic fool, for it is in the hidden branches of the ignorant or selectively ignorant mind that evil seeks to builds its nest. Hence, in a world of evil manipulators naiveté becomes a dangerous liability. With the right (True) motivations and insights however, we may proactively choose to become agents for good, instead of ignorantly blundering through life as yet another possibly-unwitting agent for evil. As always (True) education is the key, and truth is her own witness.

To reiterate; evil is that which attacks the Original Archetype, the blueprint for harmonious and productive creation and existence. Always originating in, with, or through humanity, it comes in many shapes and forms. This includes personal evil, political evil, social evil, religious evil, and even scientific evil too. Splitting the atom for example has never sounded like a good idea to me. Sure, we get a lot of power from it, but at what cost? Nuclear super-bombs and radioactive waste that will be deadly for hundreds of thousands of years! Neither should the connection with cancer go unnoticed. The nuclear industry employs many people and has definitely been a boon for most of us alive today in terms of better standards of living. But that's just us – here and now. The question is, how will more enlightened generations judge us?

And what about the oil industry? If the abuses of the planet and the resulting chronic pollution isn't enough of a clue; then maybe the heavy black symbolism of toxic oil spills should touch a raw nerve? When viewing our Earth as one great living organism there seems no way to reconcile the specter of thick black oil clogging our rivers, beaches, and forests – let alone the accompanying social disruption to eco-sensitive societies. Despite the fact that eco-friendly alternatives have been available for decades, unscrupulous corporations continue to push their destructive agendas. As long as there are profits to be made they obviously intend to storm on regardless of the real cost to the planet, to our health, and to that of future generations. By any definition that values the health and harmony of humanity and the natural balance of the planet, both the tobacco and oil industries comprise a grave threat. Just as authoritarian ideologies threaten the mental health of society, these aggressive and callous industries are a menace to our collective physical health. Both are driven by a forceful and noxious (red-black) consumerism that destroys as they proliferate. The symbolic parallels with cancer are self-evident; black and red-black malignant industries "..that multiplies indiscriminately, feeding on surrounding tissue which it destroys as it grows." If we replace the word "tissue" with 'Earth and her inhabitants' the analogy is proved. Both in regard to physical agencies destroying our planet and our bodies – as well as divisive socio-political and religious ideologies that would prey on human hearts and minds.

If we can agree upon the summation that whatever interferes with the cosmic balance of our world is intrinsically evil, then the business of eradicating sectarianism in religion is no longer a matter of mere choice or perspective; it becomes a matter of moral duty. Just like global pollution poisons the planet, sectarianism is a contaminant of the mind – a social cancer that society en masse needs to urgently confront and eradicate. No longer tied solely to empirical data, psychologists in particular may now advance with compassionate confidence into the realms of religion and spirituality, for the immutable principles reflected in the psychospiritual composition of the triadic archetype simply cannot be denied – at least not by reasonable, rational persons. Those religions that continue to promote their own sectarian agendas in opposition to the united spirit of the family of mankind and in defiance of the Golden Rule (to unconditionally love one's

241

neighbor), no longer deserve our respect or loyalty. Indeed, such malignant institutions no longer have a place in healthy human society.

Persons of courage and integrity who feel driven by their consciences to wisely abandon these floundering institutions should be comforted by the realization that any subsequent swim in the ocean of uncertainty will be of immeasurable benefit to their emotional and spiritual health. For after all, each of the founders of the world's great religions were confronted with the very same choices in their day; to stay or to go; to lose or to choose; to sink or to swim?

As far as I know, no one has ever learned to swim without first getting wet.

CHAPTER FIFTEEN

APPROACHING A CURE

Looking at some of the practicalities of tackling 'the religious problem' in society, and suggesting a means whereby psychology and religion might meet in a productive symbiosis for the betterment of us all

In this final chapter we outline some of the theoretical principles and guidelines that may be applied in the practical approach to the problem of religious sectarianism, as well as to other psychological imbalances in society at large. Targeted mainly towards those who have the background and training for therapeutic intervention, the optimistic hope is that people in all walks of life will see the value of applying the principles of the triadic archetype to their daily lives. Rather than suggesting specific techniques or styles of intervention, it is left to each individual to best discern when, where and how to best bring their own lives, and the lives of those in their care into universal alignment. Nevertheless, we should be under no illusions about the urgency of the mission.

Addressing the social problems resulting from absolutist or delusional religious beliefs obviously requires that an accurate diagnosis be made in the first place. This has been so difficult in the past because no 'theory-of-life' existed that was comprehensive enough, provable enough, or powerful enough to compete with the exciting (or terrifying) speculations of religious theorem. Our level of understanding of our amazing universe has simply not been able to compete with the emotive power of 'religious mysteries' – nor battle the creative imaginations of superstitious theorists. Especially those magical mental gymnastics and highly speculative dogmas that are *not* rooted in either physical or noumenal reality. As noted previously, whether adopted out of ignorance or apathy, or whether born of conviction or convenience, erroneous beliefs remain erroneous in spite of our abundant pious enthusiasm. Indeed, the greater the level of pious enthusiasm – the greater the risk of erroneous or dysfunctional excesses at the individual level; pseudo-piety for example, delusional thinking, addictive behavior, disempowerment, authoritarianism, sectarianism, religious elitism, and various other debilitating psychodynamics.

Given our understanding that the application of truth to existing problems will indeed help resolve them, it is obviously imperative that we identify and isolate that which is True in religion against that which is false – to which end we explored various types of religious experiences. Dealing specifically with this topic in *Psychoanalysis and Religion,* and referring to the *Tibetan Precepts of the Gurus* social psychologist Erich Fromm records the following insightful list of the "ten errors" of religion:[1]

- Desire may be mistaken for faith
- Attachment may be mistaken for benevolence and compassion
- Cessation of thought-processes may be mistaken for the quiescence of infinite mind, which is the true goal
- Sense perceptions (or phenomena) may be mistaken for revelations (or glimpses) of Reality
- A mere glimpse of Reality may be mistaken for complete realization
- Those who outwardly profess, but do not practice religion may be mistaken for true devotees
- Slaves of passion may be mistaken for masters.. ..who have liberated themselves from all conventional laws
- Actions performed in the interest of self may be mistakenly regarded as being altruistic
- Deceptive methods may be mistakenly regarded as being prudent
- Charlatans may be mistaken for Sages

Matched against our general summary of religious problems and the hypothetical religious profiles of Chapters Two and Three, we not only see allusions to several of the same unfavorable character traits, but we also see a distinct correlation between the Buddhist concept of "Reality" and our noumenal, or collective subconscious realm that is only accessed through the True religious experience. Although all religions allude to mankind's unnatural separation from this 'holy' realm, and many eminent psychologists now accept the existence of the collective unconscious with its archetypal occupants, the fact remains that intelligible visitations into this numinous area remain the select domain of a very few exceptional individuals. Insofar as the noumenal / spiritual / collective unconscious realm remains inaccessible to the general population, we will it seems, remain vulnerable to the unscrupulous manipulations of religious frauds, or to the hollow echoes of spurious religious traditions. In other words, unless we can somehow access the Truths of the collective unconscious, egoism and ignorance will continue to tether us to the sensory realm. To understand why exactly we are in this predicament, a brief review of the psychospiritual theory should reveal some useful insights.

Viewing diagram ♣ 3, we can see that empirical science is progressively advancing into previously 'mysterious' territory as mankind's awareness of himself and his environment progresses. Using the historical analogy of medicine; we can correlate the progressive advance of human knowledge with the advance in effectiveness of physical medicine. As knowledge of physiology, biology and pathology increased, so have previous erroneous suppositions and superstitions, as well as many diseases been eradicated. First the diseases existed (red); then we gained an intellectual understanding of its properties (blue); before we applied the cure (white) – thus restoring physical wholeness. Using the same chromatic principles, we can see that *physical* disease had to be tackled first (medicine), then *mental* disease (psychiatry and psychology), and now, as science advances into the noumenal realms of the unconscious through such pioneers as Freud and Jung, and then on into the religious / spiritual realm through the hard work and inspired insights of Fromm, Rogers, Allport, and others; the details of our *spiritual* disorders are also beginning to reveal themselves right on cue and right in sequence; body, mind, and spirit; red, then blue, then white.

Such advances in knowledge however, only come about through the brave endeavors of enterprising pioneers. In the religious arena, the equivalent of such pioneers are those who can not only access the higher realms of reality through the True religious experience, but who also have the capacity; that is, the knowledge and wisdom to be able to translate such reality into the language of the conscious realm. But most importantly, to do so without any corruption of immutable Truths. This however, is where the difficulties arise. For even amongst those saints and sages who are recognized as being great spiritual or moral pioneers, the teachings they imparted have often become misinterpreted, manipulated, and twisted into the very antitheses of the founder's intentions. The most obvious example of this is the perversion of the universal 'Golden Rule' declared by practically all traditions as being central to their faiths:

"The Golden Rule"

"The best deed of a great man is to forgive and forget." Islam.

"May we look on one another with the eye of a friend." Hinduism.

"You shall love your neighbor as yourself." Judaism and Christianity.

"Do not do to others what you do not want them to do to you." Confucianism.

"One should not behave towards others in a way which is disagreeable to oneself." Buddhism.

Simply stated; we generally live our lives rooted in the (red) thinking-acting arena that is driven and characterized by our basest needs and desires. When those desires are in conflict with our neighbors' desires our religious principles are supposed to kick-in, and thus ensure that love conquers selfishness and fear. Sadly however, religion has in many cases become the very cause and justification for hating one's neighbors – even unto death. Devious manipulators pose as spiritual leaders; indoctrinators pose as educators; and murderers and terrorists are honored as saints and martyrs. Vices are thus sanctified and insidiously passed off as virtue, and religion, arguably designed as the original agency of goodness, becomes a primary source of evil, discord, and destruction in our world.

Being Truly Human
Very regrettably, lofty ideals such as the Golden Rule place a distant last to our sectarian passions, selfish desires and personal beliefs. Using the triadic archetype to understand this problem, we immediately see that the understanding and interpretation of information is naturally most complete and focused in the physical, active, and tangible (red) realm; in direct contrast to our grasp and understanding of the higher (blue and white) realms. This fact is corroborated in the lives of the great saints and sages who invariably had control of their basest (red-physical) passions before accessing the higher (blue-and-white) realms of mind and spirit.

In *The Process of Individuation (1977),* Dr. Marie Louise von Franz notes in her collaborative work with Jung that the animus and anima (the primary subconscious masculine and feminine energies) are represented in four substantial classes or character types. These archetypes rise from the basest form of instinctual relations (physical) to the highest forms of (spiritual) existence, which she describes as "rarely reached.. in the psychic development of modern man." Corroborating our psychospiritual theory, Franz begins with the "purely instinctual and biological.. Eve figure" on one side and "the wholly physical man.. Tarzan" on the other. This all-natural physical male she could equally have called 'Adam'. This is followed sequentially on the feminine side by "the romantic and aesthetic level" typified by Faust's (sexual) Helen figure; and the Virgin Mary (archetype) "who raises love *(eros)* to the heights of spiritual devotion." Finally there is Sapienta or Holy Wisdom (blue), also known as Sophia "transcending even the most holy and the most pure."

Back on the masculine side, Franz lists the "romantic man of action" as the successor to 'Tarzan-Adam'; then "the bearer of the word;" and finally "the wise guide to spiritual truth" of whom Gandhi was an example.[2] And although they have suggested four relatively discrete classifications, we can clearly see that the progression from physical, through mental-emotional, to 'spiritual and beyond' solidly upholds our psychospiritual theory (♣ 1, 2, 3, 4). Not directly mentioned by Dr Franz however, are the close comparisons with the four natural human growth progressions from childhood (i), to adolescence (ii), through adult-parenthood (iii), to old age (iv); with their associated themes of physical development, sexual development, spiritual development, and the development of wisdom respectively. In these natural parallels, we witness an ideal development that ascends in archetypal order, leading in turn to the evolution of a True human being, which at the end of the day is surely our ultimate and sacred destiny?

(iv)	Spiritual-Wisdom	Wise Guide	Sophia	Maturity
(iii)	Intellectual-Spiritual	The Word	Mary	Adulthood
(ii)	Romantic-Emotional	Man-of-Action	Helen	Adolescence
(i)	Physical-Biological	Tarzan or Adam	Eve	Childhood

Table G: Stages in the 'Process of Individuation'

For example, during the years between infancy and adolescence (i) we are preoccupied with basic physical needs, elementary explorations, and physical growth. It is quite appropriate that parents are there to make informed decisions and take adult responsibility for us – and for the most part the world about us is just one great playground. We are fundamentally selfish – which is okay, and perhaps even necessary – because we haven't yet developed our individual identity.

Then there is the stage of adolescence (ii), by which time (ideally) we will have learnt enough good habits from our parents to get us through this approach-to-independence stage, with all its emotional, intellectual, and sexual confusions. Now our minds truly wake up as we try to make sense of all the changes happening in and around us, and as we struggle with the realization that we will soon be expected to become 'responsible adults'.

If all goes well, we advance to the next stage of maturity relatively intact (iii) where as discrete individuals, our bodies now under control and our minds at peace with ourselves, we seek out a complimentary partner to complete our (yin-yang) identity. Fusing the masculine with the feminine and the feminine with the masculine, we experience a sense of holistic joy and fulfillment that possesses our very souls. In short, we discover the joys of sexual love. It is at this point − provided we are still in control of our minds and our bodies − that we glimpse our first insight into the Divine heart. We have fallen in love in other words. But although we believe we have fallen in love with the object partner of our desire, perhaps it would be more accurate to describe our state of bliss as that of being in love with life itself. Our bodies, minds and spirits have experienced True union with another in the most intimate and sacred way. What possible closer experience of the Divine could there be? Allowing the initial passions of sexual love to gradually metamorphose into altruistic or agape love, we find ourselves resonating ever more with the vibrations of Ultimate Reality.

In the fourth and final stage (iv), the roles of spouse and parenthood lead us into an ever-advancing awareness of the intrinsic familial structure of humanity; the indispensability of true love; and the perennial unity of the generations. We develop a true parental heart in other words, not only towards our own offspring, but towards all of humanity. With our physical experiences to inform us, and our powers of reason to guide us, we thus blossom onto the maturity of spiritual wisdom as we near the end of our corporeal existence... at least, that's how it's supposed to work. Clearly, except in exceptional cases, neither the social environment nor our individual development yet reflects these fundamental patterns in the progression towards true human-ness. But undoubtedly.. there has been progress.

If we can agree in principle that there is indeed a realm of absolute truth somewhere in the deep collective unconscious that is gradually being accessed by the human mind; and if we can also agree that humankind is in fact undergoing a progressive transformation from a state of intellectual and spiritual ignorance towards one of wisdom and understanding; then we can begin to account for all manner of previously inexplicable events and experiences, including a great host of religious interpretations (and misinterpretations) over the centuries. Eventually, it all boils down to an understanding of the spirit, mind, and body paradigm in context of who and what we are today. Being comprised of (i) spiritual, (ii) emotional-intellectual, and (iii) physical elements, there are certain fundamentals that we absolutely need in order to achieve even a passing pretense at functionality. In the physical (red) field for instance we need food, rest, shelter, and good health in order to stay physically alive. In the (blue) emotional-intellectual realm we need to be able to process sensory information relevant to our environment in order to be able to survive; and in the (white) spiritual realm we need to be intrinsically connected with core realities that offer purpose, meaning, and guidance to our lives. If we try to remove any one of these three stages from the process of being human, then some sort of fundamental disaster strikes: Stop eating, and we die. Stop thinking, and sooner or later we will be declared insane – or get run over by a bus. Stop connecting with core realities, and we become unwitting agents of evil – at best.

At the center of the practice of becoming truly human is a process that unites all three features, namely; the process of reasoning. Problematic once again however is the fact that we are relatively insensitive to the higher (blue and white) realms, and thus are less likely to be conscious of when we are lacking in true spirituality, or in true education. "What we don't know we don't know, doesn't bother us.." or something like that. There is a perennial 'spiritual hunger' so-to-speak that we are each somewhat conscious of, but not fully understanding what constitutes true spiritual nourishment, we generally settle for the 'fast-food' equivalent, namely; institutionalized religion. Either that, or we find some other way to quiet the spiritual hunger pangs through sex, or drugs, or rock 'n' roll. In fact, any simulating addiction will suffice, be it chocolate, cigarettes, shopping, dating, soap-operas, politics, football, our careers, our bank accounts, or our egos. Whether we choose physical stimulants or emotional-or-intellectual ones is only a matter of personal sophistication, but it could be argued that those whose distractions range more in the blue than the red areas have a somewhat more 'progressive' pathology. In many ways though, the cigarette-smoking alcoholic nymphomaniac who has no religious pretensions, is probably closer to the spiritual path than the suppressive religionist who lives either in denial of his own condition or, in a state of pious hypocrisy. This might account for Jesus' famed associations with just such 'sinful' types – whilst scorning the religionists of his day.

Being 'true' solely in body is after all just living as an animal: Eat, sleep, urinate, defecate, procreate, eat, sleep.. etc. But we humans are not just physical creatures. For some curious reason we have been gifted with fine intellects and a capacity for moral discernment. In short, we were designed to reason – and not just natural reasoning, but 'supernatural' too.

Just as we need to feed our bodies, so must we feed our minds and spirits – or, continue to live like sub-human animals, denying our core spirituality and employing our fine minds instead in the singular pursuit of carnal desires, urges, and addictions.

Natural intelligence and the power of reason should not be confused. Just as the body requires activity in order to develop physical strength, so does the intellect require training to develop the powers of reason. Just as the body is dependant upon the mind, so is the mind dependant upon the spirit for internal guidance – which in turn is dependant upon the body for corporeal existence. No one aspect of the triad can be exempted without compromising our very humanity. Unfortunately, although many of us train our minds and bodies through healthy activities and education, we can sadly neglect to care for our souls. Equally however, many religionists operate at the other extreme, sacrificing body and mind in the pursuit of 'spiritual enlightenment' whilst failing to realize that we cannot afford to neglect our minds or our bodies either. The traditional religious position that the flesh is evil, and should therefore be starved, beaten, and denied at all costs is a semi-conscious recognition of the fact that we have become disproportionately preoccupied with our (red) physical aspects, and that the imbalance somehow needs to be addressed. But there are better and worse ways to achieve this. Emptying the mind and denying the body is only one technique to give the spirit some space to breathe. But because the adherent rarely understands that such mortification and denial is ultimately harmful to healthy spiritual growth if not kept in perspective, such practices can quickly become counterproductive, leading the adherent into masochistic emotional and psychological states, and the misguided belief that one's own body is 'evil', and one's mind is not to be trusted. The teaching that Lucifer, God's most intelligent creation was a proud intellectual conveniently lends itself to overt suppressions – not unusually enforced by proud intellectual clerics – and before long the ardent devotee finds himself living in a state of denial of the 'self' – the very same 'self' that Jung identified as the "Imago Dei" in man; the image of God.

Triadic vs. Dyadic
In many prevailing religious theories the unified archetypal triad has, to all intents and purposes been reduced to an antagonistic dyad. Instead of spirit-mind-body operating in glorious and harmonious union, many religious hypotheses exclude the reasoning 'mind' from the formula, and are thus left with a disconnected view of both spirituality, and physicality. Because (blue) reason is the bridge between the (red) corporeal and the (white)

incorporeal, its unprincipled absence causes a chasm of ignorance to develop not only in the space *between* the physical and the spiritual, but also *within* these two respective fields as well. As in most dualistic religious models, a subsequent polarization typically occurs between a supposed 'good' spiritual side and a 'bad' corporeal side. Being dependant upon control and authority, authoritarian religious institutions shrewdly choose the unknown spiritual realm as their 'good' home territory, and then proceed to fill the heads of potential believers with appropriate supporting theories and doctrines – which of course cannot be disproved. The 'sinful flesh' on the other hand – of which we are all very conscious – provides abundant material for a demonic opposition to 'holy' religious theory. Consequently, many of religions' qualifying claims to 'goodness' regarding their particular interpretations of the spiritual realm are rooted in a combination of guilt and superstition. By emphasizing the 'sins of the flesh' whilst espousing utopian heavenly realms, religious dualism is formatted to both suppress and fascinate simultaneously. In this manner, religious theory can elicit the most loyal response from potential adherents and, being ultimately unscientific, is conveniently subject to subtle alterations whenever church policy requires it. When the occasional curious quester challenges such theories, the inquiry itself is just as likely to be viewed as a 'sinful' misuse of the adherent's reason, as it is to solicit further indoctrinations, cautions, or admonitions towards the 'misguided' enquirer. Hence, without a reasoned understanding of their own psychospiritual subject matter, most religionists are left with an unbalanced pseudo-religious preoccupation with the 'evil' flesh (which must be subdued at all costs), and with a pseudo-spiritual religiosity that can never truly satisfy the heart. This of course serves primarily to formulate a lifelong religious addiction whose 'cure' can only be found in the ever-promised salvation, or in the heavenly kingdom to come – which of course is a mystery that we are not actually supposed to understand, let alone question. The individual's reasoning mind; the great threat to authoritarian dogmatism is thus discounted as intrinsically suspect, and the trusting adherent, now in denial of his own self is primed to accept the dictates of his religious mentors in a relatively-mindless state of obedience. In the absence of an informed awareness that we are indeed lacking in True spiritual depth and awareness, or even in True education, we see no need to quash our increasingly addictive (pseudo-religious) passions and urges. Eventually – and now fully endorsed by our chosen belief system – we pursue the three pernicious 'Ps' of power, prestige, and possessions at the expense of our own souls; of our neighbors' well-being; of our environment; and of the hopes of future generations.

This, in a rather large nutshell is the main cause of human evil and of its social and environmental repercussions; the suppression of the (blue) collective 'mind' of humanity by self-serving authoritarian agencies. Perhaps we can now better understand the historical dichotomy between the more mystically-oriented pioneers of True spirituality and their more materially-inclined successors who, in their subjective fears and lack of True spiritual awareness, have typically felt the need to build impregnable, dogmatic, political, bricks-and-mortar citadels to their respective religious beliefs. Founded as much upon the blood and tears of their 'pagan' neighbors as upon their own sweat and fears, such defensive yet equally aggressive institutions audaciously presume to herald "the coming Kingdom" or "the ideal time" or "final judgment" etc.. no doubt unawares that any True *eschatology*[*] must by definition predict the end of religion as we have known it – and hence their own demise.

Thus we see a distinct connection between preoccupation with 'external things' (red) and a resultant inaccessibility to the unconscious, or spiritual realms (blue-white). The more we live in the realm of desires, wants and urges, the less able we are to access the 'higher' or deeper realms of the psyche. Conversely, as energy flows to us from those higher realms the more likely it is to become affected (or infected) by the selfish needs of the ego. Indeed, it is no coincidence that TRE's and other mystical experiences only occur under those circumstances where the distractions of the physical realm have been minimized. The processes of contemplation or meditation such as in Zen Buddhism for example, are founded upon the principle of separation from the ego, and as we previously noted many other traditional religious practices such as fasting, celibacy, or asceticism are also directly linked to denial of the ego urges in order to access the higher realms. It is no coincidence that Buddha, Moses, Jesus, and Muhammad to name but a few, advanced upon their public missions only after extended periods 'in the wilderness' – overcoming the (red) temptations of the flesh. Noteworthy is Jesus' case where his three classic temptations even aligned with the body-mind-spirit paradigm: First the bread temptation to satisfy his physical hunger (red); then the appeal-to-the-ego temptation to prove that angels would save him (blue); and finally the spiritual temptation to bow down and worship Satan (changing 'holy' white to black).[3]

All this strongly supports our findings that religious beliefs or practices that pander to the lower realms of the desires, urges, and emotions, are by definition anti-spiritual, and are therefore a-religious in a purely

---

[*] Eschatology; the branch of theology that deals with the end of the world themes

technical sense – an interesting observation when we consider the fact that the more militant religions in history carry no blue symbolism and a preponderance of reds and blacks. Likewise, common to us all are the base emotions and characteristics associated with 'the flesh' (red), whilst higher ideals, standards, virtues and values, such as those of humanitarians, vocationalists, philanthropists, conscientious scholars, and sincere religionists are much more rare. Obviously, the future psycho-spiritual health of society depends upon this imbalance being progressively reversed until it is a majority, and not a minority, that adheres to such higher ideals. This will have the cumulative effect of controlling society's base and selfish passions, and through the subsequent empowering of our minds and spirits, open the way for the True liberation of humanity.

Although we can arguably already see this progression advancing systematically along the formulaic lines of the historical triadic archetype inasmuch as the Industrial Age (red) has been succeeded by the Information Age (blue) which may in turn now be succeeded by the (white) Psychospiritual Age perhaps?.. the territorial claims of a materially-preoccupied religious world over the noumenal realm remains a major obstacle to that progression, and therefore must be addressed.

Qualifying Truth

To better clarify our approach to these assorted social problems, a brief reassessment of the central findings of this work is now appropriate:

- The universe is fundamentally unitive, albeit comprised of interdependent symbiotic units, themes, and entities
- Man is both a macrocosim of atomic law, and a microcosim of the universe
- One cannot accurately nor comprehensively determine the true 'value' of any paricular entity, unless viewed from the 'universally-enlightened' position
- The urge to be Truly human (integrated spirit, mind, and body) is at the heart of all human drives, and its unfulfillment is at the source of all human unhappiness, dysfunction, and dis-ease
- 'God' in His many names and forms is interpreted by religious founders and mystics in symbolism that parallels the core precepts of the triadic archetype
- The combined proofs of the triadic archytype and True religious experiences suggests nouminal forces of abundant

and intelligent proportions 'guiding' or influencing human existence on an interminable scale

- Disrupting the tantric or triadic order results in repercussive damage throughout all interconnected relationships
- In order to ensure human fulfillment, all human endeavors (not just religion) need to adjust to align with these archetypal principles
- Currently, the scientific world is better aligned with metaphysical principles than most traditional religious orthodxies
- The key to understanding universal truth lies in humanity's true willingness and ability to access the higher realms of existence, known variously as 'the spirtual realm', 'the collective consciousness' or 'the soul' – the apparent home of universal archetypes and connecting point with 'God'

This formal recognition of a higher realm of truth, and the many counterfeit expressions of the same, leads us back to that place where we acknowledge that access to these higher realms, although perhaps the *primogeniture*[*] of mankind has, as we have seen, only been accessible to a very select and well-prepared few. But we shouldn't forget that this includes intellectual as well as spiritual preparation, for few if any sages would have marked history with their passing had they been ignorant simpletons – transcendental mystics or not. Evidence of mystical access thus remains our best guarantee of the moral credibility of any supposed 'spiritual' guide. Such individuals, having encountered the noumenal realm through a definitive and personal experience – an experience undeniably reflected in their personal values and morals – are surely the best qualified to be leading the quest for the collective understanding of "Ultimate Reality" as implied in the aforementioned Tibetan Precepts.

Based upon this premise, and in recognition of society's continued psychological need for religious expression; surely it is about time that we demanded such demonstrable personal credentials from those who would presume to direct the minds and hearts of humanity? Indeed, is it not now time to ask why we have allowed so-called religious institutions to self-regulate their own internal standards, when such license is not even extended to the genuine professionals of society such as doctors, lawyers, and teachers? Such professionals must adhere to strict ethical norms and

---

[*] Primogeniture; the right of inheritance

stringent accountability procedures, or face disbarment or prosecution. But senior career religionists on the other hand, who so often are entrusted with the minds, hearts, and bodies of our children, indeed with their very souls – have superciliously exempted themselves from such public accountability based presumably, upon the longstanding and illustrious tradition of saints and heroes to which they claim to belong. Hoping that the fallacy of this fairytale needs no further exposition in this work, and in light of the tragic clerical abuses of recent times, let us now courageously admit that it is indeed time to reassess the criteria for admission to this 'holiest' of professions, and subject all potential career ecclesiasts to the same exacting standards required of all professionals in society. By testing the suitability of would-be ministers against known science – which now includes the principles of the triadic archetype – the task of isolating the charlatans from the genuine articles should be no more difficult than interviewing for any specialized vocation.

As the only other respected body that approaches the noumenal realm in its professional activities, and as a science based almost wholly upon informed reasoning, psychology in particular should be foremost in assessing the personalities of ministry candidates. Thereafter to ensure that those who are genuinely motivated in the first place undergo intensive psycho-spiritual preparation for their intended ministries; preparation that would obviously incorporate standard professional ethics as well as the objective study of other religions, science, and psychology. Those showing distinctive obsessive-compulsive tendencies, or who display poor reasoning skills, or who express sectarian prejudices in any of its subtle forms should, just like professional counselors, be sent for further training or, prohibited from holding a pastoral license. Equally, any ethical or moral breaches would come under legal charge without any interference from senior clerics. Such accountability would greatly reduce the myriad pretenders, abusers, charlatans, and manipulators from the ecclesiastical ranks, whilst restoring public confidence in those who remain at the helm, and thus reconstruct institutionalized religion to better host the values and declared objectives of its noble and inspired founder(s).

Separating the clearly neurotic, psychotic, and criminal operatives from their *inappropriate* positions of authority in religious institutions, and relocating them where they truly belong as patrons of our psychotherapy clinics, psychiatric hospitals, and jails respectively; will serve to help clean up the field of religion and restore public faith in this, the one social institution uniquely qualified to represent the transcendent and metaphysical dimensions. Before this can possibly happen of course, the public must be made clinically aware of the true character of religious institutions today, and must then be prepared to take whatever civil action is necessary to strip these corporations of their unprincipled powers. Thus may we begin to dismantle those structures, policies, and behaviors that restrict the development of genuine social virtues; that foster pernicious social diseases; and continue to block access to the True religious experience.

In short, religious society must resolve to cure itself from the roots up – even if that means chopping off it's own head (metaphorically speaking) – for the head has too often proven itself unworthy of the membership. As Jesus said, "It is better for thee to enter into life with one eye, rather than having two eyes to be cast into hell fire." (Matt 5: 29)

Given the presumed success of any such social revolution the big question is, who do we now entrust with these remedial tasks, and who then do we look to for spiritual and moral guidance? Who indeed will step into the social void created by the removal of corrupt career religionists?

Interestingly enough, the answer is 'religious people' – as in *Truly* religious people (with a capital 'T'). For, despite the dismal condition of contemporary religious institutions many genuine individuals therein remain sincerely on the quest for truth and ultimate values. In religious circles, that group of people is represented by the 'cream' of admirable motivations at the top of the hypothetical character lists of Chapter Three – a selection of traits that neatly dovetails our aforementioned intrinsic / quest / humanistic categories which incidentally, converge in a triad to produce the environments where practically all incidences of True religious experiences occur. This clearly indicates that whatever core values we can discern in modern religious institutions will likely be found amongst the small but select groups of 'intrinsic humanitarian questers' who have personally encountered the True religious experience, and who remain sincerely committed to the genuine search for truth. Obviously, it is from within the ranks of these, and not from the ranks of compromised career religionists that we should seek a new spiritual elite.

Conclusion: The Psychospiritual Reformation

If the collective mental health of society is to be protected, healthcare professionals at large – and psychologists in particular can no longer ignore, or treat with disdain the pathological effects of authoritarian and sectarian religion in society. Indeed, if the field of psychology is to maintain its hard-won standing as a social service of integrity and effectiveness, it can do no other but prepare itself for the task of recovering that crucial territory lost to religious speculation over the centuries, most especially in recent years. In order to achieve this goal however, several courageous and revolutionary practical steps must be taken:

Firstly, the criteria for acceptance as a professional psychologist should now include theological training. To ignore the fact that most, if not all of the clients one sees are mentally affected by religious beliefs in one form or another is simply an unethical avoidance of responsibility to the client. Just as the physician of integrity will learn the pathologies and prognoses of local diseases, so must psychologists be better informed of the psycho-spiritual dynamics of the various faith traditions – for how indeed can we begin to treat such crippling psychological disorders without some direct knowledge of their forms and applications?

Secondly, practicing psychologists must cease any efforts to 'rehabilitate' or 'readjust' individual clientele into any social forms that do not adhere to universal norms as revealed in archetypal symbolism. In the absence of a comprehensive code of universal ethics, it has arguably been acceptable to simply alleviate the client's symptoms of disturbance and then release them – more personally content – back into the fray. In such cases quite naturally it has been the psychologist's personal-and-subjective, professional viewpoint that has been the determining factor of disturbance or mental health. In the true spirit of scientific endeavor, we need now ensure that psychologists incorporate into their procedures and goals professional directives that are compatible with the principles of the triadic archetype. [*]

Thirdly, although religion promises to produce a windfall of dysfunctional clientele for individual psychologists; the profession of psychology – putting commercial issues second to the collective health of society – should now muster its considerable professional influence and bring it to bear upon politicians, educators, and legislators for the express purpose of reforming admission and training procedures for potential career ecclesiasts. As previously mentioned, such procedures should include *at least* the same professional scrutiny of religious seminaries and such like – as that of other publicly responsible occupations – and should in any case include extensive scientific training, especially in the field of psychology. Such training would not only eradicate many who are prone to psychological imbalances, but by sorting the chaff from the wheat so-to-speak, would also enable religionists of integrity to better carry out their chosen vocations in peace, and with the trust of the public. In addition, whenever theoretical disputes arose between the religious and scientific worlds or even between differing faith traditions, there would be much more

---

[*] See *The Color of Truth Volume III: Principles to Live By*

common academic ground for fruitful debate; much more mutual respect and understanding; and consequently less fuel and ammunition for divergent attitudes.

Fourthly, psychology should formally recognize the 'True religious experience' as a scientific reality, and advance the cause for such experiences being a necessary qualifier for those who would enter the field of 'spiritual' counseling. Indeed, serious research should be undertaken with a view to 'using' such experiences as a form of psycho-spiritual training, or as intervention in therapy. Associated with this suggestion is the interesting observation that those who do genuinely encounter 'Ultimate Reality' in a symbiotic experience in a contemporary setting are invariably inclined towards unitive, vs. sectarian precepts. Thus, whilst we are busy reforming the rest of the religious world, we might as well outlaw authoritarian sectarianism in any socio-political form as an intolerable social institution. For, being fundamentally opposed to unitive psychospirituality, it is consequently out-of-synch with the triadic archetype which, although displaying systematic divisions of its own through its various symbolic manifestations, is nevertheless universally integrated. In other words, the very structure of the triadic archetype is in itself a testament to the universal and symbiotic incorporation of existence, and by implication, an indictment of dichotomic religious thought.

Finally, conscientious psychologists who are sincerely concerned with the general mental health of society should immediately volunteer their resources to the task of counseling any and all religionists who are in need of psychological assistance. Using the considerable influence and resources of the profession, every effort should be made to inform the general public of psychology's proactive concern with the current social crisis concerning faith and religion-related stresses. Just like the proverbial 'church doors' that offered sanctuary from physical persecution – so should psychologists now open their office doors too – to those who have suffered physical and psychological abuses; ironically, this time at the hands of the Church(es) themselves.

With the evidence of the triadic archetype as a blueprint, and in the void created by immoral religionists, ethical psychologists now have an excellent opportunity to influence on a historic scale, the collective health of future generations. Indeed, just as physics had to be rewritten to accommodate Einstein's theory of relativity, so perhaps might we consider realigning the operational paradigms of psychology to accommodate these newly discovered truths. In taking such a bold step whilst public confidence in institutionalized religion is rightfully declining, true 'doctors of the soul' may seize this providential opportunity to nurse humanity out of its child-like state of dependence upon manipulative institutions and superstitious beliefs, and towards the promising and liberating realm of knowledge, wisdom, and Ultimate Reality. Hopefully, we will not then be found wanting for courage to amend our existing beliefs and practices.

*   *   *

As a closing note, and in deference to any potential misinterpretations of the symbolism exposed through this work, it should be reiterated that archetypal symbols are ultimately 'merely' metaphorical language forms that convey information – albeit in this case, information apparently from the realm of the (previously) Great Unknown. Furthermore, the very fact that these truths are now being brought to light has profound implications as to the future of religion as we have known it.

In the words of Abbé Dominique Georges Piré, Belgian priest, and winner of the 1958 Nobel Prize for Peace: "What matters is not the difference between believers and unbelievers, but between those who care and those who do not care."

And finally, in the wise and penetrating words of Erich Fromm;

> ..the question is not whether man returns to religion and
> believes in God but whether he lives love and thinks truth.
> If he does so the symbol systems he uses are of secondary
> importance. If he does not they are of no importance.

ENDNOTES AND REFERENCES

CHAPTER ONE

1 *People of the Lie* by M. Scott Peck © 1983 Touchstone Books, New York - p199

2 *The Common Enemy* by Karl Menninger. Article appearing in Personality and Religion edited by William A. Sadler, Jr. © 1970 SCM Press Ltd, London. – p239

3 Extract from Norman Cousins' *In Place of Folly* (New York: Harper and Row, 1961) and quoted in: *The Common Enemy* by Karl Menninger (2 above) – p239

4 *Psychology and Religion* by Carl Gustav Jung© 1938 Yale University Press - p63

5 *Paradoxes of Religious Belief* by Milton Rokeach. Article appearing in Personality and Religion (2 above)

6 Ibid– pp227-228

7 Ibid– p228

8 Ibid– p228

9 Thomas Szasz (b. 1920), U.S. psychiatrist. *The Second Sin,"Mental Illness"* (1973).

10 *Psychoanalysis and Religion* by Erich Fromm © 1950 Yale University Press pp78-79

11 Henry S. Canby (1878–1961), U.S. author, editor , and *'Book-of-the-Month-Club'* originator. Alma Mater, ch. 5 (1936).

CHAPTER TWO

1 Excerpted from *The American Heritage Dictionary, 3rd Edition* Copyright © 1992 by Houghton Mifflin Company

2 Microsoft Bookshelf 99

3 P*sychology of Religion – An Empirical Approach* by Hood, Spilka, Hunsberger, & Gorsuch 2nd ed.© 1996 – p25

4 Ibid– p23

5 Ibid– p292

6 Saint Ignatius of Loyola (1491–1556), founder of The Society of Jesus. *Spiritual Exercises*, no. 365 (1548).

7 See http://www.sofn.org.uk/doctrine/catholiccases.htm for more details on Fox, Balasuriy, and De Mello.

8 *Priesthood Not a Profession but a Vocation*; The Irish Catholic (news article) Thursday Oct 16th, 2003

CHAPTER THREE

1 *Mysticism and Philosophy* by W.T.Stace. Philadelphia: J.B. Lippincott. – p131

2 *The Tantric Mysticism of Tibet* by J. Blofeld © 1974. New York: E.P. Dutton.

3 *The Psychology of Religion – An Empirical Approach* by Hood, Spilka, Hunsberger, & Gorsuch 2nd ed.© 1996 The Guildford Press, New York. – See Chapter 6; Religious Experience, especially p 192, the findings of Schachter and Singer in *Physiological Arousal and Religious Experience*.

4 *Legio Mariae* (official handbook of the Legion of Mary) © 1993 Concilium Legionis Mariae

CHAPTER FOUR

1 Oscar Wilde (1854 – 1900), Anglo-Irish playwright, author. *Phrases and Philosophies for the Use of the Young*, (Dec. 1894)

2 George Bernard Shaw (1856–1950), Anglo-Irish playwright, critic. *Androcles and the Lion*, Preface (1916).

CHAPTER FIVE

1 Carroll, M.P. (1986). *The cult of the Virgin Mary: Psychological Origins*, Princeton, N.J: Princeton University Press. Perry, N., & Echeverria, L. (1988). *Under the heal of Mary*. London: Routlefge and Kegan Paul. Warner, M. (1976). *Alone of all her sex: The myth and cult of the Virgin Mary*. New York: Knopf. Carroll, M.P. (1983). *Vision of the Virgin Mary: The effects of family structures on Marian apparitions*. Journal for the Scientific Study of Religion. 22, 205-221

2 *Psychology of Religion – An Empirical Approach* by Hood, Spilka, Hunsberger, & Gorsuch 2nd ed.© 1996 – p205

3 Ibid– pp455-521

4 Ibid – p2

5 *Counseling Psychology* by Charles J. Gelso and Bruce R. Fretz © 1992 by Holt, Rhinehart and Wilson. Harcourt Brace College Publishers, Orlando, FL USA – pp51-80

6 Ibid - p51

7 *The American Heritage Dictionary of the English Language, Third Edition* Copyright © 1992 by Houghton Mifflin Co.

8 *The Duality of Human Existence* by David Bakan© 1966 by Rand McNally & Company - p5

9 *The Power of Myth* by Joseph Campbell © 1988 Apostrophe S Productions – p243

CHAPTER SIX

1 *Psychology of Religion – An Empirical Approach* by Hood, Spilka, Hunsberger, & Gorsuch 2nd ed.© 1996 – p192

2 *Memories, Dreams, Reflections* by C.G.Jung © 1965 Random House Inc. – p392

3 Ibid. – p392

4 *Psychology of Religion – An Empirical Approach* by Hood, Spilka, Hunsberger, & Gorsuch 2nd ed.© 1996 – p193

CHAPTER SEVEN

1 See *"Color"* Microsoft Encarta Reference Suite 99

2 (i) Luscher Color Systems @ www.luscher-color.com (ii) *The Color Code – A new way to see yourself, your relationships, and your life* by Taylor Hartman © 1998 Fireside – Simon and Schuster

3 *The Color of Truth Vols I, II & III* by S.T.Manning PhD © 2002-2006

4 *Light, Color, and the Environment* by Faber Birren. © 1969 New York: Van Nostrand Rheinhold Co Inc.

5 *The Secret Language of Symbols* by David Fontana © 1993 Duncan Baird Publishers – p67

6 Reported in; *Color and Human Response* by Faber Birren. © 1978 New York: Van Nostrand Rheinhold Co Inc.

7 *The Secret Language of Symbols* by David Fontana © 1993 Duncan Baird Publishers – p66

8 *The Healing Power of Color* by Betty Wood © 1998 Destiny Books pp50, 51, & 105

9 *Auras* by Edgar Cayce © 1973 Association for Research and Enlightenment, Inc.

10 Ibid – p66

CHAPTER EIGHT

1 http://www.pha.jhu.edu/~kgb/cosspec/

1 *Holy Bible*, old testament; Genesis & Exodus (Moses); Samuel I; Samuel II; Chronicles I; Psalms;

2 *The Encarta 99 Desk Encyclopedia* Copyright © 1998 Microsoft Corporation.

3 *The Secret Language of Symbols* by David Fontana © 1993 Duncan Baird Publishers - p 183

4 Ibid - p 54

5 Painting by Botticelli (1445-1510)

6 *The Secret Language of Symbols* by David Fontana © 1993 Duncan Baird Publishers - p120

7 *The Color of Truth Vols I, II & III* by S.T.Manning PhD © 2002-2006

CHAPTER NINE

1 *Man and His Symbols* by Carl Gustav Jung © 1964 Aldus Books, London – p 214

2 *Holy Bible*: II Kings 19: 21, Psalms 9: 14, Isahia 1: 8, 10: 32, 16: 1, 37: 22, 52: 2, 62: 11, Jeremiah 4: 31, 6: 2, 6: 23, Lamentations 1: 6, 2:13, Micah 1: 13, Micah 4: 10, Zephania 3: 14, Zechariah 9: 9

CHAPTER ELEVEN

1 See websites: "POCM" (The Pagan Origins of the Christ Myth), and The-Color-of-Truth.com by this author

2 *The Mathnavi of Rumi*, Vol 6. (E.H.Whinfeld translation)

3 *Auras* by Edgar Cayce © 1973 Association for Research and Enlightenment, Inc.

4 *The Healing Power of Color* by Betty Wood © 1998 Destiny Books

5 *The Mathnavi of Rumi*, Vol 1. (E.H.Whinfeld translation)

6 *The Healing Power of Color* by Betty Wood © 1998 Destiny Books. p94

CHAPTER TWELVE

1 *In Praise of Tara: Songs to the Saviouress* by Martin Willson, Wisdom Pub. (see Amitabha Buddhist Centre web-p)

2 From the teachings of Ven Lama Thubten Yeshe (see website of Amitabha Buddhist Centre)

3 *Upanishads vol. 2, Brihadaranyaka-Upanishad Part 3, verse 9.*

3 *World's Religions* by Huston Smith © 1994 Harper Collins Publishers - p135

4 *In Defense of the Faith* by David Hunt (Publisher Unknown) - P37 & 38

5 For a comprehensive exploration of the feminine archetypal role in relation to Mariological doctrines please see *Mariology – Resolving the Confusion* – a master's thesis by this author http://color-of-truth.com

CHAPTER FOURTEEN

1 *Encyclopedia of Psychological Problems* by Clyde M. Narramore © 1966 Zondervan Pub., Michigan, USA – p267

2 Wilfred M. McClay, educator, author. *The Masterless: Self and Society in Modern America*, University of North Carolina Press (1994). Excerpted from *The Columbia Dictionary of Quotations* Copyright © 1993, 1995, 1997, 1998 by Columbia University

3 *The Varieties of Religious Experience* by William James. New American Library

4 *Memories, Dreams, Reflections* by C.G.Jung © 1965 Random House Inc. – p395

5 *The American Heritage Dictionary of the English Language*, Third Edition Copyright © 1992 by Houghton Mifflin Co.

6 Robert Altman (b. 1925), U.S. filmmaker. Quoted in: *Halliwell's Filmgoer's Companion* (ed. John Walker, 1993)

7 Tom Wolfe (b. 1931), U.S. journalist, author. *In Our Time*, ch. 2, "Jonestown" (1980)

8 Sigmund Freud (1856-1939), Austrian psychiatrist. *The Future of an Illusion*, ch. 8 (1927; repr. In *Complete Works*, vol. 21, ed. By James Strachey and Anna Freud, 1961

9 *Psychoanalysis and Religion* by Erich Fromm © 1950 Yale University Press – p83

CHAPTER FIFTEEN

1 Ibid – p78

2 *Man and His Symbols* by Carl Gustav Jung © 1964 Aldus Books, London – p195, 205

3 *Holy Bible*; KJV; Matthew 4:1-12

RUNNING GLOSSARY
(IN ALPHABETICAL ORDER)

Agnostic: One who accepts the *possibility* that God exists, but believes there can be no formal proof thereof

Anastomotic: An integrated network of systems such as blood vessels

Androgynous: Being neither distinguishable as masculine or feminine

Atheist ('a'-without / 'theos'-of God): One who denies the existence of God(s)

Atheistic nihilism: (in context here) A sceptical philosophy denying the existence of God, gods, or anything non-substantive, that also rejects all moral or religious values

Brahman: The Hindu name for Ultimate Reality

Collective unconscious: In Jungian psychology a part of the unconscious mind, shared by a society, a people, or all humankind. The product of ancestral experience, it contains concepts of science, religion, and morality

Consentient: Agreeing, concurrent, assenting

Conterminous: Having boundaries in common; similar in scope

Cosmogonic: Pertaining to a theory of the origins and evolution of the universe

Credulous: Having the capacity to believe; disposed to believe too readily; gullible

Diagnosis: Assessment; evaluation; critical analysis of the nature of something

Dichotomy: Division into two usually-contradictory parts

Ectopic: Abnormally positioned, deformed – a violation of the norm

Endemic: Prevalent in a particular location, place, or people

Endogenous: Originating, produced or growing from within

Eschatology: The branch of theology that deals with 'end of the world' themes

Esoteric: Intended for, or only understood by a particular group

Etymology: Branch of linguistics that deals with the origin of words

Extraneous (in context here): Coming from the outside; extrinsic

Geopolitical: To do with geographics, politics, demographics, and economics

Hypothesis: A tentative explanation; a theory; an assumption

Hz: Abbreviation of 'hertz'; a unit of frequency, or cycle such as in light waves

Imago Dei: Latin term for what may be equated with the True religious experience in context of this work

Immutable: Not subject or susceptible to change

Imperspicuous: Unclear; obtuse; hazy; not transparent

Inimical: Injurious or harmful to; adverse; hostile

Insalubrious: Unwholesome; unsavory; unhealthy

Lexicon: Dictionary or stock of terms used for a particular language

Loquacious: Very talkative; garrulous; repetitive

Lorelei: In Germanic legend, a female siren that lured sailors to their deaths

Machiavellian: Suggestive of political expediency, deceit, moral indifference, or cunning. Named for the political writings of Niccoló Machiavelli (1469-1527), esp. *The Prince* (1514)

Metaphysical: Immaterial; incorporeal; highly abstract; beyond the physical

Monotheistic ('mono'-one, 'theos'-God): The doctrine or belief that there is only one God

Neuropsychological; to do with the relationship between the nervous system and cerebral or mental functions such as language, memory, and perception

Neurosis: Any of various mental or emotional disorders arising from no apparent organic lesion, involving symptoms such as insecurity, anxiety, depression, and irrational fears

Nonmaleficence: To do no harm; cause no injury

Noumenal: That which can only be intuited by the intellect; not sensory

Objective (in this context): Of the collective, broader, or universal view – vs. the subjective-personal view

Omneity: Wholeness, integrality, completeness

Omnipresent: Present everywhere simultaneously

Ontology: The branch of metaphysics that deals with the nature of being

Orthodox Adhering to the accepted tradition

Orthopraxis: The activity of putting ones faith into action

Paedophile: An adult who is sexually attracted to children

Parochial: Narrowly restricted in scope or outlook

Pathogenesis: The development of a diseased or morbid condition

Phenomenology: A realism-based system of philosophy

Portentous: Ominous, threatening, foreboding, weighty; marked by a pretentious pomposity

Preternatural: Beyond nature; supernatural

Primogeniture: The right of inheritance

Prognosis: A prediction of the probable course or outcome of a disease

Psychobiology (or biopsychology): Study of the biological functions of the mind, emotions, and mental processes

Psychomancy: Associated with occultism, the raising of spirits, sorcery etc

Psychopathology: Study of the origin and development of personality disorders

Psychosis: A severe mental disorder, characterized by derangement of personality, loss of contact with reality, and causing deterioration of normal social functioning

Psychosomatic: Of or relating to the physical symptoms of a mental disorder

Psychotomimetic: Tending to induce hallucinations, delusions, or other psychotic symptoms

Rational humanism: A rational philosophy based on a humanistic belief in the innate dignity of the individual

Scholasticism: Christian philosophy of the Middle Ages based on the authority of Aristotle, the Bible, and the Latin Church fathers

Sciolistic: A pretentious attitude of scholarship; superficial knowledgeability

Semantics: The study of meaning in words and language symbol forms

Solecistic: An impropriety, a mistake, a misnomer

Subjective (in this context): Of the individual; of the personal perspective; limited; not universal

Sycophant; a toady; a flatterer; one who grovels or butters-up to their superiors

Taxonomy: A systematic classification system

Theist: One who believes in a personal God

Transcendental (in context here): Supernatural-extraneous; beyond the sensory-cognitive; not endogenous

TRE: True Religious Experience; see Chapter Three for a full explanation

Untermensch;('under-men'): German word for the lower classes or sub-species

BIBLIOGRAPHY by BOOK TITLE, AUTHOR, & PUBLISHER

A Handbook of Greek Mythology H.J.Rose © 1964 University Paperbacks
A History of Pagan Europe Jones and Pennick © 1995 Barnes & Noble
A Mind Awake; an Anthology of C.S.Lewis edited Clyde S.Kilby © 1968 Harvest /
HBJ Books, New York & London
An Introduction To Color Energy Inger Naess c 1998 Color Energy Corp.
Antichrist- Two Thousand Years of the Human Fascination with Evil Bernard
McGinn © 1994 Harper Collins Publishers, New York
Aristotle on God Joseph Owens, C.Ss. R. 1977 Learned Publications Inc.
Auras Edgar Cayce © 1973 Assn. for Research and Enlightenment, Inc.
Behind The Sex of God Carol Ochs c 1977 Beacon Press.
Bernadette and Lourdes Michel de Saint-Pierre © 1954 Farrar, Straus & Young, Inc
Bible Almanac Anna Trimiew © 1988 Publications International Ltd, USA
Care of the Soul Thomas Moore © 1992. Harper Collins, New York
Christ, A Symbol of the Self Carl G. Jung
Collaborative Ministry Loughlan Sofield & Caroll Juliano © 1987 Ave Maria Press
Collected Works of C.G.Jung (abstracts of) edited Carrie Lee Rothgeb 1978. USA
DHEW Publication No. (ADM)78-743
Color and Culture John Gage © 1999. University of California Press
Color and Meaning John Gage © 1999. University of California Press
Color Codes Charles A. Riley II © 1995 University Press of New England
Color Therapy Vijaya Kumar © 2004 New Dawn Press
Counseling Psychology Charles J. Gelso and Bruce R. Fretz © 1992 Holt, Rhinehart
and Wilson. Harcourt Brace College Publishers, Orlando, FL USA
Coming to Terms With Death David Bakan. Article appearing in *Personality and
Religion* edited William A. Sadler, Jr. © 1970 SCM Press Ltd, London.
Crises in Personality Development Anton Boisen. Article appearing in *Personality
and Religion* edited William A. Sadler, Jr. © 1970 SCM Press Ltd, London.
Death-of-God Theology Eric C. Meyer, C.P. 1977 Learned Publications Inc. N.Y
Eerdmans' Handbook to the History of Christianity © 1977 Lion Publishing
Encyclopedia of Psychological Problems Clyde M. Narramore © 1966 Zondervan
Publishing, Michigan, USA
Essays in Radical Empiricism William James, Ch 2 "A World of Pure Experience".
Longman Green and Co (1912) New York.
Ethics – a brief introduction Robert C. Solomon © 1984 McGraw-Hill
Explaining Unification Thought Sang Hun Lee © 1981 Unification Thought Inst.
Exposition of The Divine Principle Sun Myung Moon © 1996 HSAUWC
Faith, Religion, and Theology Brennan R. Hill, Paul Knitter & William Madges ©
1997 Twenty-Third Publications, Mystic, CT
Fascinating Bible Facts David M. Howard and Gary M. Burge © 1988 Pub's. Int.
Father and Son in Christianity and Confucianism Robert N. Bellah. Article in
Personality and Religion ed. William A. Sadler, Jr. © 1970 SCM Press Ltd. UK.

266

Formation of the Need to Achieve David C. McCelland. Article appearing in
Personality and Religion edited William A. Sadler, Jr. © 1970 SCM Press Ltd. UK
Gandhi Louis Fischer © 1954, 1982 Penguin Books
Gleanings From the Writings of Baha'u'llah translated Shogi Effendi © 1976
National Spiritual Assembly of the Baha'is of the United States
God in African Thought and Life Charles E. Fuller 1977 Learned Pub's Inc. NY
God in Analytic Philosophy David Stagaman, S.J. 1977 Learned Publications Inc.
God in the Biblical-Rabbinic Tradition Simon Greenberg 1977 Learned Pub's. Inc.
Healing and The Mind Bill Moyers © 1993 Bantam Doubleday Dell Publishing
Hellenistic Religions Luther H. Martin © 1987 Oxford University Press Inc.
History of Doctrines Vol II K. R. Hagenbach © MDCCCLIX
Holy Bible, King James Version © 1989 – 1994 Franklin Electronic Publisher
In Defense of the Faith David Hunt (Publisher Unknown)
Insight on the Scriptures © 1988 Watchtower Bible and Tract Society of
Pennsylvania, published Brooklyn, New York
Individual and Social Narcissism Erich Fromm. Article appearing in *Personality
and Religion* edited William A. Sadler, Jr. © 1970 SCM Press Ltd, London.
Inneractions Stephen C. Paul © 1992 Harper Collins, New York
Illuminations Stephen C. Paul © 1991 Harper Collins, New York
Is the Virgin Mary Dead or Alive? Danny Vierra © 1997 Modern Manna Ministries
Knowledge of God in Islam Robert E. Carter 1977 Learned Publications Inc. NY
Legio Mariae (official handbook of the Legion of Mary) © 1993 C. Legionis Mariae
Life Colors Pamela Oslie © 1991 New World Library
Light, Color, & the Environment Faber Birren. © 1969 Van Nostrand Rheinhold Co
Man and His Symbols Carl Gustav Jung © 1964 Aldus Books, London, UK
Maria Legionis Vol. 43, No.3, 2000
Mary and Modern Man Thomas Burke S.J. © 1954 The America Press
Memories, Dreams, Reflections C.G.Jung © 1965 Random House Inc.
Models of Religious Education Harold W. Burgess © 1996 Victor Books
Muhammad: His Life Based on the Earliest Sources. © 1983 Martin Lings. George
Allen & Unwin. London.
Mysticism: St. John of the Cross Robert A. Herrera 1977. Learned Publications Inc.
Mythology Edith Hamilton © 1940, 1969 Penguin Books
New American Bible © 1991 Confraternity of Christian Doctrine, Washington D.C.
New World Translation of Holy Scriptures © 1984 Watchtower Bible & Tract Soc.
Obsessive Actions and Religious Practices Sigmund Freud. Article appearing in
Personality and Religion edited William A. Sadler, Jr. © 1970 SCM Press Ltd. UK
On Becoming a Counselor Eugene Kennedy and Sara C. Charles © 1990 The
Continuum Publishing Company, New York
Paradoxes of Religious Belief Milton Rokeach. Article appearing in *Personality and
Religion* edited William A. Sadler, Jr. © 1970 SCM Press Ltd, London.
Paul J. Tillich on Natural Theology Joseph Fitzer 1977 Learned Publications Inc.
People of the Lie M. Scott Peck © 1983 Touchstone Books, New York

Personality and Religion ed; William A, Sadler, Jr. © 1970. SCM Press Ltd. UK
Platonic and Christian Theism John P. Rowan 1977 Learned Publications Inc. NY
Practical Ethics for You Eiji Uehiro, Japan (publisher unknown)
Psychoanalysis and Religion Erich Fromm © 1950 Yale University Press
Psychology and Religion Carl Gustav Jung© 1938 Yale University Press
Psychology, Symbolism, & the Sacred S. T. Manning © 2006 CheckPoint Press
Psychometric Testing Philip Carter and Ken Russell © 2001 John Wiley & Sons UK
Quantum Healing Deepak Chopra © 1990 Bantam books
Religion in Times of Social Distress Thomas F. O'Dea. Article appearing in
Personality and Religion edited William A. Sadler, Jr. © 1970 SCM Press Ltd. UK
Religious Aspects of Peak Experiences Abraham H. Maslow. Article appearing in
Personality and Religion edited William A. Sadler, Jr. © 1970 SCM Press Ltd. UK
Religious Education As A Second Language Gabriel Moran © 1989 Rel. Ed. Press
Reshaping Religious Education Harris and Moran © 1998. Westminister John Knox
Press, Kentucky USA
Science and Health Mary Baker Eddy © 1934 Christian Science Board of Directors
Sects, 'Cults' and Alternative Religions David V. Barrett © 1996 Blandford
Publishing UK, & Sterling Publishing, New York
Shrines to Our Lady Zsolt Aradi © 1954 Murray Printing Company
Symbols of Freemasonry Daniel Beresniak © 2000 Assouline Publishing, New York
Symbols of Islam Malek Chebel © 2000 Assouline Publishing, New York
Tales of a Magic Monastery Theophane the Monk © 1981 Cistercian Abbey of
Spencer Inc. Crossroads Publishing Company, New York
The Battle for God Karen Armstrong © 2002. Ballantines Publishing Group
The Book of Mormon translated by Joseph Smith Jr. © 1981 Intellectual Reserve Inc
The Bulletproof George Washington David Barton
The Christian Science Way of Life Dewitt John © 1990 Christian Science Pub. Soc.
The Color Code – A Revolutionary Eating Plan for Optimum Health by James A.
Joseph, Daniel A. Nadeau, and Anne Underwood © 2002 The Philip Lief Group
The Color Code – A new way to see yourself, your relationships, and your life
Taylor Hartman © 1998 Fireside – Simon and Schuster
The Common Enemy Karl Menninger. Article appearing in *Personality and Religion*
edited William A. Sadler, Jr. © 1970 SCM Press Ltd, London.
The Complete Idiot's Guide to Philosophy Jay Stevenson © 1998 Alpha Books
The Complete Idiot's Guide to Psychology Joni E. Johnston, © 2000 Alpha Books
The Complete Idiot's Guide to The World's Religions Brandon Toropov and Fr.
Luke Buckles © 1997 Alpha Books
The Complete Book of Bible Lists H.L.Willmington © 1987 Tyndale House Pub's
The Concept of God in Confucian Thought Te-Sheng Meng and P.K. Sih 1977
Learned Publications Inc. New York
The Concept of God in the Reformation Tradition Geddes MacGregor 1977 (Ibid)
The Creed Bernard Marthaler© 1993. Twenty-Third Publications, Mystic, CT
The Demon-Haunted World Carl Sagan ©1996. Ballantine Publishing USA
The Duality of Human Existence David Bakan© 1966 Rand McNally & Company

268

The Existence of God edited John Hick © 1964 Macmillan Publishing co., Inc.

The Feminine Dimension of the Divine Joan Chamberlain Engelsman © 1979 Westminster Press

The Growth of Medieval Theology Jaroslav Pelikan © 1978 University of Chicago

The Healing Power of Color Betty Wood © 1998 Destiny Books

The Hindu Concept of God Francis W. Vineeth 1977 Learned Publications Inc.

The Holy Qu'ran Published Amana Corporation © 1989 Maryland USA

The Illustrated Book of Myths Neil Philip © 1995 Dorling Kindersly

The Illuminated Rumi © 1997 Barks and Green. Broadway Books, Doubleday, NY

The Jesuits: The Society of Jesus and the Betrayal of the Roman Catholic Church by Malachi Martin © 1987 Touchstone Books, Simon and Schuster

The Left Hand of God Adolf Holl © 1997 Bantam Books

The Luscher Color Test Translated and Edited Ian A. Scott © 1969 Max Luscher. Washington Square Press. New York.

The Millionaire Course Marc Allen © 2003 New World Library

The Myth Behind The Sex of God Carol Ochs © 1977 Beacon Press

The Origin of Satan Elaine Pagels © 1995 Random House Inc. New York

The Oxford Study Bible © 1992 Oxford University Press

The Portable Thoreau edited Carl Bode © 1947, 1975 Viking Penguin Inc.

The Possible Human Jean Houston © 1982 J.P. Tarcher, Inc, CA

The Power of Myth Joseph Campbell © 1988 Apostrophe S Productions

The Power of Now Eckhart Tolle © 1999. New World Library, CA, USA

The Prophet Kahlil Gibran © 1923 & 1951 Random House, New York

The Prophet Max Weber. Article appearing in *Personality and Religion* edited William A. Sadler, Jr. © 1970 SCM Press Ltd, London.

The Psychologist's Book of Self-Tests Louis Janda © 1996 Berkley Publishing NY

The Psychology of Religion – An Empirical Approach Hood, Spilka, Hunsberger, & Gorsuch 2nd ed.© 1996 The Guildford Press, New York *(see sub-quotes at end)*

The Religious Context of Prejudice Gordon W. Allport. Article appearing in *Personality and Religion* edited William A. Sadler, Jr. © 1970 SCM Press Ltd. UK

The Religious Dimension of Human Experience Dorothy Lee. Article appearing in *Personality and Religion* edited William A. Sadler, Jr. © 1970 SCM Press Ltd,. UK

The Scientific Study of Religion and Personality Article appearing in *Personality and Religion* edited by William A. Sadler, Jr. © 1970 SCM Press Ltd, London.

The Scientist in the Crib Gopnik, Meltzoff, & Kuhl © 1999 William Morrow & Co.

The Secret Language of Dreams David Fontana © 1994 Duncan Baird Publishers

The Secret Language of Symbols David Fontana © 1993 Duncan Baird Publishers

The Selected Writings of Ralph Waldo Emerson Ed; Brooks Atkinson © 1992 Random House.

The Shining Wilderness Thomas Merton © 1988 Darton, Longman & Todd Ltd. UK

The Story of Christianity Vol. 1 Justo L.Gonzalez © 1985 HarperCollins

The Story of Christianity Vol. 2 Justo L.Gonzalez © 1985 HarperCollins

The Symbolism of Color Faber Birren © 1988 Citadel Press, N.J. USA

The Timetables of History Bernard Grun © 1991 Simon & Schuster Inc.

The Varieties of Religious Experience William James. New American Library
The Wanderer Kahlil Gibran © 1932 & 1960 Mary Gibran. Random House
The World's First Love Bishop Fulton Sheen © 1952 McGraw-Hill Book Co
Thought Organization in Religion Paul Pruyser. Article appearing in *Personality and Religion* edited William A. Sadler, Jr. © 1970 SCM Press Ltd, London.
Unconditional Life Deepak Chopra © 1991 Bantam books
Unification Thought © 1973 Unification Thought Institute, New York
What Is Islam? Dr. Muhammad Ansart, Islamic Federation of New Jersey, Inc. USA
What is Scientology? (L.Ron Hubbard) © 1998 Church of Scientology
When Religion becomes Evil Charles Kimball© 2002. HarperCollins New York
When Science Meets Religion Ian G. Barbour © 2000. HarperCollins, New York
Who's Who in the Bible © 1988 Publications International Ltd, USA
Who's Who in the Bible © 1994 Reader's Digest Association
Who's Who of Religions edited John R. Hinnells © Macmillan Press 1991
Wisdom's Book, The Sophia Anthology Arthur Versluis © 2000 Paragon House US
Woman and the History of Philosophy Nancy Tuana © 1992 Paragon House USA
World History edited Jeremy Black © 1999 Parragon Publishing, Bath, UK
World Religions Vol. 1; Living Religions of the Middle East Young Oon Kim ©
World Religions Vol. 2; India's Religious Quest Young Oon Kim © 1976 (Ibid)
World Religions Vol. 3; Faiths of the Far East Young Oon Kim © 1976 HSAUWC
World's Religions Huston Smith © 1994 Harper Collins Publishers
World Scripture, A Comparative Anthology of Sacred Texts Andrew Wilson © 1995 Paragon House Publishing, USA.

Psychology of Religion sub-quotes:
* Carroll, M.P. (1986). *The cult of the Virgin Mary: Psychological Origins*, Princeton, N.J: Princeton University Press.
* Perry, N., & Echeverria, L. (1988). *Under the heal of Mary*. London: Routlefge and Kegan Paul.
* Warner, M. (1976). *Alone of all her sex: The myth and cult of the Virgin Mary*. New York: Knopf.
* Carroll, M.P. (1983). Vision of the Virgin Mary: The effects of family structures on Marian apparitions. *Journal for the Scientific Study of Religion. 22, 205-221*

Websites:
Color of Truth - http://color-of-truth.com
Colour Energy - www.colourenergy.com
Allen Wood - http://www.allentwood.com/
Paul Volk - http://www.newstartplus.org/
Luscher Color Testing - www.luscher-color.com
Baha'I Faith - http://www.bahaifaith.net/kabbalah.htm
Flags of the World - http://www.crwflags.com/fotw/flags/
Tony Badillo; Solomon's Temple - http://home.earthlink.net/~tonybadillo

ABOUT THE AUTHOR

Stephen Manning is a widely-travelled educator with qualifications and experience in several fields. He has lived, worked and studied in Europe, Asia and the Americas, and during the past decade has taught a variety of subjects at schools, colleges and universities worldwide.

Specialising in teacher-training, life-skills and language instruction, his formal religious training has also generated a keen interest in the psychology of religion, and the resolution of 'the religious problem'.

Deeply concerned by the harmful effects of partisan attitudes and elitist religious beliefs, he continues to research the history and development of human society with a view to identifying common, and therefore unifying truths throughout.

He now lives with his wife and children in the remote and beautiful West of Ireland, where he spends his time researching, writing and publishing books which he believes have "..something to say."

A volunteer with the local Mountain Rescue Team, and a soccer coach and referee, in his spare time he enjoys exploring the spartan mountain environment with his pet billy-goat Jacob.

For further information or to enquire about availability for speaking engagements, please visit the website; http://color-of-truth.com